Get the eBooks FREE!

(PDF, ePub, Kindle, and liveBook all included)

We believe that once you buy a book from us, you should be able to read it in any format we have available. To get electronic versions of this book at no additional cost to you, purchase and then register this book at the Manning website.

Go to https://www.manning.com/freebook and follow the instructions to complete your pBook registration.

That's it!
Thanks from Manning!

Real-World Machine Learning

Real-World Machine Learning

HENRIK BRINK
JOSEPH W. RICHARDS
MARK FETHEROLF

MANNING
SHELTER ISLAND

For online information and ordering of this and other Manning books, please visit www.manning.com. The publisher offers discounts on this book when ordered in quantity. For more information, please contact

Special Sales Department
Manning Publications Co.
20 Baldwin Road
PO Box 761
Shelter Island, NY 11964
Email: orders@manning.com

Manning Publications Co.
20 Baldwin Road
PO Box 761
Shelter Island, NY 11964

Development editor: Susanna Kline
Technical development editor: Al Scherer
Review editors: Olivia Booth, Ozren Harlovic
Project editor: Kevin Sullivan
Copyeditor: Sharon Wilkey
Proofreader: Katie Tennant
Technical proofreader: Valentin Crettaz
Typesetter: Dennis Dalinnik
Cover designer: Marija Tudor

ISBN: 9781617291920
Printed in the United States of America
7 8 9 10 – SP – 21 20 19

brief contents

contents

foreword

Machine learning (ML) has become big business in the last few years: companies are using it to make money, applied research has exploded in both industrial and academic settings, and curious developers everywhere are looking to level up their ML skills. But this newfound *demand* has largely outrun the *supply* of good methods for learning how these techniques are used in the wild. This book fills a pressing need.

Applied machine learning comprises equal parts mathematical principles and tricks pulled from a bag—it is, in other words, a true craft. Concentrating too much on either aspect at the expense of the other is a failure mode. Balance is essential.

For a long time, the best—and the only—way to learn machine learning was to pursue an advanced degree in one of the fields that (largely separately) developed statistical learning and optimization techniques. The focus in these programs was on the core algorithms, including their theoretical properties and bounds, as well as the characteristic domain problems of the field. In parallel, though, an equally valuable lore was accumulated and passed down through unofficial channels: conference hallways, the tribal wisdom of research labs, and the data processing scripts passed between colleagues. This lore was what actually allowed the work to get done, establishing which algorithms were most appropriate in each situation, how the data needed to be massaged at each step, and how to wire up the different parts of the pipeline.

Cut to today. We now live in an era of open source riches, with high-quality implementations of most ML algorithms readily available on GitHub, as well as comprehensive and well-architected frameworks to tie all the pieces together. But in the midst of this abundance, the unofficial lore has remained stubbornly inaccessible. The authors of this book provide a great service by finally bringing this dark knowledge together in one place; this is a key missing piece as machine learning moves from esoteric academic discipline to core software engineering skillset.

Another point worth emphasizing: most of the machine-learning methods in broad use today are far from perfect, meeting few of the desiderata we might list, were we in a position to design the perfect solution. The current methods are picky about the data they will accept. They are, by and large, happy to provide overly confident predictions if not carefully tended. Small changes in their input can lead to large and mysterious changes in the models they learn. Their results can be difficult to interpret and further interrogate. Modern ML engineering can be viewed as an exercise in managing and mitigating these (and other) rough edges of the underlying optimization and statistical learning methods.

This book is organized exactly as it should be to prepare the reader for these realities. It first covers the typical workflow of machine-learning projects before diving into extended examples that show how this basic framework can be applied in realistic (read: messy) situations. Skimming through these pages, you'll find few equations (they're all available elsewhere, including the many classic texts in the field) but instead much of the hidden wisdom on how to go about implementing products and solutions based on machine learning.

This is, far and away, the best of times to be learning about this subject, and this book is an essential complement to the cornucopia of mathematical and formal knowledge available elsewhere. It is that crucial *other* book that many old hands wish they had back in the day.

BEAU CRONIN
HEAD OF DATA, 21 INC.
BERKELEY, CA

preface

As a student of physics and astronomy, I spent a significant proportion of my time dealing with data from measurements and simulations, with the goal of deriving scientific value by analyzing, visualizing, and modeling the data. With a background as a programmer, I quickly learned to use my programming skills as an important aspect of working with data. When I was first introduced to the world of machine learning, it showed not only great potential as a new tool in the data toolbox, but also a beautiful combination of the two fields that interested me the most: data science and programming.

Machine learning became an important part of my research in the physical sciences and led me to the UC Berkeley astronomy department, where statisticians, physicists, and computer scientists were working together to understand the universe, with machine learning as an increasingly important tool.

At the Center for Time Domain Informatics, I met Joseph Richards, a statistician and coauthor of this book. We learned not only that we could use our data science and machine-learning techniques to do scientific research, but also that there was increasing interest from companies and industries from outside academia. We co-founded Wise.io with Damian Eads, Dan Starr, and Joshua Bloom to make machine learning accessible to businesses.

For the past four years, Wise.io has been working with countless companies to optimize, augment, and automate their processes via machine learning. We built a large-scale machine-learning application platform that makes hundreds of millions of predictions every month for our clients, and we learned that data in the real world is messy in ways that continue to surprise us. We hope to pass on to you some of our knowledge of how to work with real-world data and build the next generation of intelligent software with machine learning.

Mark Fetherolf, our third coauthor, was a founder and CTO of multiple startups in systems management and business analytics, built on traditional statistical and quantitative methods. While working on systems to measure and optimize petrochemical refining processes, he and his team realized that the techniques they were using for process manufacturing could be applied to the performance of databases, computer systems, and networks. Their distributed systems management technologies are embedded in leading systems management products. Subsequent ventures were in the measurement and optimization of telecommunications and customer interaction management systems.

A few years later, he got hooked on Kaggle competitions and became a machine-learning convert. He led a cable television recommender project and by necessity learned a lot about big-data technologies, adapting computational algorithms for parallel computing, and the ways people respond to recommendations made by machines. In recent years, he has done consulting work in the application of machine learning and predictive analytics to the real-world applications of digital advertising, telecommunications, semiconductor manufacturing, systems management, and customer experience optimization.

HENRIK BRINK

acknowledgments

We wish to thank Manning Publications and everyone there who contributed to the development and production of the book, in particular Susanna Kline, for her patient and consistent guidance throughout the writing process.

Our thanks to Beau Cronin, for writing the foreword. Thanks also to Valentin Crettaz, who gave all chapters a thorough technical proofread. Many other reviewers provided us with helpful feedback along the way: Alain Couniot, Alessandrini Alfredo, Alex Iverson, Arthur Zubarev, David H. Clements, Dean Iverson, Jacob Quant, Jan Goyvaerts, Kostas Passadis, Leif Singer, Louis Luangkesorn, Massimo Ilario, Michael Lund, Moran Koren, Pablo Domínguez Vaselli, Patrick Toohey, Ravishankar Rajagopalan, Ray Lugo, Ray Morehead, Rees Morrison, Rizwan Patel, Robert Diana, and Ursin Stauss.

Mark Fetherolf thanks Craig Carmichael for sharing his machine-learning obsession; and his wife, Patricia, and daughter, Amy, for many years of tolerance.

Henrik Brink would like to thank the founders and the rest of the team at Wise.io for their shared passion for using machine learning to solve real-world problems. He thanks his parents, Edith and Jonny, and his brother and sister for passing on a passion for knowledge and words, and—most important—he'd like to thank his wife, Ida, and his son, Harald, for their love and support.

Joseph Richards also thanks the Wise.io team for their shared enthusiasm for machine learning and endless commitment and energy, which makes coming in to work every day a real treat. He would like to especially thank his parents, Susan and Carl, for teaching him the joy of life-long learning and for instilling in him the values of hard work and empathy. And, most important, he thanks his wife, Trishna, for her endless love, compassion, and support.

about this book

Real-World Machine Learning is a book for people who want to apply machine learning (ML) to their own real-world problems. It describes and explains the processes, algorithms, and tools that mainstream ML comprises. The focus is on the practical application of well-known algorithms, not building them from scratch. Each step in the process of building and using ML models is presented and illustrated through examples that range from simple to intermediate-level complexity.

Roadmap

Part 1, "The machine-learning workflow," introduces each of the five steps of the basic machine-learning workflow with a chapter:

- Chapter 1, "What is machine learning?" introduces the field of machine learning and what it's useful for.
- Chapter 2, "Real-world data," dives into common data processing and preparation steps in the ML workflow.
- Chapter 3, "Modeling and prediction," introduces how to build simple ML models and make predictions with widely used algorithms and libraries.
- Chapter 4, "Model evaluation and optimization," dives deeper into your ML models to evaluate and optimize their performance.
- Chapter 5, "Basic feature engineering," introduces the most common ways to augment your raw data with your knowledge of the problem.

Part 2, "Practical application," introduces techniques for scaling your models and extracting features from text, images, and time-series data to improve performance on many modern ML problems. This part also includes three full example chapters.

- Chapter 6, "Example: NYC taxi data," is the first full example chapter. You'll try to predict the tipping behavior of passengers.
- Chapter 7, "Advanced feature engineering," covers advanced feature engineering processes that allow you to extract value out of natural-language text, images, and time-series data.
- Chapter 8, "Advanced NLP example: movie review sentiment," uses your advanced feature engineering knowledge to try to predict the sentiment of online movie reviews.
- Chapter 9, "Scaling machine-learning workflows," presents techniques for scaling ML systems to larger volumes of data, higher prediction throughput, and lower prediction latency.
- Chapter 10, "Example: digital display advertising," builds a model on large amounts of data, predicting online digital display advertisement click behavior.

How to use this book

If you're new to machine learning, chapters 1 through 5 will guide you through the processes of data preparation and exploration, feature engineering, modeling, and model evaluation. Our Python examples use the popular data manipulation and machine-learning libraries pandas and scikit-learn. Chapters 6 through 10 include three practical machine-learning examples along with advanced topics in feature engineering and optimization. Because the libraries encapsulate most of the complexity, our code samples can easily be adapted to your own ML applications.

Intended audience

This book will enable programmers, data analysts, statisticians, data scientists, and others to apply machine learning to practical problems, or simply to understand it. They'll gain practical experience with real-world data, modeling, optimization, and deployment of machine-learning systems without deep theoretical derivations of specific algorithms. The mathematical basis of machine learning is discussed for those who are interested, some algorithms are explained at a high level, and references are provided for those who would like to dig deeper. The focus is on getting practical results to solve the problems at hand.

Code conventions, downloads, and software requirements

This book contains many examples of source code both in numbered listings and inline with normal text. In both cases, source code is formatted in a `fixed-width font like this` to separate it from ordinary text.

Source code listings use Python, pandas, and scikit-learn. iPython notebooks for each chapter are available on GitHub at https://github.com/brinkar/real-world-machine-learning and on the Manning website at https://www.manning.com/books/real-world-machine-learning.

Notebook files (.ipynb) correspond to each chapter. Sample data is included in a data directory within the repository so all the notebooks can be executed if the prerequisite libraries have been installed along with iPython. Graphics are generated using the pyplot module of matplotlib and Seaborn.

In some cases, graphics generated in the iPython notebooks are extracted and presented as figures in the text. (Some have been modified to improve visual quality in the print and eBook.)

Finally, some graphics are best viewed in color. Readers of the black-and-white print book may wish to refer to the color graphics in the eBook version (available in PDF, ePub, and Kindle formats), which they can get for free by registering their print book at https://www.manning.com/books/real-world-machine-learning.

Author Online

Purchase of *Real-World Machine Learning* includes free access to a private web forum run by Manning Publications, where you can make comments about the book, ask technical questions, and receive help from the authors and from other users. To access the forum and subscribe to it, point your web browser to https://www.manning.com/books/real-world-machine-learning. This page provides information on how to get on the forum after you're registered, what kind of help is available, and the rules of conduct on the forum.

Manning's commitment to our readers is to provide a venue where a meaningful dialogue between individual readers and between readers and the authors can take place. It isn't a commitment to any specific amount of participation on the part of the authors, whose contribution to the AO forum remains voluntary (and unpaid). We suggest you try asking the authors some challenging questions, lest their interest stray!

The AO forum and the archives of previous discussions will be accessible from the publisher's website as long as the book is in print.

about the authors

Henrik Brink is a data scientist and software developer with extensive ML experience in industry and academia.

Joseph Richards is a senior data scientist with expertise in applied statistics and predictive analytics. Henrik and Joseph are co-founders of Wise.io, a leading developer of machine learning solutions for industry.

Mark Fetherolf is founder and president of Numinary Data Science, a data management and predictive analytics company. He has worked as a statistician and analytics database developer in social science research, chemical engineering, information systems performance, capacity planning, cable television, and online advertising applications.

about the cover illustration

The figure on the cover of *Real-World Machine Learning* is captioned "Chinois Combattant" or "Chinese fighter." The illustration is taken from a nineteenth-century edition of Sylvain Maréchal's four-volume compendium of regional dress customs published in France. Each illustration is finely drawn and colored by hand. The rich variety of Maréchal's collection reminds us vividly of how culturally apart the world's towns and regions were just 200 years ago. Isolated from each other, people spoke different dialects and languages. Whether on city streets, in small towns, or in the countryside, it was easy to identify where they lived and what their trade or station in life was just by their dress.

Dress codes have changed since then and the diversity by region and class, so rich at the time, has faded away. It is now hard to tell apart the inhabitants of different continents, let alone different towns or regions. Perhaps we have traded cultural diversity for a more varied personal life—certainly for a more varied and fast-paced technological life.

At a time when it is hard to tell one computer book from another, Manning celebrates the inventiveness and initiative of the computer business with book covers based on the rich diversity of regional life of two centuries ago, brought back to life by Maréchal's pictures.

Part 1

The machine-learning workflow

In this first part of the book, we introduce the basic machine-learning workflow. Each chapter covers one step of the workflow.

Chapter 1 introduces machine learning, what it's useful for, and why you should be reading this book.

In chapter 2, you'll dive into the data-processing step of the basic ML workflow. You'll look at common ways to clean up and extract value from real-world and messy data.

In chapter 3, you'll start building simple ML models as you learn about a few modeling algorithms and how they're used in common implementations.

In chapter 4, you'll take a deeper look at our ML models to evaluate and optimize their performance.

Chapter 5 is dedicated to basic feature engineering. Extracting features from data can be an extremely important part of building and optimizing the performance of an ML system.

1 What is machine learning?

This chapter covers

- Machine-learning basics
- Advantages of machine learning over traditional approaches
- Overview of the basic machine-learning workflow
- Overview of advanced methods for improving model performance

In 1959, an IBM computer scientist named Arthur Samuel wrote a computer program to play checkers. Each board position was assigned a score based on its likelihood of leading to a win. At first, scores were based on a formula using factors such as the number of pieces on each side and the number of kings. It worked, but Samuel had an idea about how to improve its performance. He had the program play thousands of games against itself and used the results to refine the positional scoring. By the mid-1970s, the program had achieved the proficiency of a respectable amateur player.[1]

[1] Jonathan Schaeffer, *One Jump Ahead: Computer Perfection at Checkers* (New York: Springer, 2009).

Samuel had written a computer program that was able to improve its own performance through experience. It learned—and machine learning (ML) was born.

The aim of this book isn't to describe the gory mathematical details of machine-learning algorithms (although we'll peel back a few layers of the onion to provide insight into the inner workings of the most common ones). Rather, the book's primary purpose is to instruct non-experts on important aspects and common challenges when integrating machine learning into real-world applications and data pipelines. In this first chapter, we present a real business problem—reviewing loan applications—to demonstrate the advantages of using machine learning over some of the most common alternatives.

1.1 Understanding how machines learn

When we talk about human learning, we distinguish between rote learning, or memorization, and true intelligence. Memorizing a telephone number or a set of instructions is undoubtedly learning. But when we say *learning*, we frequently mean something more.

When children play in groups, they observe how others respond to their actions. Their future social behaviors are informed by this experience. But they don't rewind and replay their past. Rather, certain recognizable features of their interactions—playground, classroom, Mom, Dad, siblings, friends, strangers, adults, children, indoors, outdoors—provide clues. They assess each new situation based on the features it has in common with past situations. Their learning is more than gathering knowledge. They're building what might be called *insight*.

Imagine teaching a child the difference between dogs and cats by using flashcards. You show a card, the child makes a choice, and you place the card in one of two piles for right and wrong choices, respectively. As the child practices, his performance improves. Interestingly, it isn't necessary to first teach the child techniques for cat and dog recognition. Human cognition has built-in classification mechanisms. All that's needed are *examples*. After the child is proficient with the flashcards, he'll be able to classify not only the images on the flashcards, but also most any cat or dog image, not to mention the real thing. This ability to *generalize*, to apply knowledge gained through training to new unseen examples, is a key characteristic of both human and machine learning.

Of course, human learning is far more sophisticated than even the most advanced machine-learning algorithms, but computers have the advantage of greater capacity to memorize, recall, and process data. Their experience comes in the form of historical data that's processed—using the techniques described in this book—to create and optimize, through experience, algorithms that embody, if not true insight, at least the ability to generalize.

Analogies between human and machine learning naturally bring to mind the term *artificial intelligence* (AI) and the obvious question, "What's the difference between AI and machine learning?" There's no clear consensus on this matter, but most (not all) agree that ML is one form of AI, and that AI is a far broader subject encompassing such areas as robotics, language processing, and computer vision systems. To increase the ambiguity even further, machine learning is being applied in many of these adjacent AI fields with increasing frequency. We can say that the discipline of machine learning refers to *a specific body of knowledge and an associated set of techniques.* It's fairly clear what is, and what isn't, machine learning, whereas the same can't always be said for artificial intelligence. Paraphrasing Tom Mitchell's often-cited definition, a computer program is said to learn if its performance of a certain task, as measured by a computable score, improves with experience.[2]

Kaggle, a machine-learning consultancy, ran a competition for the most accurate program for classifying whether images depicted a dog or cat.[3] Competitors were provided 25,000 example images for training. Each was labeled to indicate the species depicted. After all the competitors had trained their algorithms, they were tested on their ability to classify 12,500 unlabeled test images.

When we explain the Kaggle competition to people, they often respond by reflecting on the sorts of rules one might apply to accomplish dog and cat recognition. Cats' ears are triangular and stand up; dogs' ears are floppy—but not always. Try to imagine how you might explain to a person who had never seen a dog or a cat how to tell the difference, without showing any examples.

People use a variety of methods involving shapes, colors, textures, proportions, and other features to learn, and to generalize, from examples. Machine learning also employs a variety of strategies, in various combinations, depending on the problem at hand.

These strategies are embodied in collections of algorithms developed over the course of recent decades by academics and practitioners in disciplines ranging from statistics, computer science, robotics, and applied mathematics, to online search, entertainment, digital advertising, and language translation. They are diverse and have various strengths and weaknesses. Some of them are classifiers. Others predict a numeric measurement. Some measure the similarity or difference of comparable entities (for example, people, machines, processes, cats, dogs). What the algorithms have in common is learning from examples (experience) and the capacity to apply what they've learned to new, unseen cases—the ability to generalize.

In the cats and dogs competition, during the learning phase, competitors' programs tried over and over to perform correct classifications using many algorithms. In each of the millions of iterations of the learning process, the programs performed the classification, measured their results, and then adjusted the process ever so slightly, searching for incremental improvements. The winner classified 98.914% of the unseen test images correctly. That's pretty good, considering the human error rate

---

2 Tom Mitchell, *Machine Learning* (McGraw Hill, 1997), 2. "A computer program is said to learn from experience E with respect to some class of tasks T and performance measure P, if its performance at tasks in T, as measured by P, improves with experience E."

3 See "Dogs vs. Cats" at www.kaggle.com/c/dogs-vs-cats.

is around 7%. Figure 1.1 illustrates the process. The machine-learning process analyzes labeled images and builds a model that is, in turn, used by the *recall* (prediction) process to classify unlabeled images. There's one mislabeled cat in the example.

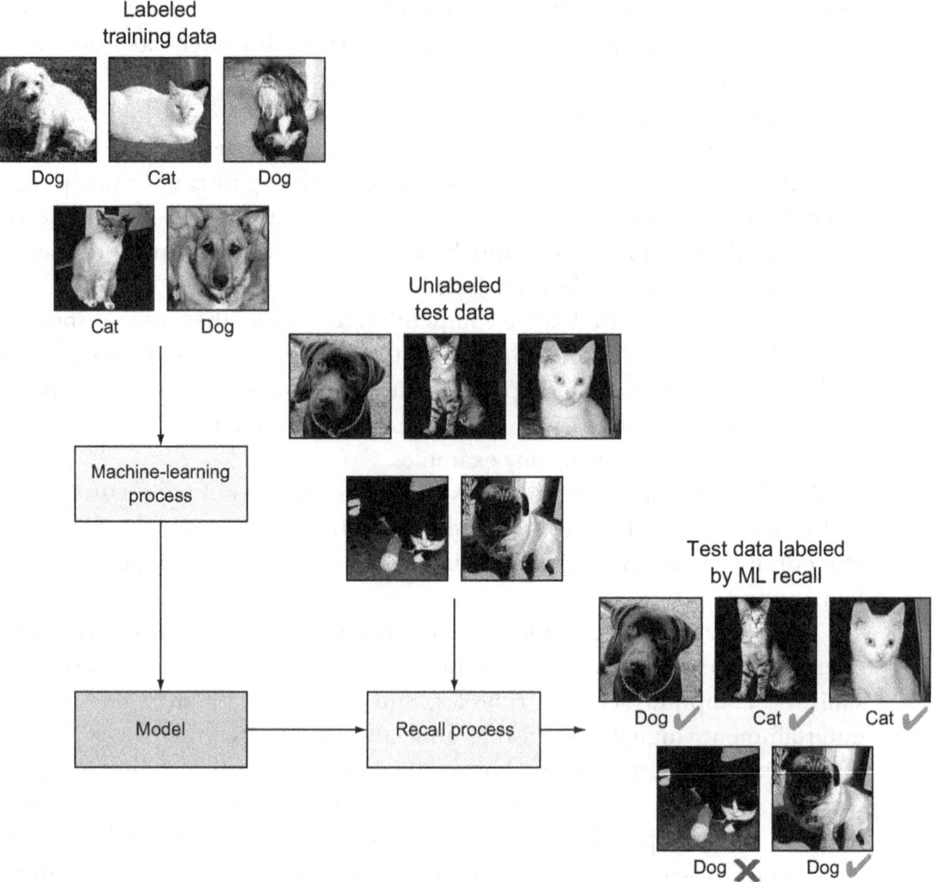

Figure 1.1 Machine-learning process for the cats and dogs competition

Please note that what we've described here is *supervised* machine learning, and it's not the only type of ML. We discuss other types later.

Machine learning can be applied to a wide range of business problems, from fraud detection, to customer targeting and product recommendation, to real-time industrial monitoring, sentiment analysis, and medical diagnosis. It can take on problems that can't be managed manually because of the huge amount of data that must be processed. When applied to large datasets, ML can sometimes find relationships so subtle that no amount of manual scrutiny would ever discover them. And when many such "weak" relationships are combined, they become strong predictors.

The process of learning from data, and subsequently using the acquired knowledge to inform future decisions, is extremely powerful. Indeed, machine learning is rapidly becoming the engine that powers the modern data-driven economy.

Table 1.1 describes widely used supervised machine-learning techniques and some of their practical applications. This isn't an exhaustive list, as the potential use cases could stretch across several pages.

Table 1.1 Use cases for supervised machine learning, organized by the type of problem

Problem	Description	Example use cases
Classification	Determine the discrete class to which each individual belongs, based on input data	Spam filtering, sentiment analysis, fraud detection, customer ad targeting, churn prediction, support case flagging, content personalization, detection of manufacturing defects, customer segmentation, event discovery, genomics, drug efficacy
Regression	Predict the real-valued output for each individual, based on input data	Stock-market prediction, demand forecasting, price estimation, ad bid optimization, risk management, asset management, weather forecasting, sports prediction
Recommendation	Predict which alternatives a user would prefer	Product recommendation, job recruiting, Netflix Prize, online dating, content recommendation
Imputation	Infer the values of missing input data	Incomplete patient medical records, missing customer data, census data

1.2 Using data to make decisions

In the following example, we describe a real-world business problem that can benefit from a machine-learning approach. We'll run through the various alternatives that are commonly used and demonstrate the advantages of the ML approach.

Imagine that you're in charge of a microlending company that provides loans to individuals who want to start small businesses in troubled communities. Early on, the company receives a few applications per week, and you're able in a few days' time to manually read each application and do the necessary background checks on each applicant to decide whether to approve each loan request. The schematic of this process is shown in figure 1.2. Your early borrowers are pleased with your short turnaround time and personal service. Word of your company starts to spread.

As your company continues to gain popularity, the number of applicants begins to increase. Soon you're receiving hundreds of applications per week. You try to stay up with the increased rate of applications by working extra hours, but the backlog of applications continues to grow. Some of your applicants grow weary of waiting and seek loans from your competitors. It's obvious to you that manually processing each application by yourself isn't a sustainable business process and, frankly, isn't worth the stress.

So what should you do? In this section, you'll explore several ways to scale up your application-vetting process to meet your increasing business needs.

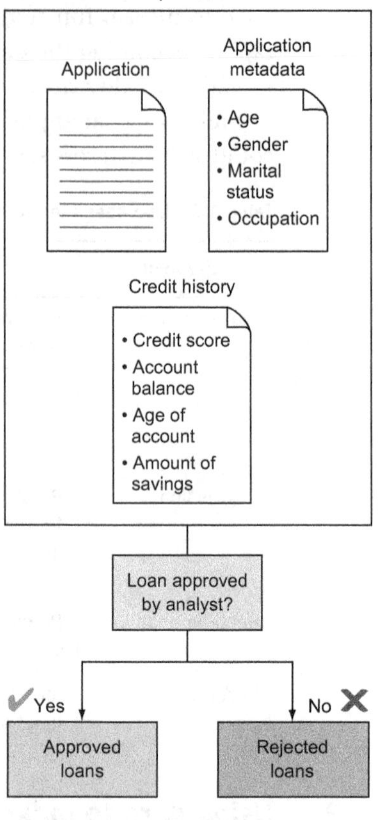

Figure 1.2 The loan-approval process for the microlending example

1.2.1 Traditional approaches

Let's explore two traditional data analysis approaches as applied to the application-vetting process: manual analysis and business rules. For each approach, we'll walk through the process of implementing the technique and highlight the ways in which it falls short of enabling you to build a scalable business.

HIRE MORE ANALYSTS

You decide to hire another analyst to help you out. You aren't thrilled with the idea of spending some of your profit on a new hire, but with a second person vetting applications, you can process roughly twice as many applications in the same amount of time. This new analyst allows you to flush out the application backlog within a week.

For the first couple of weeks, the two of you stay up with demand. Yet the number of applications continues to grow, doubling within a month to 1,000 per week. To keep up with this increased demand, you now must hire two more analysts. Projecting forward, you determine that this pattern of hiring isn't sustainable: all of your increased revenue from new loan applicants is going directly to your new hires instead of to more-critical areas such as your microlending fund. *Hiring more analysts as demand increases hinders the growth of your business.* Further, you find that the hiring process is lengthy and expensive, sapping your business of more of its revenue. Finally, each new hire is less experienced and slower at processing applications than the last, and the added stress of managing a team of individuals is wearing on you.

Aside from the obvious disadvantage of increased cost, people bring all sorts of conscious and unconscious biases to the decision-making process. To ensure consistency, you might develop detailed guidelines for the approval process and implement an extensive training program for new analysts, but this adds still more cost and probably doesn't eliminate the bias.

EMPLOY BUSINESS RULES

Imagine that of the 1,000 loans whose repayment date has passed, 70% were repaid on time. This is shown in figure 1.3.

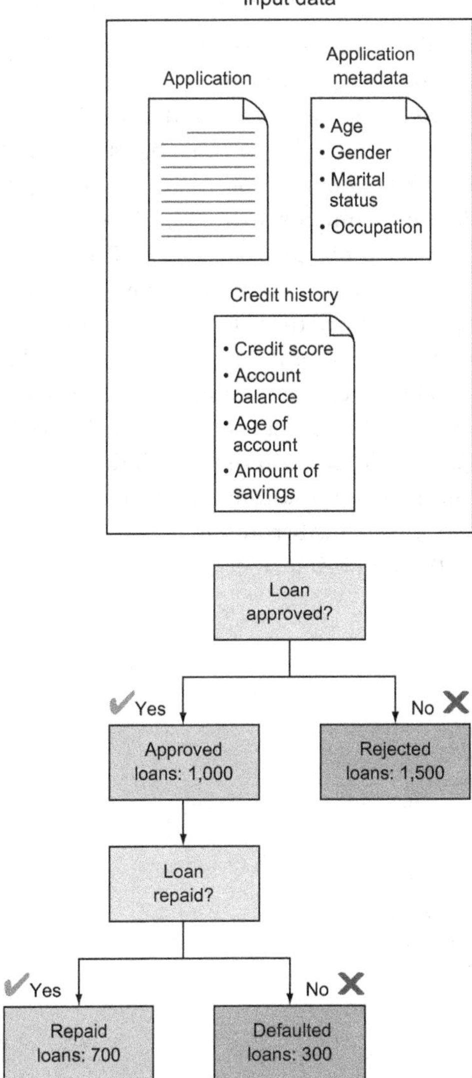

Figure 1.3 After a few months of business and 2,500 loan applications, 1,000 were approved, of which 700 applicants repaid the loan on time and the other 300 defaulted. This initial set of observed information is critical to start building automation into your loan-approval process.

You're now in a position to begin looking for trends between the applicant data and incidence of loan repayment. In particular, you perform a manual search for a set of filtering rules that produces a subset of "good" loans that were primarily paid on time. Through the process of manually analyzing hundreds of applications, you've gained extensive experience about what makes each application good or bad.[4] Through some introspection and back-testing of loan repayment status, you've noticed a few trends in the credit background checks data:[5]

- Most borrowers with a credit line of more than $7,500 defaulted on their loan.
- Most borrowers who had no checking account repaid their loan on time.

Now you can design a filtering mechanism to pare down the number of applications that you need to process manually through those two rules.

Your first filter is to automatically reject any applicant with a credit line of more than $7,500. Looking through your historical data, you find that 44 of the 86 applicants with a credit line of more than $7,500 defaulted on their loan. Roughly 51% of these high-credit-line applicants defaulted, compared to 28% of the rest. This filter seems like a good way to exclude high-risk applicants, but you realize that only 8.6% (86 out of 1,000) of your accepted applicants had a credit line that was so high, meaning that you'll still need to manually process more than 90% of applications. You need to do more filtering to get that number down to something more manageable.

Your second filter is to automatically accept any applicant who doesn't have a checking account. This seems to be an excellent filter, as 348 of the 394 (88%) applicants without a checking account repaid their loans on time. Including this second filter brings the percentage of applications that are automatically accepted or rejected up to 45%. Thus, you need to manually analyze only roughly half of the new incoming applications. Figure 1.4 demonstrates these filtering rules.

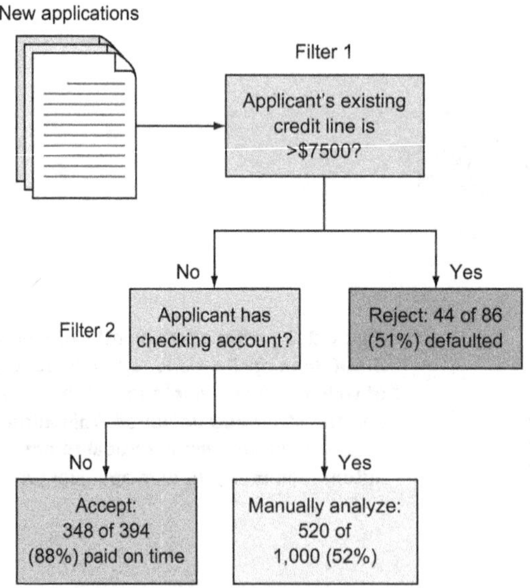

Figure 1.4 Filtering new applications through two business rules enables you to reduce manual analysis to only 52% of the incoming applications.

[4] You could also use statistical correlation techniques to determine which input data attributes are most strongly associated with the outcome event of loan repayment.

[5] In this example, we use the German Credit Data dataset. You can download this data from http://mng.bz/95r4.

With these two business rules, you can scale your business up to twice the amount of volume without having to hire a second analyst, because you now need to manually accept or reject only 52% of new applications. Additionally, based on the 1,000 applications with known outcome, you expect your filtering mechanism to erroneously reject 42 out of every 1,000 applications (4.2%) and to erroneously accept 46 of every 1,000 applications (4.6%).

As business grows, you'd like your system to automatically accept or reject a larger and larger percentage of applications without increasing losses from defaults. To do this, you again need to add more business rules. You soon encounter several problems:

- Manually finding effective filters becomes harder and harder—if not impossible—as the filtering system grows in complexity.
- The business rules become so complicated and opaque that debugging them and ripping out old, irrelevant rules becomes virtually impossible.
- The construction of your rules has no statistical rigor. You're pretty sure that better "rules" can be found by better exploration of the data, but can't know for sure.
- As the patterns of loan repayment change over time—perhaps due to changes in the population of applicants—the system doesn't adapt to those changes. To stay up to date, the system needs to be constantly adjusted.

All these drawbacks can be traced to a single debilitating weakness in a business rules approach: the system doesn't automatically learn from data.

Data-driven systems, from simple statistical models to more-sophisticated machine-learning workflows, can overcome these problems.

1.2.2 The machine-learning approach

Finally, you decide to look into an entirely automated, data-driven approach to your microlending application-vetting process. Machine learning is an attractive option because the completely automated nature of the process will allow your operation to keep pace with the increasing inflow of applications. Further, unlike business rules, ML learns the optimal decisions *directly from the data* without having to arbitrarily hard-code decision rules. This graduation from rules-based to ML-based decision making means that your decisions will be more accurate and will improve over time as more loans are made. You can be sure that your ML system produces optimized decisions with minimal handholding.

In machine learning, the data provides the foundation for deriving insights about the problem at hand. To determine whether to accept each new loan application, ML uses historical *training data* to predict the best course of action for each new application. To get started with ML for loan approval, you begin by assembling the training data for the 1,000 loans that have been granted. This training data consists of the input data for each loan application, along with the known outcome of whether each loan was repaid on time. The input data, in turn, consists of a set of *features*—numerical or categorical metrics that capture the relevant aspects of each application—such as the applicant's credit score, gender, and occupation.

In figure 1.5 historical data trains the machine-learning model. Then, as new loan applications come in, predictions of the probability of future repayment are generated instantaneously from the application data.

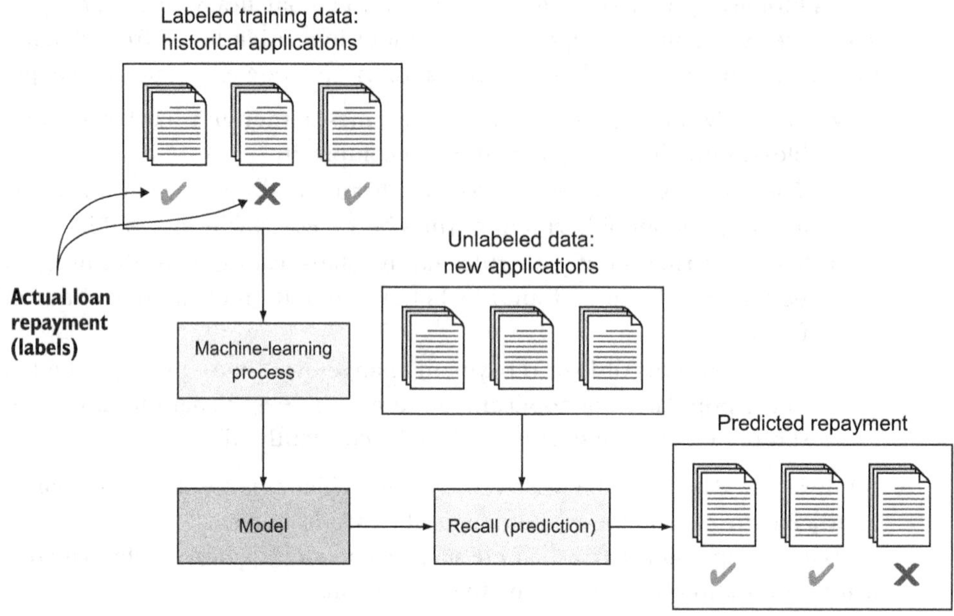

Figure 1.5 Basic ML workflow, as applied to the microloan example

ML modeling, then, determines how the input data for each applicant can be used to *best predict* the loan outcome. By finding and using patterns in the training set, ML produces a model (you can think of this as a black box, for now) that produces a prediction of the outcome for each new applicant, based on that applicant's data.

The next step is to select an ML algorithm to use. Machine learning comes in many flavors, ranging from simple statistical models to more-sophisticated approaches. Here, we compare two examples: the first is a simple parametric model, and the second a nonparametric ensemble of classification trees. Don't let the terminology scare you. Machine learning employs a lot of algorithms and lots of ways to categorize them, as you'll soon see.

Most traditional statistical business models fall into the first category. These parametric models use simple, fixed equations to express the relationship between the outcome and the inputs. Data is then used to learn the best values of the unknown terms in the equation. Approaches such as linear regression, logistic regression, and autoregressive models all fit under this category. Regression models are covered in more detail in chapter 3.

In this example, you could use logistic regression to model the loan-approval process. In logistic regression, the logarithm of the odds (the *log odds*) that each loan is repaid is modeled as a linear function of the input features. For example, if each new application contains three relevant features—the applicant's credit line, education level, and age—then logistic regression attempts to predict the log odds that the applicant will default on the loan (we'll call this y) via this equation:

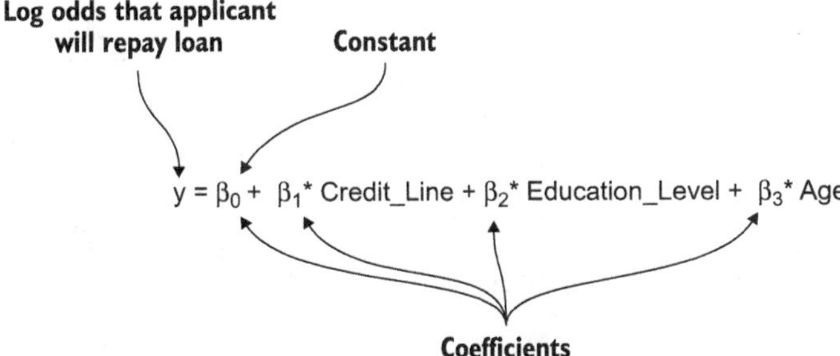

> **Log odds**
>
> The odds ratio is one way of expressing probability. You've undoubtedly heard someone say that a (favorite) team's chance of winning is 3 to 1. Odds are the probability of success (for example, winning) divided by the probability of failure (losing). Mathematically, this can be expressed as follows:
>
> Odds(A) = P(A) / P(~A) = The probability of A divided by the probability of not A
>
> So 3-to-1 odds is equivalent to 0.75 / 0.25 = 3 and log(3) = 0.47712...
>
> If A were a fair coin toss, the odds of heads would be 0.5 / 0.5 = 1. Log(1) = 0. It turns out that the log(Odds) can take on any real-valued number. A log odds value near $-\infty$ denotes a highly unlikely event. A value near ∞ indicates near certainty, and log(1) = 0 indicates an even random change. Using log-odds instead of regular probabilities is a mathematical trick that makes certain computations easier, because unlike probabilities, they're not limited to values between 0 and 1.

The optimal values of each coefficient of the equation (in this case, β_0, β_1, β_2, and β_3) are learned from the 1,000 training data examples.

When you can express the relationship between inputs and outputs in a formula like this one, predicting the output (y) from the inputs (credit line, education level, and age) is easy. All you have to do is figure out which values of β_1, β_2, and β_3 yield the best result when using your historical data.

But when the relationship between the inputs and the response are complicated, models such as logistic regression can be limited. Take the dataset in the left panel of figure 1.6, for example. Here, you have two input features, and the task is to classify each data point into one of two classes. The two classes are separated in the two-dimensional feature space by a nonlinear curve, the *decision boundary* (depicted by the curve in the figure). In the center panel, you see the result of fitting a logistic regression model on this dataset. The logistic regression model comes up with a straight line that separates the two regions, resulting in many classification errors (points in the wrong region).

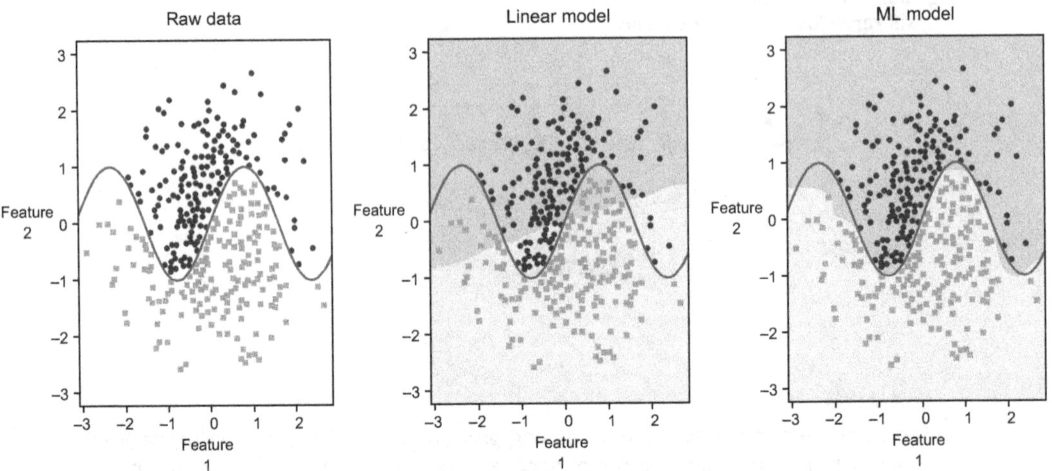

Figure 1.6 In this two-class classification, individual data points can belong to either the round class or the square class. This particular data lies in a two-dimensional feature space having a nonlinear decision boundary that separates the classes, denoted by the curve. Whereas a simple statistical model does quite poorly at accurately classifying the data (center), an ML model (right) is able to discover the true class boundary with little effort.

The problem here is that the model depicted in the center panel is attempting to explain a complicated, nonlinear phenomenon with a simple *parametric* model. The formal definition of parametric versus nonparametric models is complex and too mathematical for this book, but the gist is that parametric models work well when you have prior understanding of the relationship between your inputs and the response you're trying to predict. If you know enough about the nonlinear relationship, you may be able to transform your inputs or response variables so that a parametric model will still work. For example, if the rate at which a certain disease is observed within a population is higher for older people, you might find a linear relationship between the probability of contracting the disease and the square of the subject's age. But in the real world, you're often presented with problems for which such transformations aren't possible to guess.

What you need are more flexible models that can automatically discover complex trends and structure in data without being told what the patterns look like. This is where *nonparametric* machine-learning algorithms come to the rescue. In the right-hand panel of figure 1.6, you see the result of applying a nonparametric learning algorithm (in this case, a *random forest classifier*) to the problem. Clearly, the predicted decision boundary is much closer to the true boundary, and as a result, the classification accuracy is much higher than that of the parametric model.

Because they attain such high levels of accuracy on complicated, high-dimensional, real-world datasets, nonparametric ML models are the approach of choice for many data-driven problems. Examples of nonparametric approaches include some of the most widely used methods in machine learning, such as k-nearest neighbors, kernel smoothing, support vector machines, decision trees, and ensemble methods. We describe all of these approaches later in the book, and the appendix provides an overview of some important algorithms. Linear algorithms have other properties that make them attractive in some cases, though. They can be easier to explain and reason about, and they can be faster to compute and scale to larger datasets.

Further reading

The textbook *An Introduction to Statistical Learning* by Gareth James et al. (Springer, 2013) provides a detailed introduction to the most commonly used approaches in machine learning, at a level that's accessible to readers without a background in statistics or mathematics. A PDF version is available on the author's website (www-bcf.usc.edu/~gareth/ISL/).

Returning to the microlending problem, the best choice for scaling up your business is to employ a nonparametric ML model. The model may find the exact same rules as those you initially found manually, but chances are that they'll be slightly different in order to optimize the statistical gains. Most likely, the ML model will also automatically find other and deeper relationships between input variables and the desired outcome that you otherwise wouldn't have thought about.

In addition to providing an automated workflow, you may also attain higher accuracy, which translates directly to higher business value. Imagine that a nonparametric ML model yields 25% higher accuracy than a logistic regression approach. In this case, your ML model will make fewer mistakes on new applications: accepting fewer applicants who won't repay their loan and rejecting fewer applicants who would have repaid their loan. Overall, this means a higher average return on the loans that you do make, enabling you to make more loans overall and to generate higher revenues for your business.

We hope this gives you a taste of the power that machine learning can bring you. Before we move on to defining our basic machine-learning workflow, we'll enumerate a few advantages of machine learning, as well as a few challenges with this approach.

1.2.3 Five advantages to machine learning

To wrap up our discussion of the microlending example, we list some of the most prominent advantages to using a machine-learning system, as compared to the most common alternatives of manual analysis, hardcoded business rules, and simple statistical models. The five advantages of machine learning are as follows:

- *Accurate*—ML uses data to discover the optimal decision-making engine for your problem. As you collect more data, the accuracy can increase automatically.
- *Automated*—As answers are validated or discarded, the ML model can learn new patterns automatically. This allows users to embed ML directly into an automated workflow.
- *Fast*—ML can generate answers in a matter of milliseconds as new data streams in, allowing systems to react in real time.
- *Customizable*—Many data-driven problems can be addressed with machine learning. ML models are custom built from your own data, and can be configured to optimize whatever metric drives your business.
- *Scalable*—As your business grows, ML easily scales to handle increased data rates. Some ML algorithms can scale to handle large amounts of data on many machines in the cloud.

1.2.4 Challenges

Naturally, achieving these benefits involves a few challenges. Depending on the size and shape of the business problem, the degree of attendant difficulty ranges from child's-play trivial to Hannibal-crossing-the-Alps colossal.

Most prominent is acquiring data in a usable form. It has been estimated that data scientists spend 80% of their time on data preparation.[6] You've undoubtedly heard that businesses capture vastly greater quantities of data than ever before, and they do. You also may have heard this data referred to as the "exhaust" of business processes. In other words, our new treasure trove of data wasn't designed to meet the input needs of our ML systems. Extracting useful data from the residue can be tedious and messy work.

A related challenge is formulating the problem so that machine learning can be applied, and will yield a result that's actionable and measurable. In our example, the goal is clear: predict who will repay and who will default. The classification is easy to apply, and the outcome is easily measured. Fortunately, some real-world problems are this simple; for example, given everything we know about prospective customers (and we have a lot of data), predict whether they'll purchase our product. This is low-hanging fruit.

A more difficult example might be along these lines: find the optimum media mix and combination of advertising units to increase brand awareness for a new product line. Simply formulating the problem requires constructing a way of measuring brand

---

[6] Steve Lohr, "For Big-Data Scientists, 'Janitor Work' Is Key Hurdle to Insights," *New York Times*, August 17, 2014, http://mng.bz/7W8n.

awareness, an understanding of the alternative media options under consideration, and data that reflects pertinent experience with the alternatives and associated outcomes.

When the outcome you're trying to predict is complicated, choosing the algorithm and how to apply it may be an enormous effort in itself. Cardiology researchers working to predict the likelihood of postoperative complications have a mind-boggling set of data for each patient, but ML algorithms don't naturally slurp up electrocardiography (EKG) data and DNA sequences. *Feature engineering* is the process of transforming inputs such as these into predictive features.

We'd be remiss if we didn't mention the bane of the predictive modeler's existence: a model that fits the training data perfectly, but falls flat on its face when it's used to do real predictions on data that isn't in the training set. The problem is most often *overfitting*.

You'll see that machine learning can solve a great variety of problems, some much more easily than others. You may also notice that the value of the solution isn't always proportional to the effort required. And indeed, ML isn't a silver bullet for any problem. But as you'll see in this book, machine learning is the perfect choice for many real-world, data-driven problems.

1.3 Following the ML workflow: from data to deployment

In this section, we introduce the main workflow for integrating machine-learning models into your applications or data pipelines. The *ML workflow* has five main components: data preparation, model building, evaluation, optimization, and predictions on new data. The application of these steps has an inherent order, but most real-world machine-learning applications require revisiting each step multiple times in an iterative process. These five components are detailed in chapters 2 through 4, but we outline them in this introduction to whet your appetite for getting started. Figure 1.7

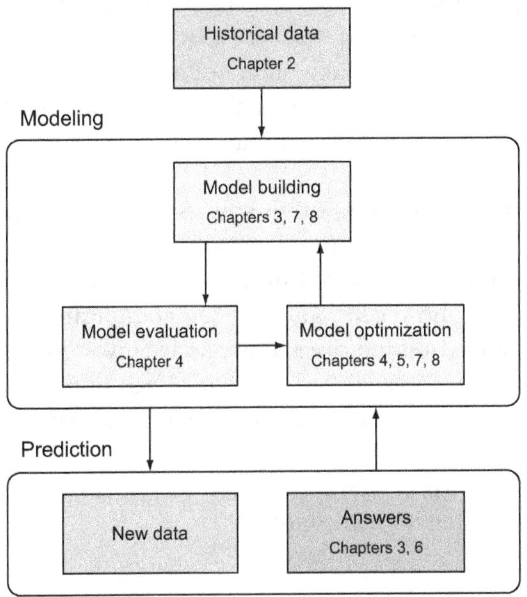

Figure 1.7 The workflow of real-world machine-learning systems. From historical input data you can build a model using an ML algorithm. You then need to evaluate the performance of the model, and optimize accuracy and scalability to fit your requirements. With the final model, you can make predictions on new data.

outlines this workflow, and the following sections introduce these concepts from top to bottom. You'll see this figure a lot throughout the book as we introduce the various components of the ML workflow.

1.3.1 Data collection and preparation

Collecting and preparing data for machine-learning systems usually entails getting the data into a tabular format, if it's not already. Think of the tabular format as a spreadsheet in which data is distributed in rows and columns, with each row corresponding to an *instance* or *example* of interest, and each column representing a measurement on this instance. A few exceptions and variations exist, but it's fair to say that most machine-learning algorithms require data in this format. Don't worry; you'll deal with the exceptions as you encounter them. Figure 1.8 shows a simple dataset in this format.

Features in columns

Person	Name	Age	Income	Marital status
1	Jane Doe	24	81,200	Single
2	John Smith	41	121,000	Married

Examples in rows

Figure 1.8 In a tabular dataset, rows are called *instances* and columns represent *features*.

The first thing to notice about tabular data is that individual columns usually include the same type of data, and rows typically include data of various types. In figure 1.8, you can already identify four types of data: *Name* is a string variable, *Age* is an integer variable, *Income* is a floating-point variable, and *Marital status* is a categorical variable (taking on a discrete number of categories). Such a dataset is called *heterogeneous* (in contrast to homogeneous), and in chapter 2 we explain how and why we'll coerce some of these types of data into other types, depending on the particular machine-learning algorithm at hand.

Real-world data can be "messy" in a variety of other ways. Suppose that a particular measurement is unavailable for an instance in the data-gathering phase, and there's no way of going back to find the missing piece of information. In this case, the table will contain a *missing value* in one or more cells, and this can complicate both model building and subsequent predictions. In some cases, humans are involved in the data-gathering phase, and we all know how easy it is to make mistakes in repetitive tasks such as data recording. This can lead to some of the data being flat-out wrong, and you'll have to be able to handle such scenarios, or at least know how well a particular algorithm behaves in the presence of misleading data. You'll look closer at methods for dealing with missing and misleading data in chapter 2.

1.3.2 Learning a model from data

The first part of building a successful machine-learning system is to ask a question that can be answered by the data. With this simple Person table, you could build an ML model that could predict whether a person is married or single. This information would be useful for showing relevant ads, for example.

In this case, you'd use the *Marital status* variable as the *target*, or *label*, and the remaining variables as *features*. The job of the ML algorithm will then be to find how the set of input features can successfully predict the target. Then, for people whose marital status is unknown, you can use the model to predict marital status based on the input variables for each individual. Figure 1.9 shows this process on our toy dataset.

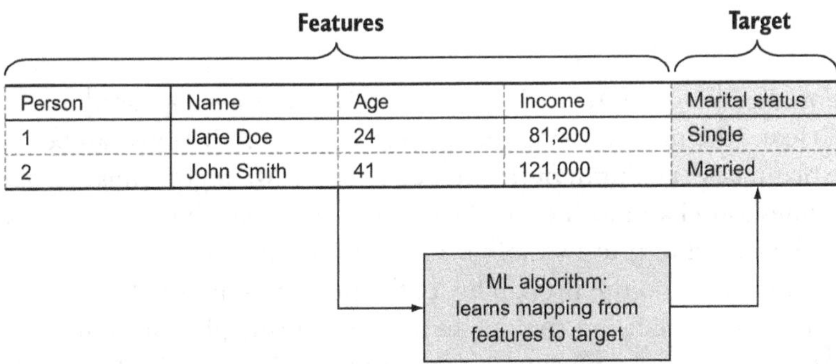

Figure 1.9 The machine-learning modeling process

At this point, think of the ML algorithm as a magical box that performs the mapping from input features to output data. To build a useful model, you'd need more than two rows. One of the advantages of machine-learning algorithms, compared with other widely used methods, is the ability to handle many features. Figure 1.9 shows only four features, of which the *Person* ID and *Name* probably aren't useful in predicting marital status. Some algorithms are relatively immune to uninformative features, whereas others may yield higher accuracy if you leave those features out. Chapter 3 presents a closer look at types of algorithms and their performance on various kinds of problems and datasets.

It's worth noting, however, that valuable information can sometimes be extracted from seemingly uninformative features. A location feature may not be informative in itself, for example, but can lead to informative features such as population density. This type of data enhancement, called *feature extraction*, is important in real-world ML projects and is the topic of chapters 5 and 7.

With our ML model in hand, you can now make predictions on new data—data for which the target variable is unknown. Figure 1.10 shows this process, using the magic-box model built in figure 1.9.

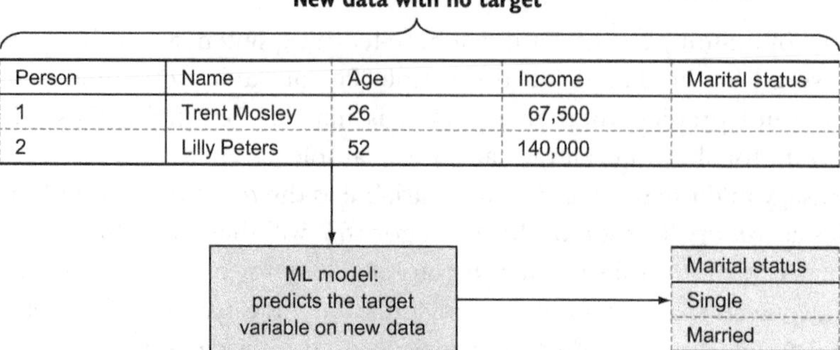

Figure 1.10 Using the model for prediction on new data

The target predictions are returned in the same form as they appeared in the original data used to learn the model. Using the model to make predictions can be seen as filling out the blank target column of the new data. Some ML algorithms can also output the probabilities associated with each class. In our married/single example, a *probabilistic* ML model would output two values for each new person: the probability of this person being married and the probability of the person being single.

We left out a few details on the way here, but in principle you've just architected your first ML system. Every machine-learning system is about building models and using those models to make predictions. Let's look at the basic machine-learning workflow in pseudocode to get another view of how simple it is.

Listing 1.1 Initial structure of an ML workflow program

```
data = load_data("data/people.csv")
model = build_model(data, target="Marital status")
new_data = load_data("data/new_people.csv")
predictions = model.predict(new_data)
```

Although we haven't programmed any of these functions yet, the basic structure is in place. By chapter 3, you'll understand these steps; the rest of the book (chapters 4 through 10) is about making sure you're building the best model for the problem at hand.

1.3.3 *Evaluating model performance*

Rarely is an ML system put to use without some kind of validation of the performance of the model. Even though we've skipped a lot of details in this chapter, let's pretend that you know how to build a model and make predictions. You can now apply a clever trick to get some sense of how well your model is working before you use it to predict on new data.

You take out some of the data and pretend that you don't know the target variable. You then build a model on the remaining data and use the held-out data (testing data) to make predictions. Figure 1.11 illustrates this model-testing process.

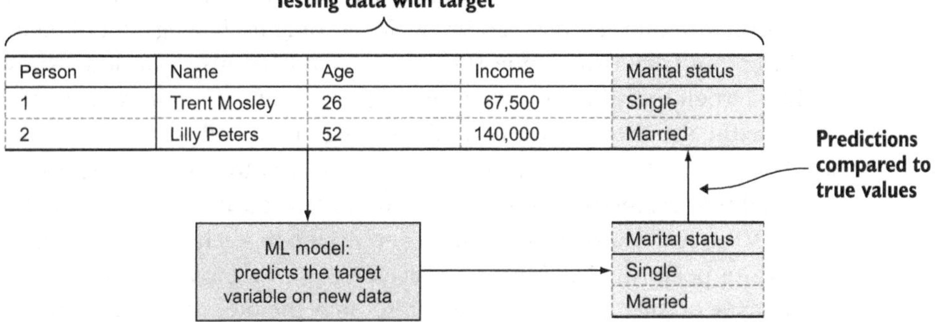

Figure 1.11 When using a testing set to evaluate model performance, you "pretend" that the target variable is unknown and compare the predictions with the true values.

Let's also look at the pseudocode for this workflow.

Listing 1.2 Our ML workflow program with model evaluation

```
data = load_data(...)
training_data, testing_data = split_data(data)
model = build_model(training_data, target="Marital status")
true_values = testing_data.extract_column("Marital status")
predictions = model.predict(testing_data)
accuracy = compare_predictions(predictions, true_values)
```

You can now compare the predicted results with the known "true" values to get a feeling for the accuracy of the model. In the pseudocode, this functionality is hidden behind the `compare_predictions` function, and most of chapter 4 is dedicated to understanding how this function looks for various types of machine-learning problems.

1.3.4 Optimizing model performance

The last piece of the essential machine-learning puzzle is also covered in chapter 4: how to use the results of your model evaluation to go back and make the model better. You can achieve better model accuracy in three ways:

- *Tuning the model parameters*—ML algorithms are configured with parameters specific to the underlying algorithm, and the optimal value of these parameters often depends on the type and structure of the data. The value of each parameter, or any of them combined, can have an impact on the performance of the model. We introduce various ways to find and select the best parameter values, and show how this can help in determining the best algorithm for the dataset in question.

- *Selecting a subset of features*—Many ML problems include a large number of features, and the noise from those features can sometimes make it hard for the algorithm to find the real signal in the data, even though they might still be informative on their own. For many ML problems, having a lot of data is a good thing; but it can sometimes be a curse. And because you don't know beforehand when this will affect your model performance, you have to carefully determine the features that make up the most general and accurate model.
- *Preprocessing the data*—If you search the internet for machine-learning datasets, you'll find easy-to-use datasets that many ML algorithms can be quickly applied to. Most real-world datasets, however, aren't in such a clean state, and you'll have to perform cleaning and processing, a process widely referred to as *data munging* or *data wrangling*. The dataset may include names that are spelled differently, although they refer to the same entity, or have missing or incorrect values, and these things can hurt the performance of the model. It may sound like edge cases, but you'll be surprised how often this happens even in sophisticated, data-driven organizations.

With the machine-learning essentials in place, you'll look briefly at more-advanced features in the next section before learning more details about the main components covered in this section.

1.4 Boosting model performance with advanced techniques

The previous section introduced the essential steps in any real-world machine-learning project, and now you'll look at additional techniques often used to improve model performance even further. Depending on the data and problem at hand, some of these techniques can provide significant gains in accuracy, but sometimes at the cost of speed in both training and prediction. These techniques are explained in more detail in chapters 5 through 10, but this section outlines the main ideas.

1.4.1 Data preprocessing and feature engineering

You'll look at various kinds of data and how to deal with common types of messiness in chapter 2. But in addition to this essential data cleaning, you can go a step further and extract additional value from the data that might improve your model performance.

In any problem domain, specific knowledge goes into deciding the data to collect, and this valuable domain knowledge can also be used to extract value from the collected data, in effect adding to the features of the model before model building. We call this process *feature engineering*, and when the previously introduced essential ML workflow has become second nature to you, you can find yourself spending almost all your time in this part of the optimization process. This is also the creative part of machine learning, where you get to use your knowledge and imagination to come up with ways to improve the model by digging into the data and extracting hidden value. You'll make extensive use of our statistically validated model evaluation and optimization steps to distinguish what seemed like a good idea at the time from what is actually useful. Here are a few important examples of feature engineering:

- *Dates and times*—You'll see a date or time variable in many datasets, but by themselves they're not useful for ML algorithms, which tend to require raw numbers or categories. The information might be valuable, though. If you want to predict which ad to show, it'll certainly be important to know the time of day, the day of the week, and the time of year. With feature engineering, this information can be extracted from the dates and times and made available to the model.

  Also, when dates and times appear in observations of repetitive activity, such as a user's repeated visits to a website over the course of a month or year, they can be used to compute interval durations that may be predictive. For example, on a shopping site, users might visit more frequently just prior to making a purchase to review and compare items and prices.
- *Location*—Location data, such as latitude/longitude coordinates or location names, is available in some datasets. This information can sometimes be used in itself, but you may be able to extract additional information that's useful for a specific problem. For example, if you want to predict election results in a county, you might want to extract the population density, mean income, and poverty rate to use as numbers in your model.
- *Digital media*—This is data such as text, documents, images, and video. The feature engineering that makes this kind of data usable is the difficult part of projects like the dogs and cats competition. Edges, shapes, and color spectra are first extracted from the images. Then these are classified using mathematical transformations, the output of which is a set of features usable by the classification algorithms.

Hopefully it's clear that feature engineering can be important for real-world ML projects. Chapters 5 and 7 go into much more detail, introducing specific feature-engineering techniques; you'll learn how these techniques feed into your ML workflow so your model performance improves without becoming too complex and prone to overfitting. Figure 1.12 illustrates feature-engineering integration into the larger ML workflow introduced in section 1.3.

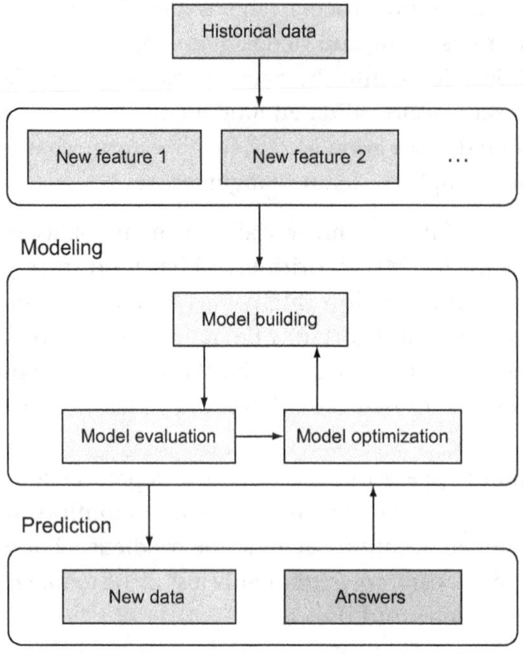

Figure 1.12 Feature-engineering phase inserted in the original ML workflow

1.4.2 Improving models continually with online methods

Most traditional ML models are static or only rarely rebuilt. But in many cases, you'll have data and predictions flowing back into the system, and you want the model to improve with time and adapt to changes in the data. Several ML algorithms support this type of *online learning*; chapter 8 introduces these algorithms and their potential pitfalls. Figure 1.13 shows how continual relearning can be integrated into the ML workflow.

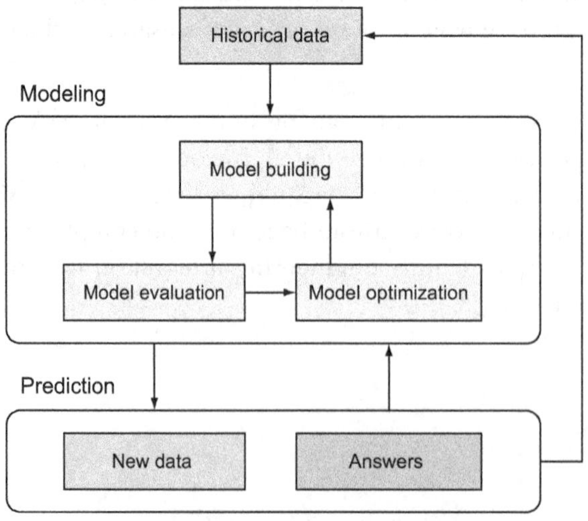

Figure 1.13 In this flow of an online ML system, predictions are fed back to the model for iterative improvements.

1.4.3 Scaling models with data volume and velocity

It's well known that datasets are increasing in size and velocity more quickly than ever. Datasets for supervised methods, in which the target answers are in the training set, have traditionally been relatively small because humans were needed in order to acquire the answers. Today, a lot of data (including answers) is produced directly by sensors, machines, or computers, and we're beginning to see requirements for scalable ML algorithms in order to handle these data volumes.

Chapter 9 presents details of machine-learning methods that are capable of scaling with growing dataset sizes; you'll see how they compare to each other and to nonscaling algorithms.

1.5 Summary

This chapter introduced machine learning as a better, more data-driven approach to making decisions. The main points to take away from this chapter are as follows:

- Machine-learning algorithms are distinguished from rule-based systems in that they create their own models based on data. Supervised ML systems generalize by learning from the features of examples with known results.
- Machine learning is often more accurate, automated, fast, customizable, and scalable than manually constructed rule-based systems.
- Machine-learning challenges include identifying and formulating problems to which ML can be applied, acquiring and transforming data to make it usable, finding the right algorithms for the problem, feature engineering, and overfitting.
- The basic machine-learning workflow consists of data preparation, model building, model evaluation, optimization, and predictions on new data.
- Online learning models continually relearn by using the results of their predictions to update themselves.

1.6 Terms from this chapter

Word	Definition
instance or example	A single object, observation, transaction, or record.
target or label	The numerical or categorical (label) attribute of interest. This is the variable to be predicted for each new instance.
features	The input attributes that are used to predict the target. These also may be numerical or categorical.
model	A mathematical object describing the relationship between the features and the target.
training data	The set of instances with a known target to be used to fit an ML model.
recall	Using a model to predict a target or label.

Word	Definition
supervised machine learning	Machine learning in which, given examples for which the output value is known, the training process infers a function that relates input values to the output.
unsupervised machine learning	Machine-learning techniques that don't rely on labeled examples, but rather try to find hidden structure in unlabeled data.
ML workflow	The stages in the ML process: data preparation, model building, evaluation, optimization, and prediction.
online machine learning	A form of machine learning in which predictions are made, and the model is updated, for each new example.

In chapter 2, you'll get into the practical matters of collecting data, preparing it for machine learning use, and using visualizations to gain the insight needed to choose the best tools and methods.

2 Real-world data

This chapter covers

- Getting started with machine learning
- Collecting training data
- Using data-visualization techniques
- Preparing your data for ML

In supervised machine learning, you use data to teach automated systems how to make accurate decisions. ML algorithms are designed to discover patterns and associations in historical training data; they learn from that data and encode that learning into a model to accurately predict a data attribute of importance for new data. Training data, therefore, is fundamental in the pursuit of machine learning. With high-quality data, subtle nuances and correlations can be accurately captured and high-fidelity predictive systems can be built. But if training data is of poor quality, the efforts of even the best ML algorithms may be rendered useless.

This chapter serves as your guide to collecting and compiling training data for use in the supervised machine-learning workflow (figure 2.1). We give general guidelines for preparing training data for ML modeling and warn of some of the common pitfalls. Much of the art of machine learning is in exploring and visualizing training data to assess data quality and guide the learning process. To that end,

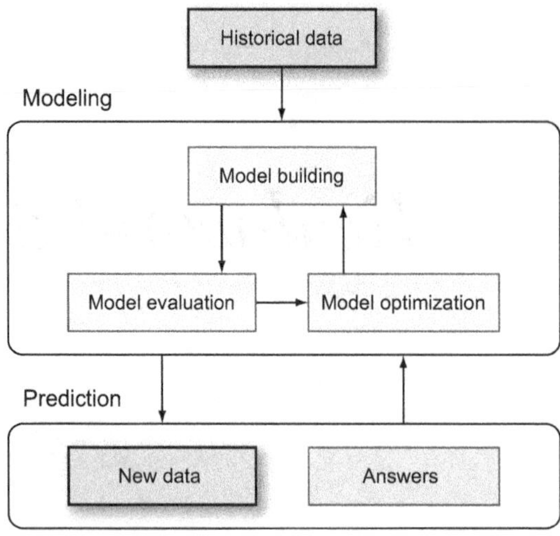

Figure 2.1 The basic ML workflow. Because this chapter covers data, we've highlighted the boxes indicating historical data and new data.

we provide an overview of some of the most useful data-visualization techniques. Finally, we discuss how to prepare a training dataset for ML model building, which is the subject of chapter 3.

This chapter uses a real-world machine-learning example: *churn prediction*. In business, *churn* refers to the act of a customer canceling or unsubscribing from a paid service. An important, high-value problem is to predict which customers are likely to churn in the near future. If a company has an accurate idea of which customers may unsubscribe from their service, then they may intervene by sending a message or offering a discount. This intervention can save companies millions of dollars, as the typical cost of new customer acquisition largely outpaces the cost of intervention on churners. Therefore, a machine-learning solution to churn prediction—whereby those users who are likely to churn are predicted weeks in advance—can be extremely valuable.

This chapter also uses datasets that are available online and widely used in machine-learning books and documentation: Titanic Passengers and Auto MPG datasets.

2.1 Getting started: data collection

To get started with machine learning, the first step is to ask a question that's suited for an ML approach. Although ML has many flavors, most real-world problems in machine learning deal with *predicting a target variable (or variables) of interest.* In this book, we cover primarily these supervised ML problems. Questions that are well suited for a supervised ML approach include the following:

- Which of my customers will churn this month?
- Will this user click my advertisement?
- Is this user account fraudulent?

- Is the sentiment of this tweet negative, positive, or neutral?
- What will demand for my product be next month?

You'll notice a few commonalities in these questions. First, they all require making assessments on one or several instances of interest. These instances can be people (such as in the churn question), events (such as the tweet sentiment question), or even periods of time (such as in the product demand question).

Second, each of these problems has a well-defined target of interest, which in some cases is binary (churn versus not churn, fraud versus not fraud), in some cases takes on multiple classes (negative versus positive versus neutral), or even hundreds or thousands of classes (picking a song out of a large library) and in others takes on numerical values (product demand). Note that in statistics and computer science, the *target* is also commonly referred to as the *response* or *dependent variable*. These terms may be used interchangeably.

Third, each of these problems can have sets of historical data in which the target is known. For instance, over weeks or months of data collection, you can determine which of your subscribers churned and which people clicked your ads. With some manual effort, you can assess the sentiment of different tweets. In addition to known target values, your historical data files will contain information about each instance that's knowable at the time of prediction. These are *input features* (also commonly referred to as the *explanatory* or *independent variables*). For example, the product usage history of each customer, along with the customer's demographics and account information, would be appropriate input features for churn prediction. The input features, together with the known values of the target variable, compose the *training set*.

Finally, each of these questions comes with an implied *action* if the target were knowable. For example, if you knew that a user would click your ad, you would bid on that user and serve the user an ad. Likewise, if you knew precisely your product demand for the upcoming month, you would position your supply chain to match that demand. The role of the ML algorithm is to use the training set to determine how the set of input features can most accurately predict the target variable. The result of this "learning" is encoded in a machine-learning model. When new instances (with an unknown target) are observed, their features are fed into the ML model, which generates predictions on those instances. Ultimately, those predictions enable the end user to taker smarter (and faster) actions. In addition to producing predictions, the ML model allows the user to draw inferences about the relationships between the input features and the target variable.

Let's put all this in the context of the churn prediction problem. Imagine that you work for a telecom company and that the question of interest is, "Which of my current cell-phone subscribers will unsubscribe in the next month?" Here, each instance is a current subscriber. Likewise, the target variable is the binary outcome of whether each subscriber cancelled service during that month. The input features can consist of any information about each customer that's knowable at the beginning of the month, such as the current duration of the account, details on the subscription plan, and usage information such as total number of calls made and minutes used in the previous month. Figure 2.2 shows the first four rows of an example training set for telecom churn prediction.

Cust. ID	State	Acct length	Area code	Int'l plan	Voicemail plan	Total messages	Total mins.	Total calls	Churned?
502	FL	124	561	No	Yes	28	251.4	104	False
1007	OR	48	503	No	No	0	190.4	92	False
1789	WI	63	608	No	Yes	34	152.2	119	False
2568	KY	58	606	No	No	0	247.2	116	True

(Features: Cust. ID through Total calls; Target: Churned?)

Figure 2.2 Training data with four instances for the telecom churn problem

The aim of this section is to give a basic guide for properly collecting training data for machine learning. Data collection can differ tremendously from industry to industry, but several common questions and pain points arise when assembling training data. The following subsections provide a practical guide to addressing four of the most common data-collection questions:

- Which input features should I include?
- How do I obtain known values of my target variable?
- How much training data do I need?
- How do I know if my training data is good enough?

2.1.1 *Which features should be included?*

In machine-learning problems, you'll typically have dozens of features that you could use to predict the target variable. In the telecom churn problem, input attributes about each customer's demographics (age, gender, location), subscription plan (status, time remaining, time since last renewal, preferred status), and usage (calling history, text-messaging data and data usage, payment history) may all be available to use as input features. Only two practical restrictions exist on whether something may be used as an input feature:

- The value of the feature must be known at the time predictions are needed (for example, at the beginning of the month for the telecom churn example).
- The feature must be numerical or categorical in nature (chapter 5 shows how non-numerical data can be transformed into features via feature engineering).

Data such as Calling History data streams can be processed into a set of numerical and/or categorical features by computing summary statistics on the data, such as total minutes used, ratio of day/night minutes used, ratio of week/weekend minutes used, and proportion of minutes used in network.

Given such a broad array of possible features, which should you use? As a simple rule of thumb, features should be included only if they're suspected to be related to the target variable. Insofar as the goal of supervised ML is to predict the target, features that obviously have nothing to do with the target should be excluded. For example, if a distinguishing identification number was available for each customer, it shouldn't be used as an input feature to predict whether the customer will unsubscribe. Such useless features make it more difficult to detect the true relationships (signals) from the random perturbations in the data (noise). The more uninformative features are present, the lower the signal-to-noise ratio and thus the less accurate (on average) the ML model will be.

Likewise, excluding an input feature because it wasn't previously known to be related to the target can also hurt the accuracy of your ML model. Indeed, it's the role of ML to discover new patterns and relationships in data! Suppose, for instance, that a feature counting the number of current unopened voicemail messages was excluded from the feature set. Yet, some small subset of the population has ceased to check their voicemail because they decided to change carriers in the following month. This signal would express itself in the data as a slightly increased conditional probability of churn for customers with a large number of unopened voicemails. Exclusion of that input feature would deprive the ML algorithm of important information and therefore would result in an ML system of lower predictive accuracy. Because ML algorithms are able to discover subtle, nonlinear relationships, features beyond the known, first-order effects can have a substantial impact on the accuracy of the model.

In selecting a set of input features to use, you face a trade-off. On one hand, throwing every possible feature that comes to mind ("the kitchen sink") into the model can drown out the handful of features that contain any signal with an overwhelming amount of noise. The accuracy of the ML model then suffers because it can't distinguish true patterns from random noise. On the other extreme, hand-selecting a small subset of features that you already know are related to the target variable can cause you to omit other highly predictive features. As a result, the accuracy of the ML model suffers because the model doesn't know about the neglected features, which are predictive of the target.

Faced with this trade-off, the most practical approach is the following:

1. Include all the features that you suspect to be predictive of the target variable. Fit an ML model. If the accuracy of the model is sufficient, stop.
2. Otherwise, expand the feature set by including other features that are less obviously related to the target. Fit another model and assess the accuracy. If performance is sufficient, stop.
3. Otherwise, starting from the expanded feature set, run an ML *feature selection algorithm* to choose the best, most predictive subset of your expanded feature set.

We further discuss feature selection algorithms in chapter 5. These approaches seek the most accurate model built on a subset of the feature set; they retain the signal in the feature set while discarding the noise. Though computationally expensive, they can yield a tremendous boost in model performance.

To finish this subsection, it's important to note that in order to use an input feature, that feature doesn't have to be present for each instance. For example, if the ages of your customers are known for only 75% of your client base, you could still use age as an input feature. We discuss ways to handle missing data later in the chapter.

2.1.2 *How can we obtain ground truth for the target variable?*

One of the most difficult hurdles in getting started with supervised machine learning is the aggregation of training instances with a known target variable. This process often requires running an existing, suboptimal system for a period of time, until enough training data is collected. For example, in building out an ML solution for telecom churn, you first need to sit on your hands and watch over several weeks or months as some customers unsubscribe and others renew. After you have enough training instances to build an accurate ML model, you can flip the switch and start using ML in production.

Each use case will have a different process by which ground truth—the actual or observed value of the target variable—can be collected or estimated. For example, consider the following training-data collection processes for a few selected ML use cases:

- *Ad targeting*—You can run a campaign for a few days to determine which users did/didn't click your ad and which users converted.
- *Fraud detection*—You can pore over your past data to figure out which users were fraudulent and which were legitimate.
- *Demand forecasting*—You can go into your historical supply-chain management data logs to determine the demand over the past months or years.
- *Twitter sentiment*—Getting information on the true intended sentiment is considerably harder. You can perform manual analysis on a set of tweets by having people read and opine on tweets (or use crowdsourcing).

Although the collection of instances of known target variables can be painful, both in terms of time and money, the benefits of migrating to an ML solution are likely to more than make up for those losses. Other ways of obtaining ground-truth values of the target variable include the following:

- Dedicating analysts to manually look through past or current data to determine or estimate the ground-truth values of the target
- Using crowdsourcing to use the "wisdom of crowds" in order to attain estimates of the target
- Conducting follow-up interviews or other hands-on experiments with customers
- Running controlled experiments (for example, A/B tests) and monitoring the responses

Each of these strategies is labor-intensive, but you can accelerate the learning process and shorten the time required to collect training data by collecting only target variables for the instances that have the most influence on the machine-learning model. One example of this is a method called *active learning*. Given an existing (small) training set and a (large) set of data with unknown response variable, active learning identifies the subset of instances from the latter set whose inclusion in the training set would yield the most accurate ML model. In this sense, active learning can accelerate the production of an accurate ML model by focusing manual resources. For more information on active learning and related methods, see the 2009 presentation by Dasgupta and Langford from ICML.[1]

2.1.3 How much training data is required?

Given the difficulty of observing and collecting the response variable for data instances, you might wonder how much training data is required to get an ML model up and running. Unfortunately, this question is so problem-specific that it's impossible to give a universal response or even a rule of thumb.

These factors determine the amount of training data needed:

- The complexity of the problem. Does the relationship between the input features and target variable follow a simple pattern, or is it complex and nonlinear?
- The requirements for accuracy. If you require only a 60% success rate for your problem, less training data is required than if you need to achieve a 95% success rate.
- The dimensionality of the feature space. If only two input features are available, less training data will be required than if there were 2,000 features.

One guiding principle to remember is that, as the training set grows, the models will (on average) get more accurate. (This assumes that the data remains *representative* of the ongoing data-generating process, which you'll learn more about in the next section.) More training data results in higher accuracy because of the data-driven nature of ML models. Because the relationship between the features and target is learned entirely from the training data, the more you have, the higher the model's ability to recognize and capture more-subtle patterns and relationships.

Using the telecom data from earlier in the chapter, we can demonstrate how the ML model improves with more training data and also offer a strategy to assess whether more training data is required. The telecom training dataset consists of 3,333 instances, each containing 19 features plus the binary outcome of unsubscribed versus renewed. Using this data, it's straightforward to assess whether you need to collect more data. Do the following:

1. Using the current training set, choose a grid of subsample sizes to try. For example, with this telecom training set of 3,333 instances of training data, your grid could be 500; 1,000; 1,500; 2,000; 2,500; 3,000.
2. For each sample size, randomly draw that many instances (without replacement) from the training set.

[1] See http://videolectures.net/icml09_dasgupta_langford_actl/.

3. With each subsample of training data, build an ML model and assess the accuracy of that model (we talk about ML evaluation metrics in chapter 4).
4. Assess how the accuracy changes as a function of sample size. If it seems to level off at the higher sample sizes, the existing training set is probably sufficient. But if the accuracy continues to rise for the larger samples, the inclusion of more training instances would likely boost accuracy.

Alternatively, if you have a clear accuracy target, you can use this strategy to assess whether that target has been fulfilled by your current ML model built on the existing training data (in which case it isn't necessary to amass more training data).

Figure 2.3 demonstrates how the accuracy of the fitted ML model changes as a function of the number of training instances used with the telecom dataset. In this case, it's clear that the ML model improves as you add training data: moving from 250 to 500 to 750 training examples produces significant improvements in the accuracy level. Yet, as you increase the number of training instances beyond 2,000, the accuracy

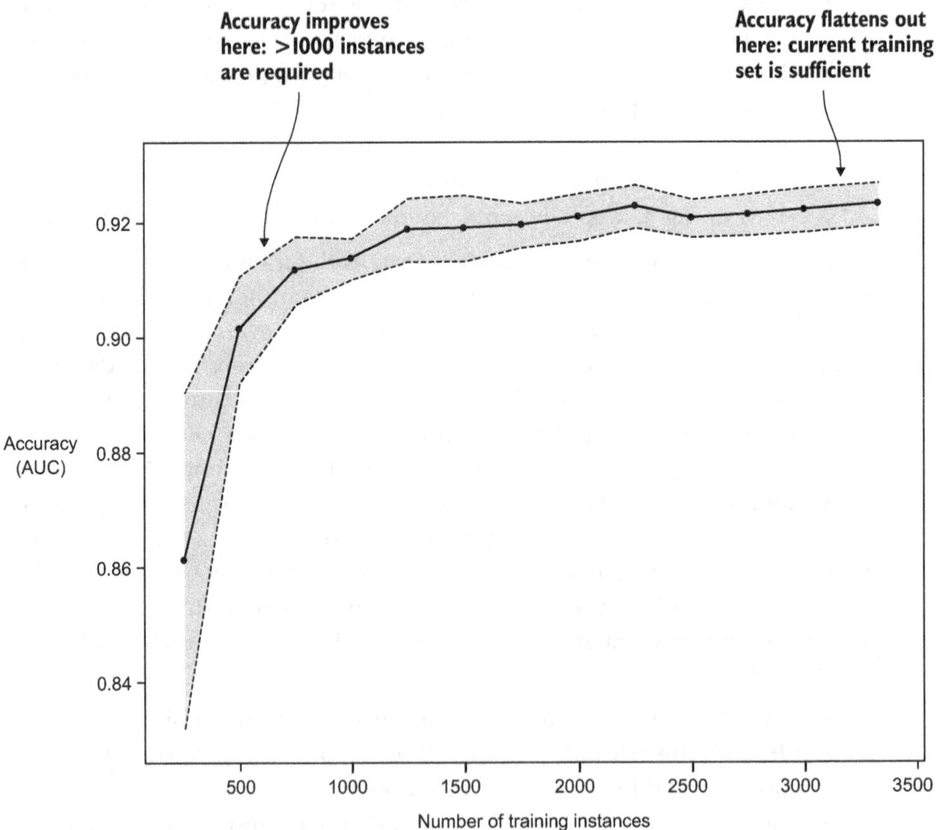

Figure 2.3 Testing whether the existing sample of 3,333 training instances is enough data to build an accurate telecom churn ML model. The black line represents the average accuracy over 10 repetitions of the assessment routine, and the shaded bands represent the error bands.

levels off. This is evidence that the ML model won't improve substantially if you add more training instances. (This doesn't mean that significant improvements couldn't be made by using more features.)

2.1.4 Is the training set representative enough?

Besides the size of the training set, another important factor for generating accurate predictive ML models is the *representativeness* of the training set. How similar are the instances in the training set to the instances that will be collected in the future? Because the goal of supervised machine learning is to generate accurate predictions on new data, it's fundamental that the training set be representative of the sorts of instances that you ultimately want to generate predictions for. A training set that consists of a nonrepresentative sample of what future data will look like is called *sample-selection bias* or *covariate shift*.

A training sample could be nonrepresentative for several reasons:

- It was possible to obtain ground truth for the target variable for only a certain, biased subsample of data. For example, if instances of fraud in your historical data were detected only if they cost the company more than $1,000, then a model trained on that data will have difficulty identifying cases of fraud that result in losses less than $1,000.
- The properties of the instances have changed over time. For example, if your training example consists of historical data on medical insurance fraud, but new laws have substantially changed the ways in which medical insurers must conduct their business, then your predictions on the new data may not be appropriate.
- The input feature set has changed over time. For example, say the set of location attributes that you collect on each customer has changed; you used to collect ZIP code and state, but now collect IP address. This change may require you to modify the feature set used for the model and potentially discard old data from the training set.

In each of these cases, an ML model fit to the training data may not extrapolate well to new data. To borrow an adage: you wouldn't necessarily want to use your model trained on apples to try to predict on oranges! The predictive accuracy of the model on oranges would likely not be good.

To avoid these problems, it's important to attempt to make the training set as representative of future data as possible. This entails structuring your training-data collection process in such a way that biases are removed. As we mention in the following section, visualization can also help ensure that the training data is representative.

Now that you have an idea of how to collect training data, your next task is to structure and assemble that data to get ready for ML model building. The next section shows how to preprocess your training data so you can start building models (the topic of chapter 3).

2.2 Preprocessing the data for modeling

Collecting data is the first step toward preparing the data for modeling, but sometimes you must run the data through a few preprocessing steps, depending on the composition of the dataset. Many machine-learning algorithms work only on numerical data—integers and real-valued numbers. The simplest ML datasets come in this format, but many include other types of features, such as categorical variables, and some have missing values. Sometimes you need to construct or compute features through feature engineering. Some numeric features may need to be rescaled to make them comparable or to bring them into line with a frequency distribution (for example, grading on the normal curve). In this section, you'll look at these common data preprocessing steps needed for real-world machine learning.

2.2.1 Categorical features

The most common type of non-numerical feature is the categorical feature. A feature is *categorical* if values can be placed in buckets and the order of values isn't important. In some cases, this type of feature is easy to identify (for example, when it takes on only a few string values, such as `spam` and `ham`). In other cases, whether a feature is a numerical (integer) feature or categorical isn't so obvious. Sometimes either may be a valid representation, and the choice can affect the performance of the model. An example is a feature representing the day of the week, which could validly be encoded as either numerical (number of days since Sunday) or as categorical (the names Monday, Tuesday, and so forth). You aren't going to look at model building and performance until chapters 3 and 4, but this section introduces a technique for dealing with categorical features. Figure 2.4 points out categorical features in a few datasets.

Person	Name	Age	Income	Marital status
1	Jane Doe	24	81,200	Single
2	John Smith	41	121,000	Married

Categorical features

PassengerId	Survived	Pclass	Gender	Age	SibSp	Parch	Ticket	Fare	Cabin	Embarked
1	0	3	Male	22	1	0	A/5 21171	7.25		S
2	1	1	Female	38	1	0	PC 17599	71.2833	C85	C
3	1	3	Female	26	0	0	STON/02. 3101282	7.925		S
4	1	1	Female	35	1	0	113803	53.1	C123	S
5	0	3	Male	35	0	0	373450	8.05		S
6	0	3	Male		0	0	330877	8.4583		Q

Figure 2.4 Identifying categorical features. At the top is the simple Person dataset, which has a Marital Status categorical feature. At the bottom is a dataset with information about Titanic passengers. The features identified as categorical here are Survived (whether the passenger survived or not), Pclass (what class the passenger was traveling on), Gender (male or female), and Embarked (from which city the passenger embarked).

Some machine-learning algorithms use categorical features natively, but generally they need data in numerical form. You can encode categorical features as numbers (one number per category), but you can't use this encoded data as a true categorical feature because you've then introduced an (arbitrary) order of categories. Recall that one of the properties of categorical features is that they aren't ordered. Instead, you can convert each of the categories into a separate binary feature that has value 1 for instances for which the category appeared, and value 0 when it didn't. Hence, each categorical feature is converted to a set of binary features, one per category. Features constructed in this way are sometimes called *dummy variables*. Figure 2.5 illustrates this concept further.

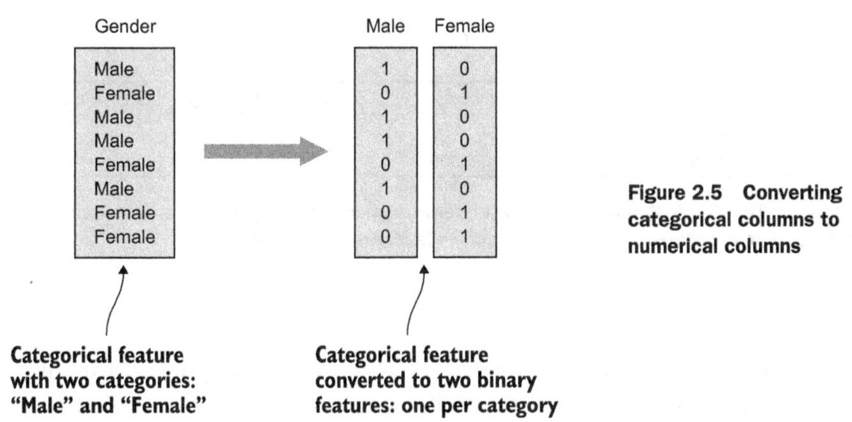

Figure 2.5 Converting categorical columns to numerical columns

The pseudocode for converting the categorical features in figure 2.5 to binary features looks like the following listing. Note that `categories` is a special NumPy type (www.numpy.org) such that `(data == cat)` yields a list of Boolean values.

Listing 2.1 Convert categorical features to numerical binary features

```
def cat_to_num(data):
    categories = unique(data)
    features = []
    for cat in categories:
            binary = (data == cat)
            features.append(binary.astype("int"))
    return features
```

NOTE Readers familiar with the Python programming language may have noticed that the preceding example isn't just pseudocode, but also valid Python. You'll see this a lot throughout the book: we introduce a code snippet as pseudocode, but unless otherwise noted, it's working code. To make the code simpler, we implicitly import a few helper libraries, such as `numpy` and `scipy`. Our examples will generally work if you include `from numpy import *`, and `from scipy import *`. Note that although this approach is convenient for trying out examples interactively, you should never use it in real applications, because the `import *` construct may cause name conflicts and unexpected results. All code samples are available for inspection and direct execution in the accompanying GitHub repository: https://github.com/brinkar/real-world-machine-learning.

The categorical-to-numerical conversion technique works for most ML algorithms. But a few algorithms (such as certain types of decision-tree algorithms and related algorithms such as random forests) can use categorical features natively. This will often yield better results for highly categorical datasets, and we discuss this further in the next chapter. Our simple Person dataset, after conversion of the categorical feature to binary features, is shown in figure 2.6.

Person	Name	Age	Income	Marital status: Single	Marital status: Married
1	Jane Doe	24	81,200	1	0
2	John Smith	41	121,000	0	1

Figure 2.6 The simple Person dataset after conversion of the categorical Marital Status feature to binary numerical features. (The original dataset is shown in figure 2.4.)

2.2.2 Dealing with missing data

You've already seen a few examples of datasets with missing data. In tabular datasets, missing data often appears as empty cells, or cells with NaN (Not a Number), N/A, or None. Missing data is usually an artifact of the data-collection process; for some reason, a particular value couldn't be measured for a data instance. Figure 2.7 shows an example of missing data in the Titanic Passengers dataset.

There are two main types of missing data, which you need to handle in different ways. First, for some data, *the fact that it's missing* can carry meaningful information that could be useful for the ML algorithm. The other possibility is that the data is missing

PassengerId	Survived	Pclass	Gender	Age	SibSp	Parch	Ticket	Fare	Cabin	Embarked
1	0	3	Male	22	1	0	A/5 21171	7.25		S
2	1	1	Female	38	1	0	PC 17599	71.2833	C85	C
3	1	3	Female	26	0	0	STON/02. 3101282	7.925		S
4	1	1	Female	35	1	0	113803	53.1	C123	S
5	0	3	Male	35	0	0	373450	8.05		S
6	0	3	Male		0	0	330877	8.4583		Q

Missing values

Figure 2.7 The Titanic Passengers dataset has missing values in the Age and Cabin columns. The passenger information has been extracted from various historical sources, so in this case the missing values stem from information that couldn't be found in the sources.

only because its measurement was impossible, and the unavailability of the information isn't otherwise meaningful. In the Titanic Passengers dataset, for example, missing values in the Cabin column may indicate that those passengers were in a lower social or economic class, whereas missing values in the Age column carry no useful information (the age of a particular passenger at the time simply couldn't be found).

Let's first consider the case of *informative* missing data. When you believe that information is missing from the data, you usually want the ML algorithm to be able to use this information to potentially improve the prediction accuracy. To achieve this, you want to convert the missing values into the same format as the column in general. For numerical columns, this can be done by setting missing values to –1 or –999, depending on typical values of non-null values. Pick a number at one end of the numerical spectrum that will denote missing values, and remember that order is important for numerical columns. You don't want to pick a value in the middle of the distribution of values.

For a categorical column with potentially informative missing data, you can create a new category called Missing, None, or similar, and then handle the categorical feature in the usual way (for example, using the technique described in the previous section). Figure 2.8 shows a simple diagram of what to do with meaningful missing data.

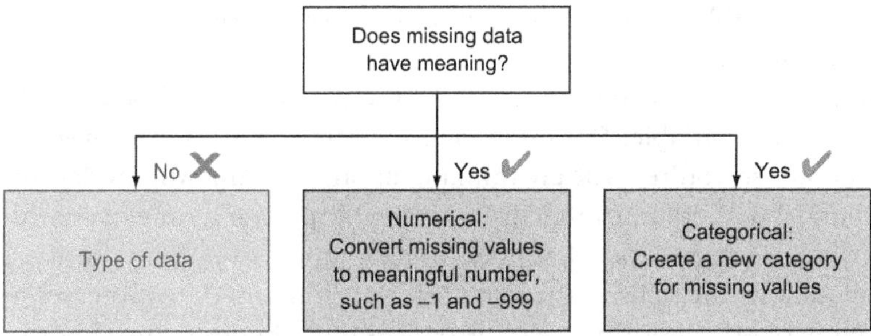

Figure 2.8 What to do with meaningful missing data

When the absence of a value for a data item has no informative value in itself, you proceed in a different way. In this case, you can't introduce a special number or category because you might introduce data that's flat-out wrong. For example, if you were to change any missing values in the Age column of the Titanic Passengers dataset to –1, you'd probably hurt the model by messing with the age distribution for no good reason. Some ML algorithms will be able to deal with these truly missing values by ignoring them. If not, you need to preprocess the data to either eliminate missing values or replace them by guessing the true value. This concept of replacing missing data is called *imputation*.

If you have a large dataset and only a handful of missing values, dropping the observations with missing data is the easiest approach. But when a larger portion of your observations contain missing values, the loss of perfectly good data in the dropped observations will reduce the predictive power of your model. Furthermore, if the observations with missing values aren't randomly distributed throughout your dataset, this approach may introduce unexpected bias.

Another simple approach is to assume some temporal order to the data instances and replace missing values with the column value of the preceding row. With no other information, you're making a guess that a measurement hasn't changed from one instance to the next. Needless to say, this assumption will often be wrong, but less wrong than, for example, filling in zeros for the missing values, especially if the data is a series of sequential observations (yesterday's temperature isn't an unreasonable estimate of today's). And for extremely big data, you won't always be able to apply more-sophisticated methods, and these simple methods can be useful.

When possible, it's usually better to use a larger portion of the existing data to guess the missing values. You can replace missing column values by the mean or median value of the column. With no other information, you assume that the average will be closest to the truth. Depending on the distribution of column values, you might want to use the median instead; the mean is sensitive to outliers. These are widely used in machine learning today and work well in many cases. But when you set all missing values to a single new value, you diminish the visibility of potential correlation with other variables that may be important in order for the algorithm to detect certain patterns in the data.

What you want to do, if you can, is use all the data at your disposal to predict the value of the missing variable. Does this sound familiar? This is exactly what machine learning is about, so you're basically thinking about building ML models in order to be able to build ML models. In practice, you'll typically use a simple algorithm (such as linear or logistic regression, described in chapter 3) to impute the missing data. This isn't necessarily the same as the main ML algorithm used. In any case, you're creating a pipeline of ML algorithms that introduces more knobs to turn in order to optimize the model in the end.

Again, it's important to realize that there's no single best way to deal with truly missing data. We've discussed a few ways in this section, and figure 2.9 summarizes the possibilities.

2.2.3 Simple feature engineering

Chapter 5 covers domain-specific and advanced feature-engineering techniques, but it's worth mentioning the basic idea of simple data preprocessing in order to make the model better.

You'll use the Titanic example again in this section. Figure 2.10 presents another look at part of the data, and in particular the Cabin feature. Without processing, the Cabin feature isn't necessarily useful. Some values seem to include multiple cabins, and even a single cabin wouldn't seem like a good categorical feature because all cabins would be separate "buckets." If you want to predict, for example, whether a certain

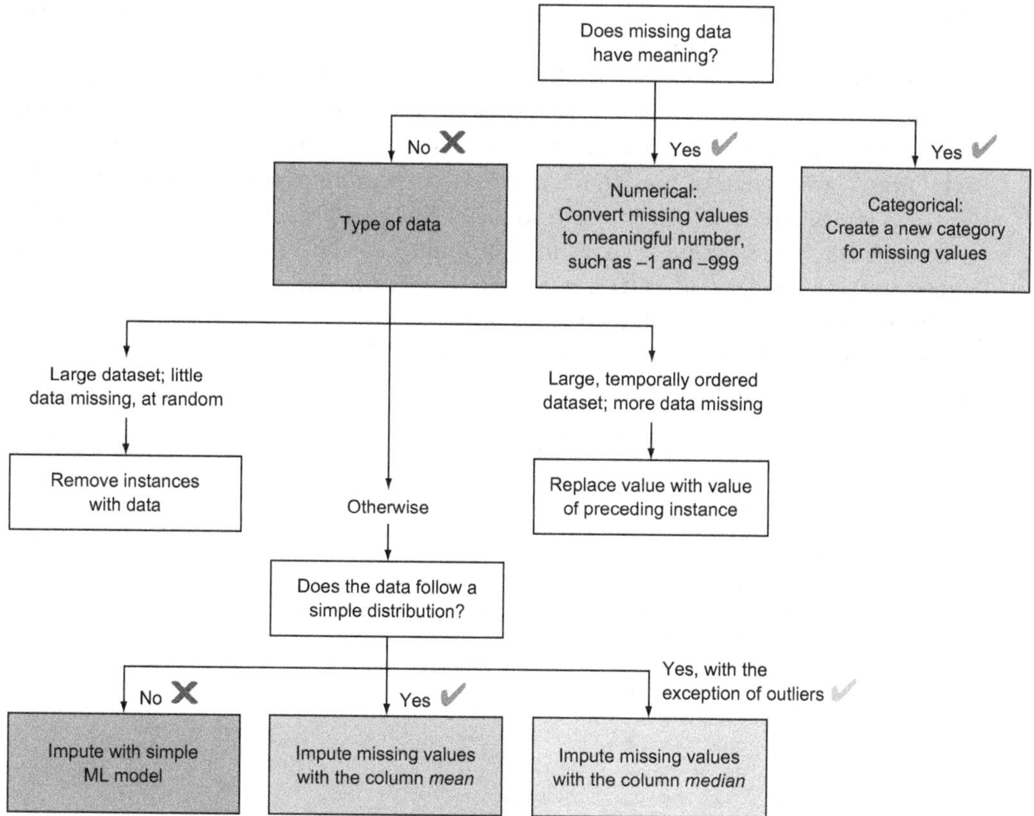

Figure 2.9 Full decision diagram for handling missing values when preparing data for ML modeling

PassengerId	Survived	Pclass	Gender	Age	SibSp	Parch	Ticket	Fare	Cabin	Embarked
1	0	3	Male	22	1	0	A/5 21171	7.25		S
2	1	1	Female	38	1	0	PC 17599	71.2833	C85	C
3	1	3	Female	26	0	0	STON/02. 3101282	7.925		S
4	1	1	Female	35	1	0	113803	53.1	C123	S
5	0	3	Male	35	0	0	373450	8.05		S
6	0	3	Male		0	0	330877	8.4583		Q

Figure 2.10 In the Titanic Passengers dataset, some Cabin values include multiple cabins, whereas others are missing. And cabin identifiers themselves may not be good categorical features.

passenger survived, living in a particular cabin instead of the neighboring cabin may not have any predictive power.

Living in a particular section of the ship, though, could be important for survival. For single cabin IDs, you could extract the letter as a categorical feature and the number as a numerical feature, assuming they denote different parts of the ship. You could even find a layout map of the Titanic and map each cabin to the level and side of the ship, ocean-facing versus interior, and so forth. These approaches don't handle multiple cabin IDs, but because it looks like all multiple cabins are close to each other, extracting only the first cabin ID should be fine. You could also include the number of cabins in a new feature, which could also be relevant.

All in all, you'll create three new features from the Cabin feature. The following listing shows the code for this simple extraction.

Listing 2.2 Simple feature extraction on Titanic cabins

```
def cabin_features(data):
    features = []
    for cabin in data:
        cabins = cabin.split(" ")
        n_cabins = len(cabins)
        # First char is the cabin_char
        try:
            cabin_char = cabins[0][0]
        except IndexError:
            cabin_char = "X"
            n_cabins = 0
        # The rest is the cabin number
        try:
            cabin_num = int(cabins[0][1:])
        except:
            cabin_num = -1
        # Add 3 features for each passanger
        features.append( [cabin_char, cabin_num, n_cabins] )
    return features
```

By now it should be no surprise what we mean by *feature engineering*: using the existing features to create new features that increase the value of the original data by applying our knowledge of the data or domain in question. As mentioned earlier, you'll look at advanced feature-engineering concepts and common types of data that need to be processed to be used by most algorithms. These include free-form text features for things such as web pages or tweets. Other important features can be extracted from images, video, and time-series data as well.

2.2.4 Data normalization

Some ML algorithms require data to be *normalized*, meaning that each individual feature has been manipulated to reside on the same numeric scale. The value range of a feature can influence the importance of the feature compared to other features. If one feature has values between 0 and 10, and another has values between 0 and 1, the weight of the first feature is 10, compared to the second. Sometimes you'll want to force a particular feature weight, but typically it's better to let the ML algorithm figure out the relative weights of the features. To make sure all features are considered equally, you need to normalize the data. Often data is normalized to be in the range from 0 to 1, or from –1 to 1.

Let's consider how this normalization is performed. The following code listing implements this function. For each feature, you want the data to be distributed between a minimum value (typically –1) and a maximum value (typically +1). To achieve this, you divide the data by the total range of the data in order to get the data into the 0–1 range. From here, you can re-extend to the required range (2, in the case of –1 to +1) by multiplying with this transformed value. At last, you move the starting point from 0 to the minimum required value (for example, –1).

Listing 2.3 Feature normalization

```
def normalize_feature(data, f_min=-1.0, f_max=1.0):
    d_min, d_max = min(data), max(data)
    factor = (f_max - f_min) / (d_max - d_min)
    normalized = f_min + (data - d_min)*factor
    return normalized, factor
```

Note that you return both the normalized data and the factor with which the data was normalized. You do this because any new data (for example, for prediction) will have to be normalized in the same way in order to yield meaningful results. This also means that the ML modeler will have to remember how a particular feature was normalized, and save the relevant values (factor and minimum value).

We leave it up to you to implement a function that takes new data, the normalization factor, and the normalized minimum value and reapplies the normalization.

As you expand your data-wrangling toolkit and explore a variety of data, you'll begin to see that each dataset has qualities that make it uniquely interesting, and often challenging. But large collections of data with many variables are hard to fully understand by looking at tabular representations. Graphical data-visualization tools are indispensable for understanding the data from which you hope to extract hidden information.

2.3 Using data visualization

Between data collection/preprocessing and ML model building lies the important step of data visualization. Data visualization serves as a sanity check of the training features and target variable before diving into the mechanics of machine learning and prediction. With simple visualization techniques, you can begin to explore the relationship between the input features and the output target variable, which will guide you in model building and assist in your understanding of the ML model and predictions.

Response variable \ Input feature	Categorical	Numerical
Categorical	Mosaic plots Section 2.3.1	Box plots Section 2.3.2
Numerical	Density plots Section 2.3.3	Scatterplots Section 2.3.4

Figure 2.11 Four visualization techniques, arranged by the type of input feature and response variable to be plotted

Further, visualization techniques can tell you how representative the training set is and inform you of the types of instances that may be lacking.

This section focuses on methods for visualizing the association between the target variable and the input features. We recommend four visualization techniques: mosaic plots, box plots, density plots, and scatter plots. Each technique is appropriate for a different type (numeric or categorical) of input feature and target variable, as shown in figure 2.11.

Further reading

A plethora of books are dedicated to statistical visualization and plotting data. If you'd like to dive deeper into this topic, check out the following:

- The classic textbook *The Visual Display of Quantitative Information* by Edward Tufte (Graphics Press, 2001) presents a detailed look into visualizing data for analysis and presentation.
- For R users, *R Graphics Cookbook* by Winston Chang (O'Reilly, 2013) covers data visualization in R, from the basics to advanced topics, with code samples to follow along.
- For Python users, *Python Data Visualization Cookbook* by Igor Milovanović, Dimitry Foures, and Giuseppe Vettigli (Packt Publishing, 2015) covers the basics to get you up and running with Matplotlib.

2.3.1 Mosaic plots

Mosaic plots allow you to visualize the relationship between two or more categorical variables. Plotting software for mosaic plots is available in R, SAS, Python, and other scientific or statistical programming languages.

To demonstrate the utility of mosaic plots, you'll use one to display the relationship between passenger gender and survival in the Titanic Passengers dataset. The mosaic plot begins with a square whose sides each have length 1. The square is then divided, by vertical lines, into a set of rectangles whose widths correspond to the proportion of the data belonging to each of the categories of the input feature. For example, in the Titanic data, 24% of passengers were female, so you split the unit square along the x-axis into two rectangles corresponding to a width 24% / 76% of the area.

Next, each vertical rectangle is split by horizontal lines into subrectangles whose relative areas are proportional to the percent of instances belonging to each category of the response variable. For example, of Titanic passengers who were female, 74% survived (this is the *conditional probability* of survival, given that the passenger was female). Therefore, the Female rectangle is split by a horizontal line into two subrectangles that contain 74% / 26% of the area of the rectangle. The same is repeated for the Male rectangle (for males, the breakdown is 19% / 81%).

What results is a quick visualization of the relationship between gender and survival. If there is no relationship, the horizontal splits would occur at similar locations on the y-axis. If a strong relationship exists, the horizontal splits will be far apart. To enhance the visualization, the rectangles are shade-coded to assess the statistical significance of the relationship, compared to independence of the input feature and response variable, with large negative residuals ("lower count than expected") shaded dark gray, and large positive residuals ("higher count than expected") shaded light gray; see figure 2.12.

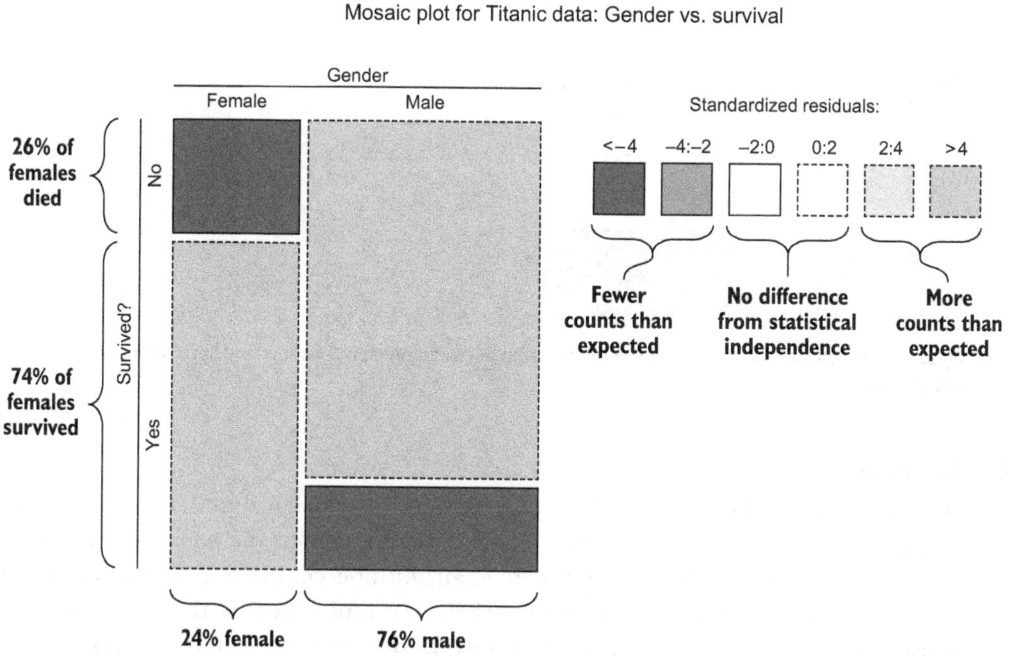

Figure 2.12 Mosaic plot showing the relationship between gender and survival on the Titanic. The visualization shows that a much higher proportion of females (and much smaller proportion of males) survived than would have been expected if survival were independent of gender. "Women and children first."

This tells you that when building a machine-learning model to predict survival on the Titanic, gender is an important factor to include. It also allows you to perform a sanity check on the relationship between gender and survival: indeed, it's common knowledge that a higher proportion of women survived the disaster. This gives you an extra layer of assurance that your data is legitimate. Such data visualizations can also help you interpret and validate your machine-learning models, after they've been built.

Figure 2.13 shows another mosaic plot for survival versus passenger class (first, second, and third). As expected, a higher proportion of first-class passengers (and a lower proportion of third-class passengers) survived the sinking. Obviously, passenger class is also an important factor in an ML model to predict survival, and the relationship is exactly as you should expect: higher-class passengers had a higher probability of survival.

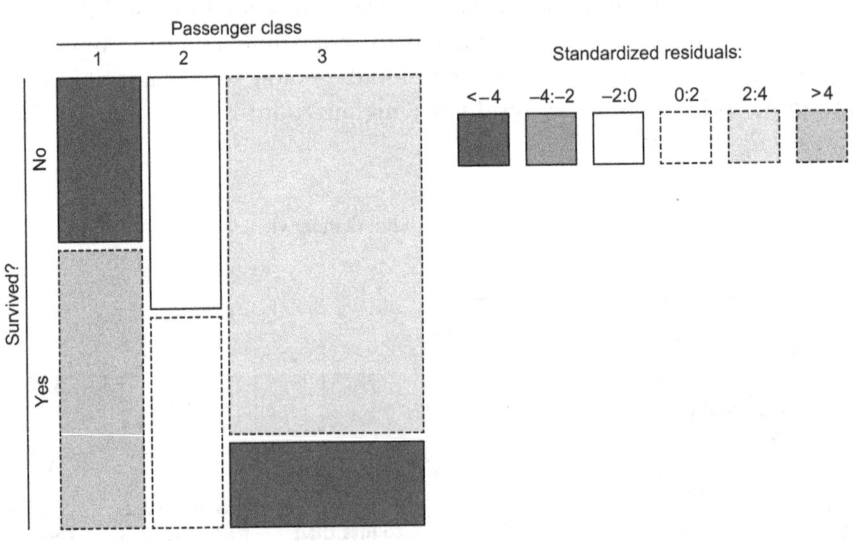

Figure 2.13 Mosaic plot showing the relationship between passenger class and survival on the Titanic

2.3.2 Box plots

Box plots are a standard statistical plotting technique for visualizing the distribution of a numerical variable. For a single variable, a box plot depicts the *quartiles* of its distribution: the minimum, 25th percentile, median, 75th percentile, and maximum of the values. Box-plot visualization of a single variable is useful to get insight into the center, spread, and skew of its distribution of values plus the existence of any outliers.

You can also use box plots to compare distributions when plotted in parallel. In particular, they can be used to visualize the difference in the distribution of a numerical feature as a function of the various categories of a categorical response variable.

Returning to the Titanic example, you can visualize the difference in ages between survivors and fatalities by using parallel box plots, as in figure 2.14. In this case, it's not clear that any differences exist in the distribution of passenger ages of survivors versus fatalities, as the two box plots look fairly similar in shape and location.

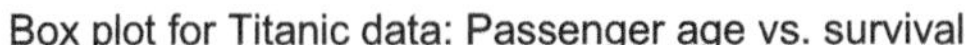

Box plot for Titanic data: Passenger age vs. survival

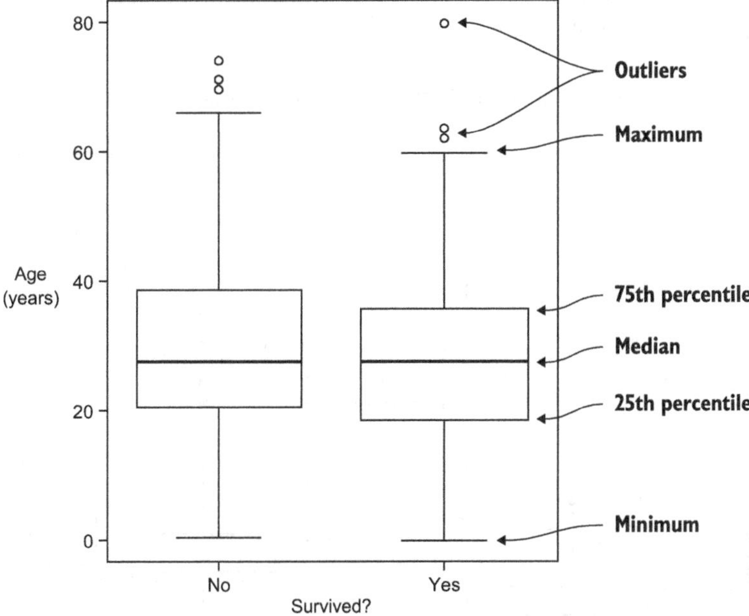

Figure 2.14 Box plot showing the relationship between passenger age and survival on the Titanic. No noticeable differences exist between the age distributions for survivors versus fatalities. (This alone *shouldn't* be a reason to exclude age from the ML model, as it may still be a predictive factor.)

It's important to recognize the limitations of visualization techniques. Visualizations aren't a substitute for ML modeling! Machine-learning models can find and exploit subtle relationships hidden deep inside the data that aren't amenable to being exposed via simple visualizations. You shouldn't automatically exclude features whose visualizations don't show clear associations with the target variable. These features could still carry a strong association with the target when used in association with other input features. For example, although age doesn't show a clear relationship with survival, it could be that for third-class passengers, age is an important predictor (perhaps for third-class passengers, the younger and stronger passengers could make their way to the deck of the ship more readily than older passengers). A good ML model will discover and expose such a relationship, and thus the visualization alone isn't meant to exclude age as a feature.

Figure 2.15 displays box plots exploring the relationship between passenger fare paid and survival outcome. In the left panel, it's clear that the distributions of fare paid are highly skewed (many small values and a few large outliers), making the differences difficult to visualize. This is remedied by a simple transformation of the fare (square root, in the right panel), making the differences easy to spot. Fare paid has an obvious relationship with survival status: those paying higher fares were more likely to survive, as is expected. Thus, fare amount should be included in the model, as you expect the ML model to find and exploit this positive association.

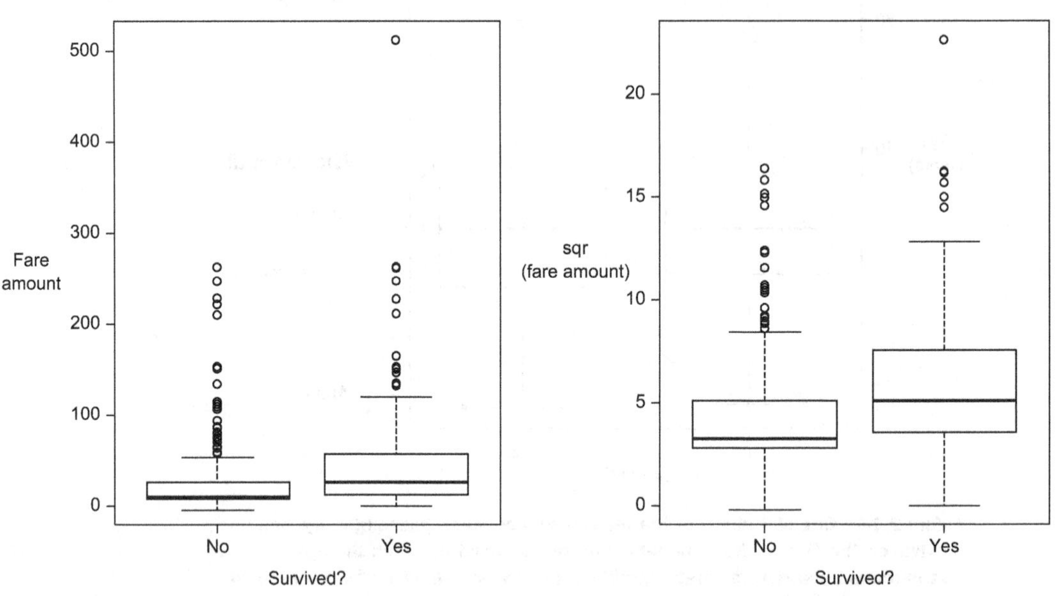

Figure 2.15 Box plots showing the relationship between passenger fare paid and survival on the Titanic. The square-root transformation makes it obvious that passengers who survived paid higher fares, on average.

2.3.3 Density plots

Now, we move to numerical, instead of categorical, response variables. When the input variable is categorical, you can use box plots to visualize the relationship between two variables, just as you did in the preceding section. You can also use density plots.

Density plots display the distribution of a single variable in more detail than a box plot. First, a smoothed estimate of the probability distribution of the variable is estimated (typically using a technique called *kernel smoothing*). Next, that distribution is plotted as a curve depicting the values that the variable is likely to have. By creating a single density plot of the response variable for each category that the input feature takes, you can easily visualize any discrepancies in the values of the response variable for differences in the categorical input feature. Note that density plots are similar to

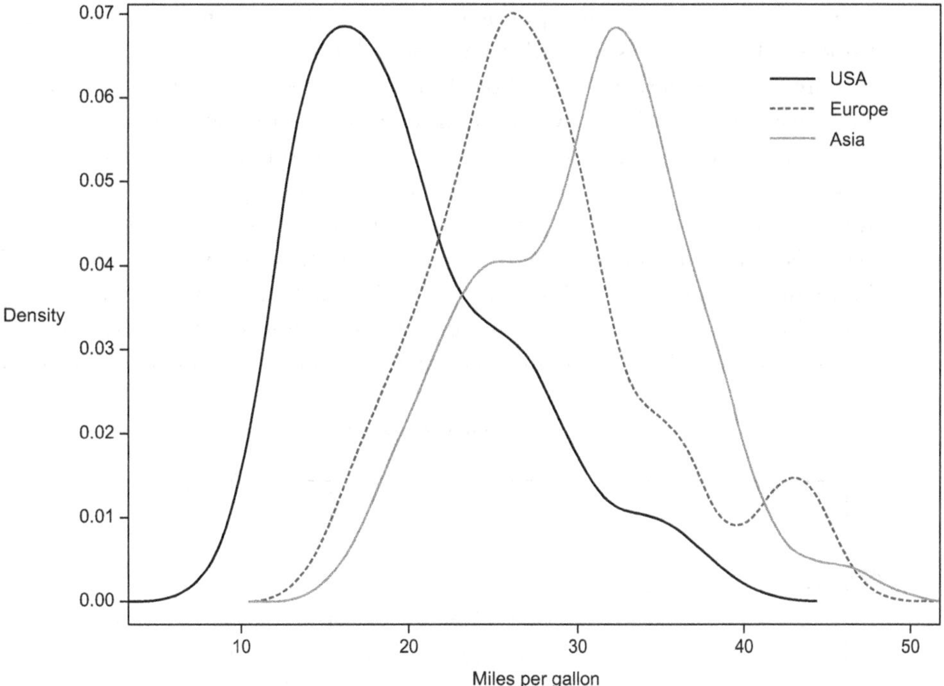

Figure 2.16 Density plot for the Auto MPG dataset, showing the distribution of vehicle MPG for each manufacturer region. It's obvious from the plot that Asian cars tend to have the highest MPG and that cars made in the United States have the lowest. Region is clearly a strong indicator of MPG.

histograms, but their smooth nature makes it much simpler to visualize multiple distributions in a single figure.

In the next example, you'll use the Auto MPG dataset.[2] This dataset contains the miles per gallon (MPG) attained by each of a large collection of automobiles from 1970–82, plus attributes about each auto, including horsepower, weight, location of origin, and model year. Figure 2.16 presents a density plot for MPG versus location of origin (United States, Europe, or Asia). It's clear from the plot that Asian cars tend to have higher MPG, followed by European and then American cars. Therefore, location should be an important predictor in our model. Further, a few secondary "bumps" in the density occur for each curve, which may be related to different types of automobile (for example, truck versus sedan versus hybrid). Thus, extra exploration of these secondary bumps is warranted to understand their nature and to use as a guide for further feature engineering.

[2] The Auto MPG dataset is available at https://archive.ics.uci.edu/ml/datasets/Auto+MPG and is standard in the R programming language, by entering `data(mtcars)`.

2.3.4 Scatter plots

A *scatter plot* is a simple visualization of the relationship between two numerical variables and is one of the most popular plotting tools in existence. In a scatter plot, the value of the feature is plotted versus the value of the response variable, with each instance represented as a dot. Though simple, scatter plots can reveal both linear and nonlinear relationships between the input and response variables.

Figure 2.17 shows two scatter plots: one of car weight versus MPG, and one of car model year versus MPG. In both cases, clear relationships exist between the input features and the MPG of the car, and hence both should be used in modeling. In the left panel is a clear banana shape in the data, showing a nonlinear decrease in MPG for increasing vehicle weight. Likewise, the right panel shows an increasing, linear relationship between MPG and the model year. Both plots clearly indicate that the input features are useful in predicting MPG, and both have the expected relationship.

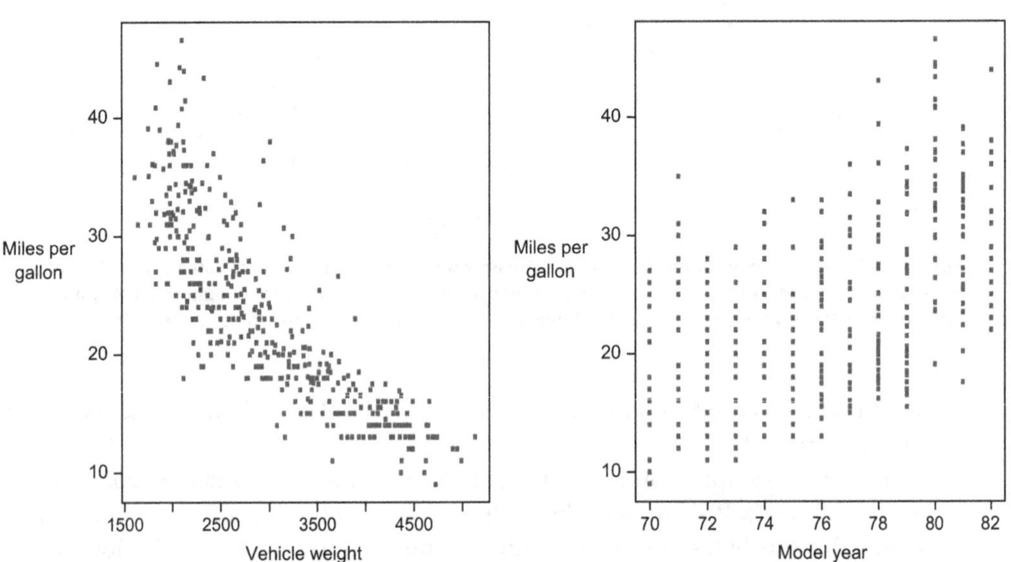

Figure 2.17 Scatter plots for the relationship of vehicle miles per gallon versus vehicle weight (left) and vehicle model year (right)

2.4 Summary

In this chapter, you've looked at important aspects of data in the context of real-world machine learning:

- Steps in compiling your training data include the following:
  - Deciding which input features to include
  - Figuring out how to obtain ground-truth values for the target variable

  - Determining when you've collected enough training data
  - Keeping an eye out for biased or nonrepresentative training data
- Preprocessing steps for training data include the following:
  - Recoding categorical features
  - Dealing with missing data
  - Feature normalization (for some ML approaches)
  - Feature engineering
- Four useful data visualizations are mosaic plots, density plots, box plots, and scatter plots:

		Input Feature	
		Categorical	Numerical
Response Variable	Categorical	Mosaic plots	Box plots
	Numerical	Density plots	Scatter plots

With our data ready for modeling, let's now start building machine-learning models!

2.5 Terms from this chapter

Word	Definition
dummy variable	A binary feature that indicates that an observation is (or isn't) a member of a category
ground truth	The value of a known target variable or label for a training or test set
missing data	Those features with unknown values for a subset of instances
imputation	Replacement of the unknown values of missing data with numerical or categorical values

3 Modeling and prediction

This chapter covers

- Discovering relationships in data through ML modeling
- Using models for prediction and inference
- Building classification models
- Building regression models

The previous chapter covered guidelines and principles of data collection, preprocessing, and visualization. The next step in the machine-learning workflow is to use that data to begin exploring and uncovering the relationships that exist between the input features and the target. In machine learning, this process is done by building statistical models based on the data. This chapter covers the basics required to understand ML modeling and to start building your own models. In contrast to most machine-learning textbooks, we spend little time discussing the various approaches to ML modeling, instead focusing attention on the big-picture concepts. This will help you gain a broad understanding of machine-learning model building and quickly get up to speed on building your own models to solve real-world problems. For those seeking more information about specific ML modeling techniques, please see the appendix.

We begin the chapter with a high-level overview of statistical modeling. This discussion focuses on the big-picture concepts of ML modeling, such as the purpose of models, the ways in which models are used in practice, and a succinct look at types of modeling techniques in existence and their relative strengths and weaknesses. From there, we dive into the two most common machine-learning models: classification and regression. In these sections, we give more details about how to build models on your data. We also call attention to a few of the most common algorithms used in practice in the "Algorithm highlight" boxes scattered throughout the chapter.

3.1 Basic machine-learning modeling

The objective of machine learning is to discover patterns and relationships in data and to put those discoveries to use. This process of discovery is achieved through the use of modeling techniques that have been developed over the past 30 years in statistics, computer science, and applied mathematics. These various approaches can range from simple to tremendously complex, but all share a common goal: to estimate the functional relationship between the input features and the target variable.

These approaches also share a common workflow, as illustrated in figure 3.1: use of historical data to build and optimize a model that is, in turn, used to make predictions based on new data. This section prepares you for the practical sections later in the chapter. You'll look at the general goal of machine learning modeling in the next section, and move on to seeing how the end product can be used and a few important aspects for differentiating between ML algorithms.

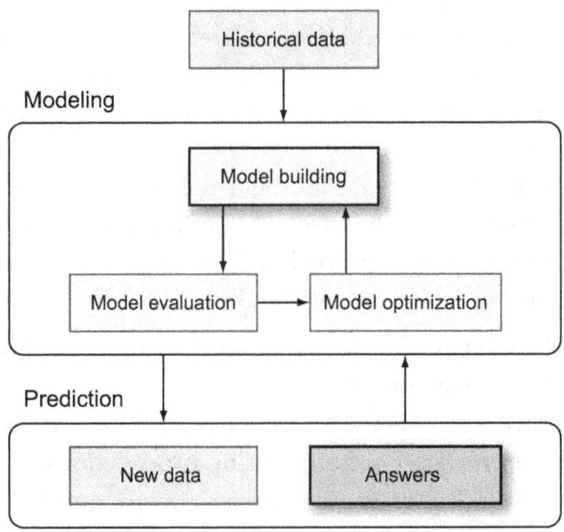

Figure 3.1 The basic ML workflow

3.1.1 Finding the relationship between input and target

Let's frame the discussion of ML modeling around an example. Recall the Auto MPG dataset from chapter 2. The dataset contains metrics about automobiles, such as manufacturer region, model year, vehicle weight, horsepower, and number of cylinders. The purpose of the dataset is to understand the relationship between the input features and a vehicle's miles per gallon (MPG) rating.

Input features are typically referred to using the symbol X, with subscripts differentiating inputs when multiple input features exist. For instance, we'll say that X_1 refers to manufacturer region, X_2 to model year, X_3 to vehicle weight, and so forth. The collection of all the input features is referred to as the bold **X**. Likewise, the target variable is typically referred to as Y.

The relationship between the inputs, **X**, and output, Y, can be succinctly represented by this simple formula:

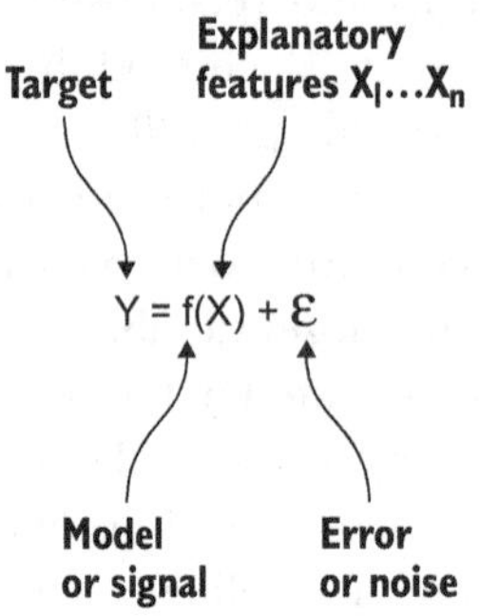

In this equation, f represents the unknown function that relates the input variables to the target, Y. The goal of ML modeling is to accurately estimate f by *using data*. The symbol ε represents random noise in the data that's unrelated to the function f. The function f is commonly referred to as the *signal*, whereas the random variable ε is called the *noise*. The challenge of machine learning is to use data to determine what the true signal is, while ignoring the noise.

In the Auto MPG example, the function f describes the true MPG rating for an automobile as a function of that car's many input features. If you knew that function perfectly, you could know the MPG rating for any car, real or fictional. But you could have numerous sources of noise, ε, including (and certainly not limited to) the following:

- Imperfect measurement of each vehicle's MPG rating caused by small inaccuracies in the measuring devices—measurement noise
- Variations in the manufacturing process, causing each car in the fleet to have slightly different MPG measurements—manufacturing process noise
- Noise in the measurement of the input features, such as weight and horsepower
- Lack of access to the broader set of features that would exactly determine MPG

Using the noisy data that you have from hundreds of vehicles, the ML approach is to use modeling techniques to find a good estimate for f. This resultant estimate is referred to as an *ML model*.

In sections 3.2 and 3.3, we describe in further detail how these ML modeling techniques work. Indeed, the bulk of the academic literature on machine learning deals with how to best estimate f.

3.1.2 The purpose of finding a good model

Assuming that you have a good estimate of f, what next? Machine learning has two main goals: *prediction* and *inference.*

PREDICTION

After you have a model, you can use that model to generate predictions of the target, Y, for new data, $\mathbf{X}_{new}$, by plugging those new features into the model. In mathematical notation, if f_{est} denotes your machine-learning estimate of f (recall that f denotes the true relationship between the features and the target), then predictions for new data can be obtained by plugging the new data into this formula:

$$Y_{pred} = f_{est}(\mathbf{X}_{new})$$

These predictions can then be used to make decisions about the new data or may be fed into an automated workflow.

Going back to the Auto MPG example, suppose that you have an ML model, f_{est}, that describes the relationship between MPG and the input metrics of an automobile. Prediction allows you to ask the question, "What would the MPG of a certain automobile with known input metrics be?" Such a predictive ability would be useful for designing automobiles, because it would allow engineers to assess the MPG rating of different design concepts and to ensure that the individual concepts meet MPG requirements.

Prediction is the most common use of machine-learning systems. Prediction is central to many ML use cases, including these:

- Deciphering handwritten digits or voice recordings
- Predicting the stock market
- Forecasting
- Predicting which users are most likely to click, convert, or buy
- Predicting which users will need product support and which are likely to unsubscribe
- Determining which transactions are fraudulent
- Making recommendations

Because of the high levels of predictive accuracy attained by machine-learning approaches and the rapid speed by which ML predictions can be generated, ML is used every day by thousands of companies for predictive purposes.

INFERENCE

In addition to making predictions on new data, you can use machine-learning models to better understand the relationships between the input features and the output target.

A good estimate of f can enable you to answer deep questions about the associations between the variables at hand. For example:

- Which input features are most strongly related to the target variable?
- Are those relationships positive or negative?
- Is f a simple relationship, or is it a function that's more nuanced and nonlinear?

These inferences can tell you a lot about the data-generating process and give clues to the factors driving relationships in the data. Returning to the Auto MPG example, you can use inference to answer questions such as these: Does manufacturer region have an effect on MPG? Which of the inputs are most strongly related to MPG? And are they negatively or positively related? Answers to these questions can give you an idea of the driving factors in automobile MPG and give clues about how to engineer vehicles with higher MPG.

3.1.3 *Types of modeling methods*

Now the time has come to dust off your statistics knowledge and dive into some of the mathematical details of ML modeling. Don't worry—we'll keep the discussion relatively broad and understandable for those without much of a statistics background!

Statistical modeling has a general trade-off between predictive accuracy and model interpretability. Simple models are easy to interpret, yet won't produce accurate predictions (particularly for complicated relationships). Complex models may produce accurate predictions, but may be black-box and hard to interpret.

In addition, the machine-learning model has two main types: parametric and nonparametric. The essential difference is that parametric models assume that f takes a specific functional form, whereas nonparametric models don't make such strict assumptions. Therefore, parametric approaches tend to be simple and interpretable, but less accurate. Likewise, nonparametric approaches are usually less interpretable but more accurate across a broad range of problems. Let's take a closer look at both parametric and nonparametric approaches to ML modeling.

PARAMETRIC METHODS

The simplest example of a parametric approach is linear regression. In linear regression, f is assumed to be a linear combination of the numerical values of the inputs. The standard linear regression model is as follows:

$$f(\mathbf{X}) = \beta_0 + X_1 \times \beta_1 + X_2 \times \beta_2 + \ldots$$

In this equation, the unknown parameters, β_0, β_1,... can be interpreted as the intercept and slope parameters (with respect to each of the inputs). When you fit a parametric model to some data, you estimate the best values of each of the unknown parameters. Then you can turn around and plug those estimates into the formula for $f(\mathbf{X})$ along with new data to generate predictions.

Other examples of commonly used parametric models include logistic regression, polynomial regression, linear discriminant analysis, quadratic discriminant analysis, (parametric) mixture models, and naïve Bayes (when parametric density estimation is used). Approaches often used in conjunction with parametric models for model selection purposes include ridge regression, lasso, and principal components regression. Further details about some of these methods are given later in this chapter, and a description of each approach is given in the appendix.

The drawback of parametric approaches is that they make strong assumptions about the true form of the function f. In most real-world problems, f doesn't assume such a simple form, especially when there are many input variables (X). In these situations, parametric approaches will fit the data poorly, leading to inaccurate predictions. Therefore, most real-world approaches to machine learning depend on nonparametric machine-learning methods.

NONPARAMETRIC METHODS

In *nonparametric* models, f doesn't take a simple, fixed function. Instead, the form and complexity of f adapts to the complexity of the data. For example, if the relationship between X and Y is wiggly, a nonparametric approach will choose a function f that matches the curvy patterns. Likewise, if the relationship between the input and output variable is smooth, a simple function f will be chosen.

A simple example of a nonparametric model is a classification tree. A *classification tree* is a series of recursive binary decisions on the input features. The classification tree learning algorithm uses the target variable to learn the optimal series of splits such that the terminal leaf nodes of the tree contain instances with similar values of the target.

Take, for example, the Titanic Passengers dataset. The classification tree algorithm first seeks the best input feature to split on, such that the resulting leaf nodes contain passengers who either mostly lived or mostly died. In this case, the best split is on the sex (male/female) of the passenger. The algorithm continues splitting on other input features in each of the subnodes until the algorithm can no longer detect any good subsequent splits.

Classification trees are nonparametric because the depth and complexity of the tree isn't fixed in advance, but rather is learned from the data. If the relationship between the target variable and the input features is complex and there's a sufficient amount of data, then the tree will grow deeper, uncovering more-nuanced patterns. Figure 3.2 shows two classification trees learned from different subsets of the Titanic Passengers dataset. In the left panel is a tree learned from only 400 passengers: the resultant model is simple, consisting of only a single split. In the right panel is a tree learned from 891 passengers: the larger amount of data enables the model to grow in complexity and find more-detailed patterns in the data.

Other examples of nonparametric approaches to machine learning include k-nearest neighbors, splines, basis expansion methods, kernel smoothing, generalized additive models, neural nets, bagging, boosting, random forests, and support vector machines. Again, more details about some of these methods are given later in this chapter, and a description of each approach is given in the appendix.

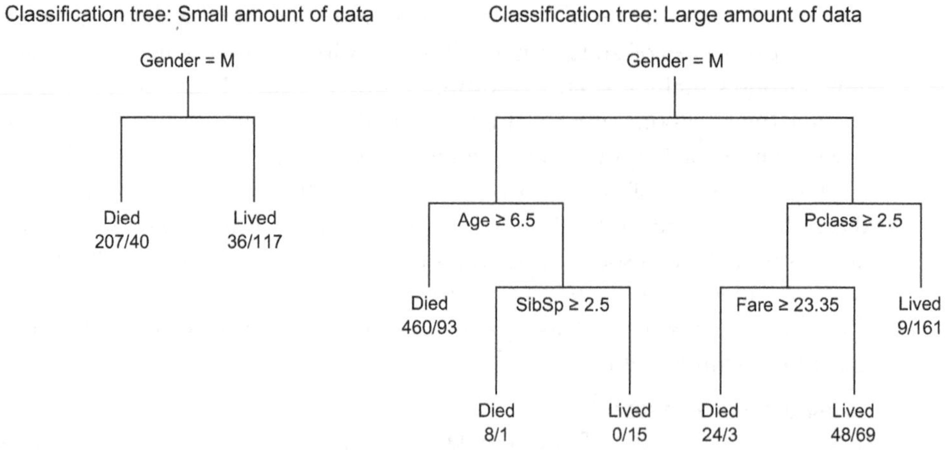

Classification tree: Small amount of data

Gender = M

Died 207/40

Lived 36/117

Classification tree: Large amount of data

Gender = M

Age ≥ 6.5

Pclass ≥ 2.5

Died 460/93

SibSp ≥ 2.5

Fare ≥ 23.35

Lived 9/161

Died 8/1

Lived 0/15

Died 24/3

Lived 48/69

Figure 3.2 A decision tree is an example of a nonparametric ML algorithm, because its functional form isn't fixed. The tree model can grow in complexity with larger amounts of data to capture more-complicated patterns. In each terminal node of the tree, the ratio represents the number of training instances in that node that died versus lived.

3.1.4 Supervised versus unsupervised learning

Machine-learning problems fall into two camps: supervised and unsupervised. *Supervised problems* are ones in which you have access to the target variable for a set of training data, and *unsupervised problems* are ones in which there's no identified target variable.

All the examples so far in this book fall in the supervised camp. These problems each contain a target of interest (Did the Titanic passenger survive? Did the customer churn? What's the MPG?) and a set of training data with known values of the target. Indeed, most problems in machine learning are supervised in nature, and most ML techniques are designed to solve supervised problems. We spend the vast majority of this book describing how to solve supervised problems.

In unsupervised learning, you have access to only input features, and don't have an associated target variable. So what kinds of analyses can you perform if there's no target available? The unsupervised learning approach has two main classes:

- *Clustering*—Use the input features to discover natural groupings in the data and to divide the data into those groups. Methods: k-means, Gaussian mixture models, and hierarchical clustering.
- *Dimensionality reduction*—Transform the input features into a small number of coordinates that capture most of the variability of the data. Methods: principal component analysis (PCA), multidimensional scaling, manifold learning.

Both clustering and dimensionality reduction have wide popularity (particularly, k-means and PCA), yet are often abused and used inappropriately when a supervised approach is warranted.

But unsupervised problems do play a significant role in machine learning, often in support of supervised problems, either to help compile training data for learning or to derive new input features on which to learn. You'll return to the topic of unsupervised learning in chapter 8.

Now, let's transition to the more practical aspects of ML modeling. Next we describe the steps needed to start building models on your own data and the practical considerations of choosing which algorithm to use. We break up the rest of the chapter into two sections corresponding to the two most common problems in machine learning: classification and regression. We begin with the topic of classification.

3.2 Classification: predicting into buckets

In machine learning, *classification* describes the prediction of new data into buckets (classes) by using a *classifier* built by the machine-learning algorithm. Spam detectors put email into Spam and No Spam buckets, and handwritten digit recognizers put images into buckets from 0 through 9, for example. In this section, you'll learn how to build classifiers based on the data at hand. Figure 3.3 illustrates the process of classification.

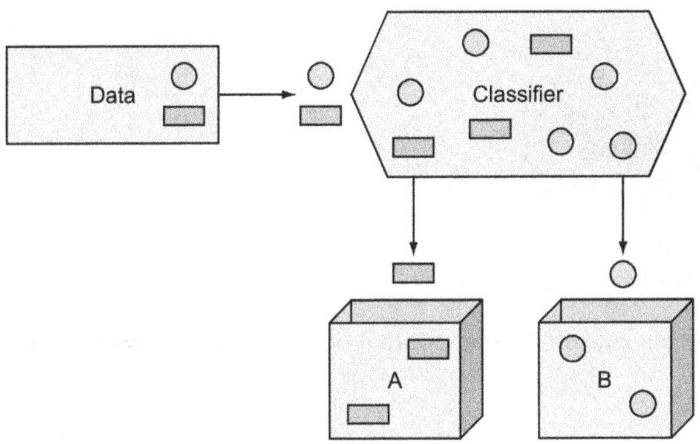

Figure 3.3 A classification process. Rectangles and circles are divided by a classifier into classes A and B. This is a case of binary classification with only two classes.

Let's again use an example. In chapter 2, you looked at the Titanic Passengers dataset for predicting survival of passengers onboard the ill-fated ship. Figure 3.4 shows a subset of this data.

PassengerId	Survived	Pclass	Gender	Age	SibSp	Parch	Ticket	Fare	Cabin	Embarked
1	0	3	Male	22	1	0	A/5 21171	7.25		S
2	1	1	Female	38	1	0	PC 17599	71.2833	C85	C
3	1	3	Female	26	0	0	STON/02. 3101282	7.925		S
4	1	1	Female	35	1	0	113803	53.1	C123	S
5	0	3	Male	35	0	0	373450	8.05		S
6	0	3	Male		0	0	330877	8.4583		Q

Figure 3.4 A subset of the Titanic Passengers dataset

As we've previously discussed, typically the best way to start an ML project is to get a feel for the data by visualizing it. For example, it's considered common knowledge that more women than men survived the Titanic, and you can see that this is the case from the mosaic plot in figure 3.5 (if you've forgotten about mosaic plots, look back at section 2.3.1).

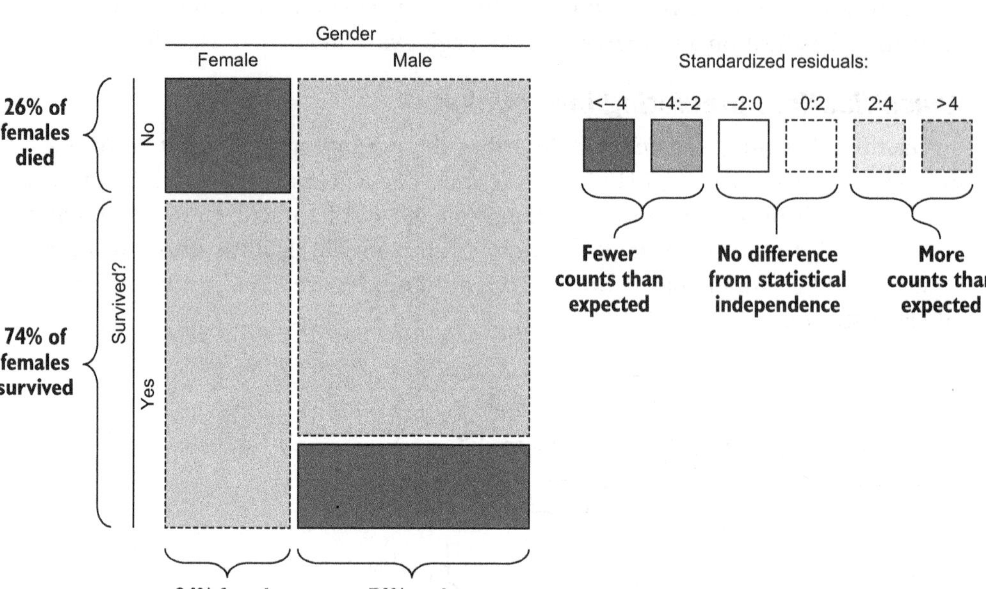

Figure 3.5 Mosaic plot showing overwhelming support for the idea that more women than men survived the disaster.

By using the visualization techniques in section 2.3, you can get a feeling for the performance of each feature in the Titanic Passengers dataset. But it's important to realize that just because a single feature looks good or bad, it doesn't necessarily show the performance of the feature in combination with one or more other features. Maybe the age together with the sex and social status divides the passengers much better than any single feature. In fact, this is one of the main reasons to use machine-learning algorithms in the first place: to find signals in many dimensions that humans can't discover easily.

The following subsections introduce the methodology for building classification models and making predictions. You'll look at a few specific algorithms and the difference between linear and nonlinear algorithms.

3.2.1 Building a classifier and making predictions

The first order of business is to choose the classification algorithm to use for building the classifier. Many algorithms are available, and each has pros and cons for different data and deployment requirements. The appendix provides a table of algorithms and a comparison of their properties. You'll use this table throughout the book for selecting algorithms to try for different problems. In this section, the choice of algorithm isn't essential; in the next chapter, you'll learn how to properly measure the performance of the algorithm and choose the best for the job.

The next step is to ready the data for modeling. After exploring some of the features in the dataset, you may want to preprocess the data to deal with categorical features, missing values, and so on (as discussed in chapter 2). The preprocessing requirements are also dependent on the specific algorithm, and the appendix lists these requirements for each algorithm.

For the Titanic survival model, you'll start by choosing a simple classification algorithm: logistic regression.[1] For logistic regression, you need to do the following:

1. Impute missing values.
2. Expand categorical features.
3. From chapter 2, you know that the Fare feature is heavily skewed. In this situation, it's advantageous (for some ML models) to transform the variable to make the feature distribution more symmetric and to reduce the potentially harmful impact of outliers. Here, you'll choose to transform Fare by taking the square root.

The final dataset that you'll use for modeling is shown in figure 3.6.

Pclass	Age	SibSp	Parch	sqrt_Fare	Gender = female	Gender = male	Embarked = C	Embarked = Q	Embarked = S
3	22	1	0	2.692582	0	1	0	0	1
1	38	1	0	8.442944	1	0	1	0	0
3	26	0	0	2.815138	1	0	0	0	1
1	35	1	0	7.286975	1	0	0	0	1
3	35	0	0	2.837252	0	1	0	0	1

Figure 3.6 The first five rows of the Titanic Passengers dataset after processing categorical features and missing values, and transforming the Fare variable by taking the square root (see the `prepare_data` function in the source code repository). All features are now numerical, which is the preferred format for most ML algorithms.

You can now go ahead and build the model by running the data through the logistic regression algorithm. This algorithm is implemented in the scikit-learn Python package, and the model-building and prediction code look like the following listing.

[1] The *regression* in logistic regression doesn't mean it's a regression algorithm. Logistic regression expands linear regression with a logistic function to make it suitable for classification.

Listing 3.1 Building a logistic regression classifier with scikit-learn

```
from sklearn.linear_model import LogisticRegression as Model

def train(features, target):
  model = Model()
  model.fit(features, target)
  return model

def predict(model, new_features):
  preds = model.predict(new_features)
  return preds

# Assume Titanic data is loaded into titanic_feats,
# titanic_target and titanic_test
model = train(titanic_feats, titanic_target)
predictions = predict(model, titanic_test)
```

Annotations:
- Imports the logistic regression algorithm
- Fits the logistic regression algorithm using features and target data
- Makes predictions on a new set of features using the model
- Returns the model built by the algorithm
- Returns predictions (0 or 1)

After building the model, you predict the survival of previously unseen passengers based on their features. The model expects features in the format given in figure 3.6, so any new passengers will have to be run through exactly the same processes as the training data. The output of the `predict` function will be 1 if the passenger is predicted to survive, and 0 otherwise.

It's useful to visualize the classifier by plotting the decision boundary. Given two of the features in the dataset, you can plot the boundary that separates surviving passengers from the dead, according to the model. Figure 3.7 shows this for the Age and square-root Fare features.

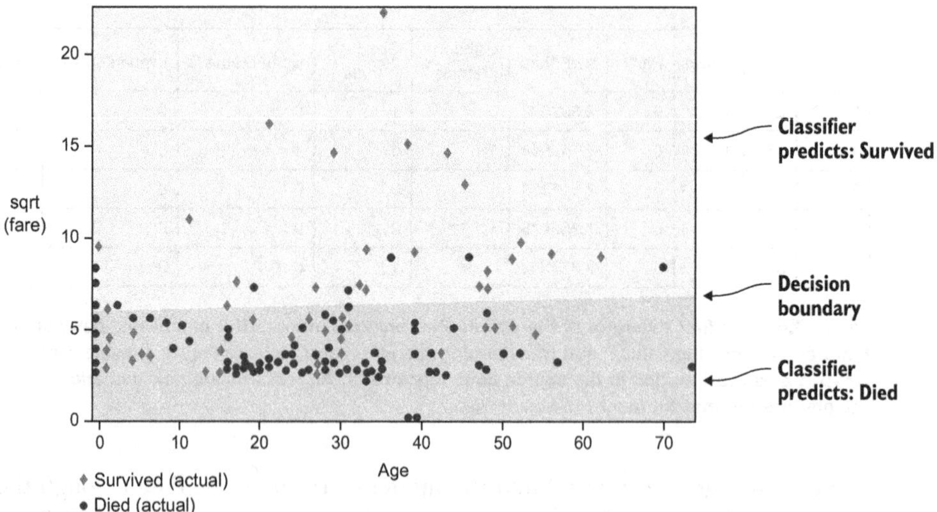

Figure 3.7 The decision boundary for the Age and sqrt(Fare) features. The diamonds show passengers who survived, whereas circles denote passengers who died. The light background denotes the combinations of Age and Fare that are predicted to yield survival. Notice that a few instances overlap the boundary. The classifier isn't perfect, but you're looking in only two dimensions. The algorithm on the full dataset finds this decision boundary in 10 dimensions, but that becomes harder to visualize.

Algorithm highlight: logistic regression

In these "Algorithm highlight" boxes, you'll take a closer look at the basic ideas behind the algorithms used throughout the book. This allows curious readers to try to code up, with some extra research, basic working versions of the algorithms. Even though we focus mostly on the use of existing packages in this book, understanding the basics of a particular algorithm can sometimes be important to fully realize the predictive potential.

The first algorithm you'll look at is the *logistic regression algorithm*, arguably the simplest ML algorithm for classification tasks. It's helpful to think about the problem as having only two features and a dataset divided into two classes. Figure 3.7 shows an example, with the features Age and sqrt(Fare); the target is Survived or Died. To build the classifier, you want to find the line that best splits the data into the target classes. A line in two dimensions can be described by two parameters. These two numbers are the parameters of the model that you need to determine.

The algorithm then consists of the following steps:

1. You can start the search by picking the parameter values at random, hence placing a random line in the two-dimensional figure.
2. Measure how well this line separates the two classes. In logistic regression, you use the statistical *deviance* for the goodness-of-fit measurement.
3. Guess new values of the parameters and measure the separation power.
4. Repeat until there are no better guesses. This is an *optimization* procedure that can be done with a range of optimization algorithms. Gradient descent is a popular choice for a simple optimization algorithm.

This approach can be extended to more dimensions, so you're not limited to two features in this model. If you're interested in the details, we strongly encourage you to research further and try to implement this algorithm in your programming language of choice. Then look at an implementation in a widely used ML package. We've left out plenty of details, but the preceding steps remain the basis of the algorithm.

Some properties of logistic regression include the following:

- The algorithm is relatively simple to understand, compared to more-complex algorithms. It's also computationally simple, making it scalable to large datasets.
- The performance will degrade if the decision boundary that separates the classes needs to be highly nonlinear. See section 3.2.2.
- Logistic regression algorithms can sometimes overfit the data, and you often need to use a technique called *regularization* that limits this danger. See section 3.2.2 for an example of overfitting.

Further reading

If you want to learn more about logistic regression and its use in the real world, check out *Applied Logistic Regression* by David Hosmer et al. (Wiley, 2013).

3.2.2 Classifying complex, nonlinear data

Looking at figure 3.7, you can understand why logistic regression is a linear algorithm: the decision boundary is a straight line. Of course, your data might not be well separated by a straight line, so for such datasets you should use a nonlinear algorithm. But nonlinear algorithms are typically more demanding computationally and don't scale well to large datasets. You'll look further at the scalability of various types of algorithms in chapter 8.

Looking again at the appendix, you can pick a nonlinear algorithm for modeling the Titanic Passengers dataset. A popular method for nonlinear problems is a support vector machine with a nonlinear kernel. Support vector machines are linear by nature, but by using a kernel, this model becomes a powerful nonlinear method. You can change a single line of code in listing 3.1 to use this new algorithm, and the decision boundary is plotted in figure 3.8:

```
from sklearn.svm import SVC as Model
```

You can see that the decision boundary in figure 3.8 is different from the linear one in figure 3.7. What you see here is a good example of an important concept in machine learning: overfitting. The algorithm is capable of fitting well to the data, almost at the single-record level, and you risk losing the ability to make good predictions on new data that wasn't included in the training set; the more complex you allow the model to become, the higher the risk of overfitting.

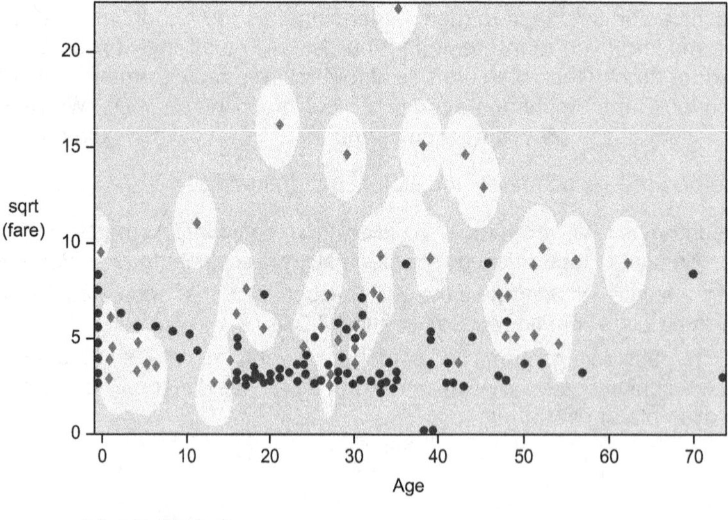

Figure 3.8 Nonlinear decision boundary of the Titanic survival support vector machine classifier with a nonlinear kernel. The light background denotes the combinations of Age and Fare that are predicted to yield survival.

Usually, you can avoid overfitting a nonlinear model by using model parameters built into the algorithm. By tweaking the parameters of the model, keeping the data unchanged, you can obtain a better decision boundary. Note that you're currently using intuition to determine when something is overfitting; in chapter 4, you'll learn how to use data and statistics to quantify this intuition. For now, you'll use our (the authors') experience and tweak a certain parameter called *gamma*. You don't need to know what gamma is at this point, only that it helps control the risk of overfitting. In chapter 5, you'll see how to optimize the model parameters without only guessing at better values. Setting gamma = 0.1 in the SVM classifier, you obtain the much improved decision boundary shown in figure 3.9.

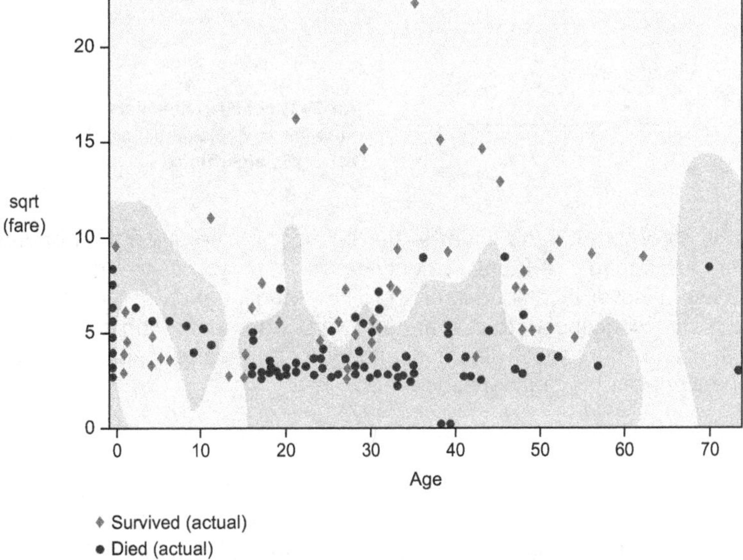

Figure 3.9 Decision boundary of nonlinear RBF-kernel SVM with gamma = 0.1

> **Algorithm highlight: support vector machines**
>
> The support vector machine (SVM) algorithm is a popular choice for both linear and nonlinear problems. It has some interesting theoretical and practical properties that make it useful in many scenarios.
>
> The main idea behind the algorithm is, as with logistic regression discussed previously, to find the line (or equivalent in higher dimensions) that separates the classes optimally. Instead of measuring the distance to all points, SVMs try to find the largest *margin* between only the points on either side of the decision line. The idea is that there's no reason to worry about points that are well within the boundary, only ones that are close. In the following image, you can see that lines H_1 and H_2 are bad separation

(continued)

boundaries, because the distance to the closest point on both sides of the line isn't the largest it can be. H_3 is the optimal line.

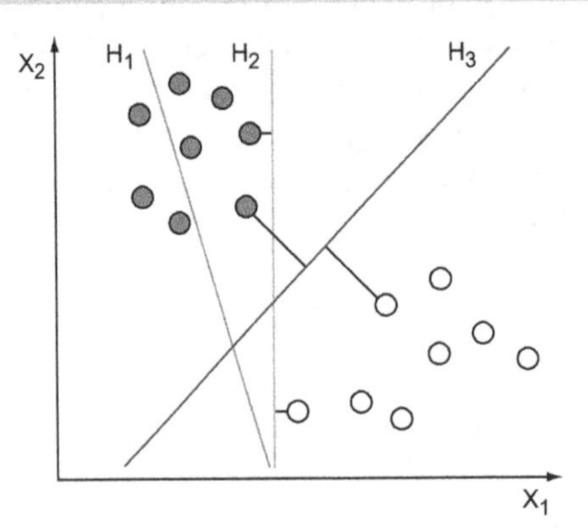

An SVM decision boundary (H_3) is often superior to decision boundaries found by other ML algorithms.

Although this algorithm is also linear in the sense that the separation boundary is linear, SVMs are capable of fitting to nonlinear data, as you saw earlier in this section. SVMs use a clever technique in order to fit to nonlinear data: the kernel trick. A *kernel* is a mathematical construct that can "warp" the space where the data lives. The algorithm can then find a linear boundary in this warped space, making the boundary nonlinear in the original space.

Further reading

Hundreds of books have been written about machine-learning algorithms, covering everything from their theoretical foundation and efficient implementation to their practical use. If you're looking for a more rigorous treatment of these topics, we recommend two classic texts on ML algorithms:

- *The Elements of Statistical Learning: Data Mining, Inference, and Prediction* by Trevor Hastie et al. (Springer, 2009).
- *Pattern Recognition and Machine Learning* by Christopher Bishop (Springer, 2007).

3.2.3 Classifying with multiple classes

Up to this point, you've looked at classification into only two classes. In some cases, you'll have more than two classes. A good real-world example of multiclass classification is the handwritten digit recognition problem. Whenever you send old-school mail to your family, a robot reads the handwritten ZIP code and determines where to send the letter, and good digit recognition is essential in this process. A public dataset, the

MNIST database,[2] is available for research into these types of problems. This dataset consists of 60,000 images of handwritten digits. Figure 3.10 shows a few of the handwritten digit images.

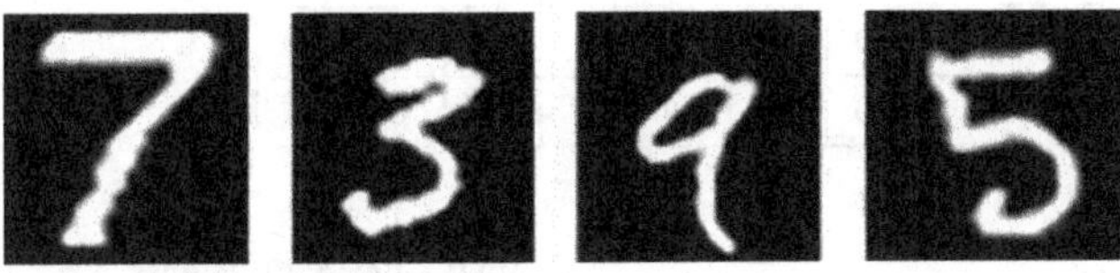

Figure 3.10 Four randomly chosen handwritten digits from the MNIST database

The images are 28 × 28 pixels each, but we convert each image into $28^2 = 784$ features, one feature for each pixel. In addition to being a multiclass problem, this is also a high-dimensional problem. The pattern that the algorithm needs to find is a complex combination of many of these features, and the problem is nonlinear in nature.

To build the classifier, you first choose the algorithm to use from the appendix. The first nonlinear algorithm on the list that natively supports multiclass problems is the k-nearest neighbors classifier, which is another simple but powerful algorithm for nonlinear ML modeling. You need to change only one line in listing 3.1 to use the new algorithm, but you'll also include a function for getting the full prediction probabilities instead of just the final prediction:

```
from sklearn.neighbors import KNeighborsClassifier as Model

def predict_probabilities(model, new_features):
  preds = model.predict_proba(new_features)
  return preds
```

Building the k-nearest neighbors classifier and making predictions on the four digits shown in figure 3.10, you obtain the table of probabilities shown in figure 3.11.

You can see that the predictions for digits 1 and 3 are spot on, and there's only a small (10%) uncertainty for digit 4. Looking at the second digit (3), it's not surprising that this is hard to classify perfectly. This is the main reason to get the full probabilities in the first place: to be able to take action on things that aren't perfectly certain. This is easy to understand in the case of a post office robot routing letters; if the robot is sufficiently uncertain about some digits, maybe we should have a good old human look at it before we send it out wrong.

[2] You can find the MNIST Database of Handwritten Digits at http://yann.lecun.com/exdb/mnist/.

	Actual value	0	1	2	3	4	5	6	7	8	9
Digit 1	7	0	0	0	0.0	0	0.0	0	1	0	0.0
Digit 2	3	0	0	0	0.7	0	0.2	0	0	0	0.1
Digit 3	9	0	0	0	0.0	0	0.0	0	0	0	1.0
Digit 4	5	0	0	0	0.0	0	0.9	0	0	0	0.1

Predicted digit

Digit 2 has a probability of 0.2 of being 5.

Figure 3.11 Table of predicted probabilities from a k-nearest neighbors classifier, as applied to the MNIST dataset

Algorithm highlight: k-nearest neighbors

The *k-nearest neighbors algorithm* is a simple yet powerful nonlinear ML method. It's often used when model training should be quick, but predictions are typically slower. You'll soon see why this is the case.

The basic idea is that you can classify a new data record by comparing it with similar records from the training set. If a dataset record consists of a set of numbers, n_i, you can find the *distance* between records via the usual distance formula:

$$d = \sqrt{n_1^2 + n_2^2 \cdots + n_n^2}.$$

When making predictions on new records, you find the *closest* known record and assign that class to the new record. This would be a 1-nearest neighbor classifier, as you're using only the closest neighbor. Usually you'd use 3, 5, or 9 neighbors and pick the class that's most common among neighbors (you use odd numbers to avoid ties).

The training phase is relatively quick, because you index the known records for fast distance calculations to new data. The prediction phase is where most of the work is done, finding the closest neighbors from the entire dataset.

The previous simple example uses the usual Euclidean distance metric. You can also use more-advanced distance metrics, depending on the dataset at hand.

K-nearest neighbors is useful not only for classification, but for regression as well. Instead of taking the most common class of neighbors, you take the average or median values of the target values of the neighbors. Section 3.3 further details regression.

3.3 Regression: predicting numerical values

Not every machine-learning problem is about putting records into classes. Sometimes the target variable takes on numerical values—for example, when predicting dollar values in a financial model. We call the act of predicting numerical values *regression*, and the model itself a *regressor*. Figure 3.12 illustrates the concept of regression.

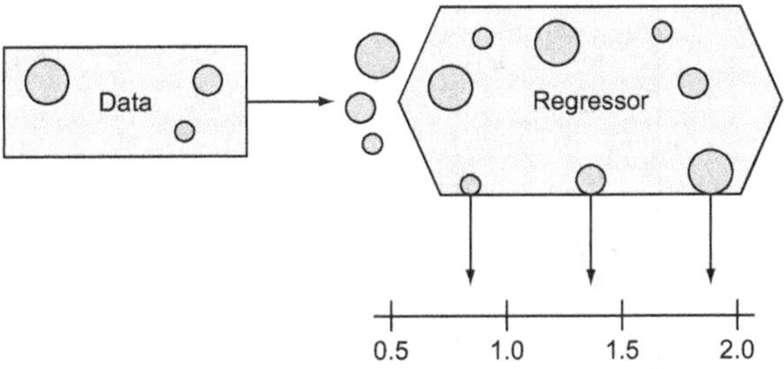

Figure 3.12 In this regression process, the regressor is predicting the numerical value of a record.

As an example of a regression analysis, you'll use the Auto MPG dataset introduced in chapter 2. The goal is to build a model that can predict the average miles per gallon of a car, given various properties of the car such as horsepower, weight, location of origin, and model year. Figure 3.13 shows a small subset of this data.

	MPG	Cylinders	Displacement	Horsepower	Weight	Acceleration	Model/year	Origin
0	18	8	307	130	3504	12.0	70	1
1	15	8	350	165	3693	11.5	70	1
2	18	8	318	150	3436	11.0	70	1
3	16	8	304	150	3433	12.0	70	1
4	17	8	302	140	3449	10.5	70	1

Figure 3.13 Small subset of the Auto MPG data

In chapter 2, you discovered useful relationships between the MPG rating, the car weight, and the model year. These relationships are shown in figure 3.14.

In the next section, you'll look at how to build a basic linear regression model to predict the miles per gallon values of this dataset of vehicles. After successfully building a basic model, you'll look at more-advanced algorithms for modeling nonlinear data.

3.3.1 *Building a regressor and making predictions*

Again, you'll start by choosing an algorithm to use and getting the data into a suitable format. Arguably, the linear regression algorithm is the simplest regression algorithm. As the name indicates, this is a linear algorithm, and the appendix shows the data preprocessing needed in order to use this algorithm. You need to (1) impute missing values and (2) expand categorical features. Our Auto MPG dataset has no missing values,

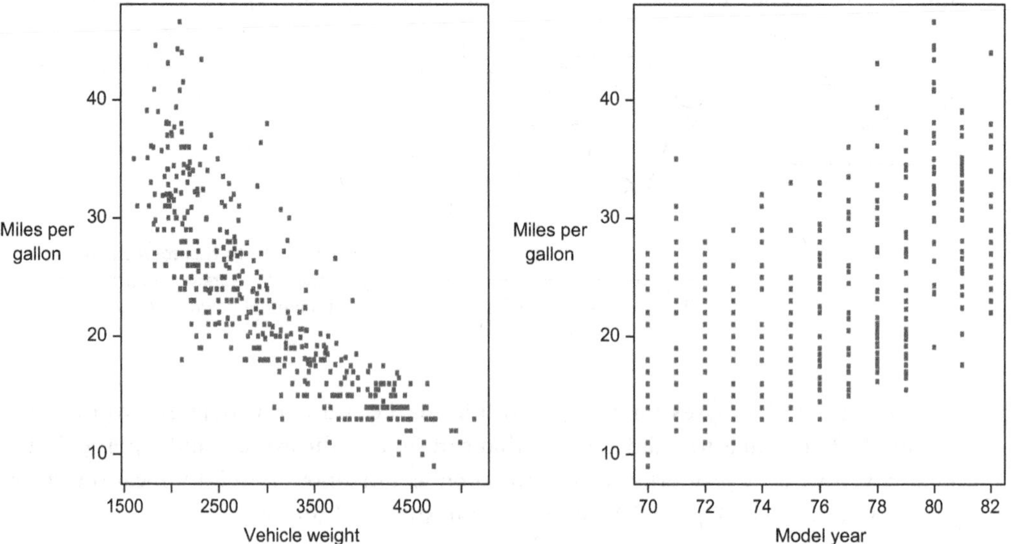

Figure 3.14 Using scatter plots, you can see that Vehicle Weight and Model Year are useful for predicting MPG. See chapter 2 for more details.

but there's one categorical column: Origin. After expanding the Origin column (as described in section 2.2.1 in chapter 2), you obtain the data format shown in figure 3.15.

You can now use the algorithm to build the model. Again, you can use the code structure defined in listing 3.1 and change this line:

```
from sklearn.linear_model import LinearRegression as Model
```

With the model in hand, you can make predictions. In this example, however, you'll split the dataset into a training set and a testing set before building the model. In chapter 4, you'll learn much more about how to evaluate models, but you'll use some

	MPG	Cylinders	Displacement	Horsepower	Weight	Acceleration	Model/year	Origin = 1	Origin = 2	Origin = 3
387	27	4	140	86	2790	15.6	82	1	0	0
388	44	4	97	52	2130	24.6	82	0	1	0
389	32	4	135	84	2295	11.6	82	1	0	0
390	28	4	120	79	2625	18.6	82	1	0	0
391	31	4	119	82	2720	19.4	82	1	0	0

Figure 3.15 The Auto MPG data after expanding the categorical Origin column

simple techniques in this section. By training a model on only some of the data while holding out a testing set, you can subsequently make predictions on the testing set and see how close your predictions come to the actual values. If you were training on all the data and making predictions on some of that training data, you'd be cheating, as the model is more likely to make good predictions if it's seen the data while training.

Figure 3.16 shows the results of making predictions on a held-out testing set, and how they compare to the known values. In this example, you train the model on 80% of the data and use the remaining 20% for testing.

Origin = 1	Origin = 3	Origin = 2	MPG	Predicted MPG
0	0	1	26.0	27.172795
1	0	0	23.8	24.985776
1	0	0	13.0	13.601050
1	0	0	17.0	15.181120
1	0	0	16.9	16.809079

Figure 3.16 Comparing MPG predictions on a held-out testing set to actual values

A useful way to compare more than a few rows of predictions is to use our good friend, the scatter plot, once again. For regression problems, both the actual target values and the predicted values are numeric. Plotting the predictions against each other in a scatter plot, introduced in chapter 2, you can visualize how well the predictions follow the actual values. This is shown for the held-out Auto MPG test set in figure 3.17. This figure

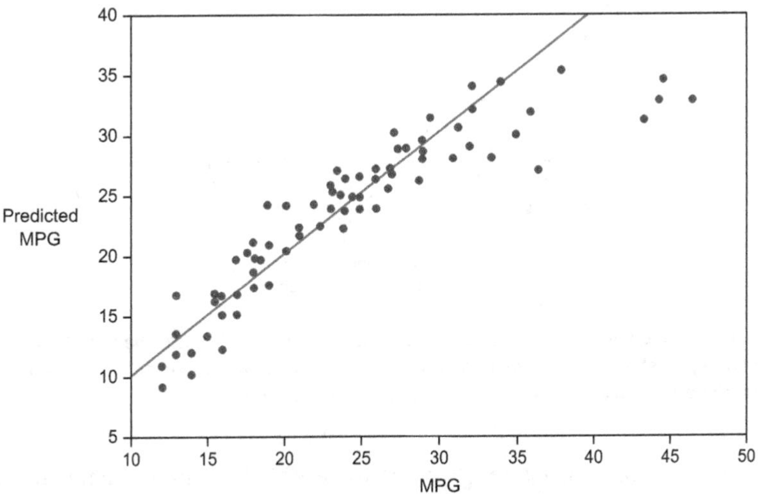

Figure 3.17 A scatter plot of the actual versus predicted values on the held-out test set. The diagonal line shows the perfect regressor. The closer all of the predictions are to this line, the better the model.

shows great prediction performance, as the predictions all fall close to the optimal diagonal line. By looking at this figure, you can get a sense of how your ML model might perform on new data. In this case, a few of the predictions for higher MPG values seem to be underestimated, and this may be useful information for you. For example, if you want to get better at estimating high MPG values, you might need to find more examples of high MPG vehicles, or you might need to obtain higher-quality data in this regime.

Algorithm highlight: linear regression

Like logistic regression for classification, *linear regression* is arguably the simplest and most widely used algorithm for building regression models. The main strengths are linear scalability and a high level of interpretability.

This algorithm plots the dataset records as points, with the target variable on the y-axis, and fits a straight line (or plane, in the case of two or more features) to these points. The following figure illustrates the process of optimizing the distance from the points to the straight line of the model.

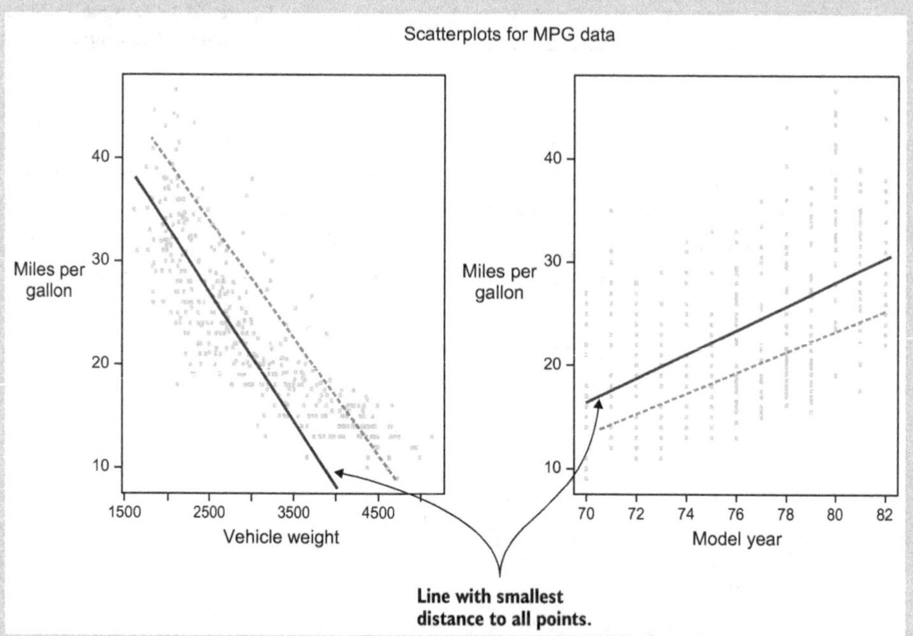

Demonstration of how linear regression determines the best-fit line. Here, the dark line is the optimal linear regression fitted line on this dataset, yielding a smaller mean-squared deviation from the data to any other possible line (such as the dashed line shown).

A straight line can be described by two parameters for lines in two dimensions, and so on. You know this from the a and b in $y = a \times x + b$ from the basic math. These parameters are fitted to the data, and when optimized, they completely describe the model and can be used to make predictions on new data.

3.3.2 *Performing regression on complex, nonlinear data*

In some datasets, the relationship between features can't be fitted by a linear model, and algorithms such as linear regression may not be appropriate if accurate predictions are required. Other properties, such as scalability, may make lower accuracy a necessary trade-off. Also, there's no guarantee that a nonlinear algorithm will be more accurate, as you risk overfitting to the data. As an example of a nonlinear regression model, we introduce the random forest algorithm. Random forest is a popular method for highly nonlinear problems for which accuracy is important. As evident in the appendix, it's also easy to use, as it requires minimal preprocessing of data. In figures 3.18 and 3.19, you can see the results of making predictions on the Auto MPG test set via the random forest model.

Origin = 1	Origin = 3	Origin = 2	MPG	Predicted MPG
0	0	1	26.0	27.1684
1	0	0	23.8	23.4603
1	0	0	13.0	13.6590
1	0	0	17.0	16.8940
1	0	0	16.9	15.5060

Figure 3.18 Table of actual versus predicted MPG values for the nonlinear random forest regression model

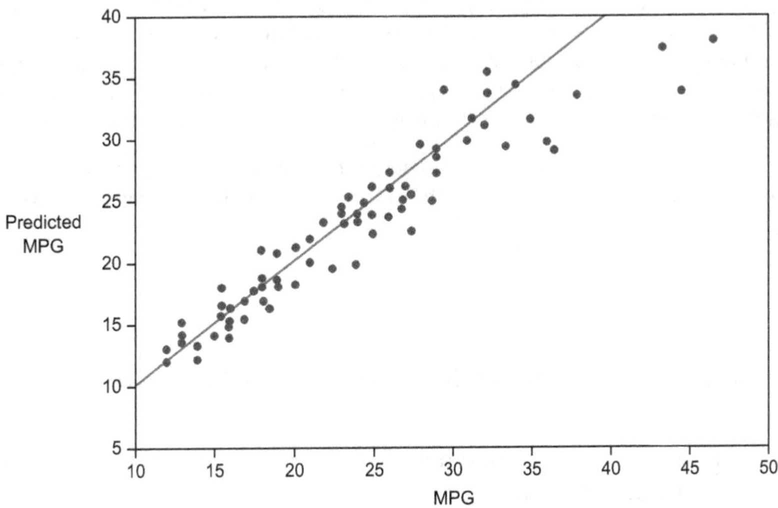

Figure 3.19 Comparison of MPG data versus predicted values for the nonlinear random forest regression model

This model isn't much different from the linear algorithm, at least visually. It's not clear which of the algorithms performs the best in terms of accuracy. In the next chapter, you'll learn how to quantify the performance (often called the *accuracy score* of the model) so you can make meaningful measurements of how good the prediction accuracy is.

Algorithm highlight: random forest

For the last algorithm highlight of this chapter, we introduce the *random forest* (RF) algorithm. This highly accurate nonlinear algorithm is widely used in real-world classification and regression problems.

The basis of the RF algorithm is the decision tree. Imagine that you need to make a decision about something, such as what to work on next. Some variables can help you decide the best course of action, and some variables weigh higher than others. In this case, you might ask first, "How much money will this make me?" If the answer is less than $10, you can choose to not go ahead with the task. If the answer is more than $10, you might ask the next question in the decision tree, "Will working on this make me happy?" and answer with a yes/no. You can continue to build out this tree until you've reached a conclusion and chosen a task to work on.

The decision tree algorithm lets the computer figure out, based on the training set, which variables are the most important, and put them in the top of the tree, and then gradually use less-important variables. This allows it to combine variables and say, "If the amount is greater than $10 and makes me happy, and amount of work less than 1 hour, then yes."

A problem with decision trees is that the top levels of the tree have a huge impact on the answer, and if the new data doesn't follow exactly the same distribution as the training set, the ability to generalize might suffer. This is where the random forest method comes in. By building a collection of decision trees, you mitigate this risk. When making the answer, you pick the majority vote in the case of classification, or take the mean in case of regression. Because you use votes or means, you can also give back full probabilities in a natural way that not many algorithms share.

Random forests are also known for other kinds of advantages, such as their immunity to unimportant features, noisy datasets in terms of missing values, and mislabeled records.

3.4 Summary

In this chapter, we introduced machine-learning modeling. Here we list the main takeaways from the chapter:

- The purpose of modeling is to describe the relationship between the input features and the target variable.
- You can use models either to generate predictions for new data (whose target is unknown) or to infer the true associations (or lack thereof) present in the data.

- There are hundreds of methods for ML modeling. Some are parametric, meaning that the form of the mathematical function relating the features to the target is fixed in advance. Parametric models tend to be more highly interpretable yet less accurate than nonparametric approaches, which are more flexible and can adapt to the true complexity of the relationship between the features and the target. Because of their high levels of predictive accuracy and their flexibility, nonparametric approaches are favored by most practitioners of machine learning.
- Machine-learning methods are further broken into supervised and unsupervised methods. Supervised methods require a training set with a known target, and unsupervised methods don't require a target variable. Most of this book is dedicated to supervised learning.
- The two most common problems in supervised learning are classification, in which the target is categorical, and regression, in which the target is numerical. In this chapter, you learned how to build both classification and regression models and how to employ them to make predictions on new data.
- You also dove more deeply into the problem of classification. Linear algorithms can define linear decision boundaries between classes, whereas nonlinear methods are required if the data can't be separated linearly. Using nonlinear models usually has a higher computational cost.
- In contrast to classification (in which a categorical target is predicted), you predict a numerical target variable in regression models. You saw examples of linear and nonlinear methods and how to visualize the predictions of these models.

3.5 Terms from this chapter

Word	Definition
model	The base product from using an ML algorithm on training data.
prediction	Predictions are performed by pulling new data through the model.
inference	The act of gaining insight into the data by building the model and not making predictions.
(non)parametric	Parametric models make assumptions about the structure of the data. Nonparametric models don't.
(un)supervised	Supervised models, such as classification and regression, find the mapping between the input features and the target variable. Unsupervised models are used to find patterns in the data without a specified target variable.
clustering	A form of unsupervised learning that puts data into self-defined clusters.
dimensionality reduction	Another form of unsupervised learning that can map high-dimensional datasets to a lower-dimensional representation, usually for plotting in two or three dimensions.
classification	A supervised learning method that predicts data into buckets.
regression	The supervised method that predicts numerical target values.

In the next chapter, you'll look at creating and testing models, the exciting part of machine learning. You'll see whether your choice of algorithms and features is going to work to solve the problem at hand. You'll also see how to rigorously validate a model to see how good its predictions are likely to be on new data. And you'll learn about validation methods, metrics, and some useful visualizations for assessing your models' performance.

Model evaluation and optimization

4

This chapter covers

- Using cross-validation for properly evaluating the predictive performance of models
- Overfitting and how to avoid it
- Standard evaluation metrics and visualizations for binary and multiclass classification
- Standard evaluation metrics and visualizations for regression models
- Optimizing your model by selecting the optimal parameters

After you fit a machine-learning model, the next step is to assess the accuracy of that model. Before you can put a model to use, you need to know how well it's expected to predict on new data. If you determine that the predictive performance is quite good, you can be comfortable in deploying that model in production to analyze new data. Likewise, if you assess that the predictive performance isn't good enough for the task at hand, you can revisit your data and model to try to improve and optimize its accuracy. (The last section of this chapter introduces simple model optimization. Chapters 5, 7, and 9 cover more-sophisticated methods of improving the predictive accuracy of ML models.)

Properly assessing the predictive performance of an ML model is a nontrivial task. We begin this chapter by introducing statistically rigorous techniques to evaluate the predictive performance of ML models, demonstrating both pictorially and with pseudocode how to perform correct validation of a model.

From there, we dive into assessment of ML classification models, focusing on the typical evaluation metrics and graphical tools used by machine-learning practitioners. Then we introduce analogous evaluation tools for regression models. Finally, we describe a simple way to optimize the predictive performance of a model through parameter tuning.

By the end of the chapter, you'll be equipped with the means and know-how to evaluate the predictive accuracy of the ML models that you built in chapter 3 and to optimize those models for predictive accuracy (see figure 4.1). This model evaluation provides the information you need to determine whether the model you built is good enough for your use case or requires further optimization.

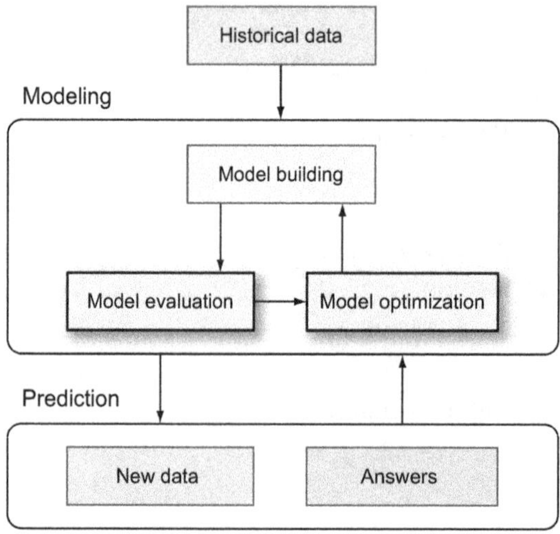

Figure 4.1 Evaluation and optimization in the ML workflow

4.1 Model generalization: assessing predictive accuracy for new data

The primary goal of supervised machine learning is accurate prediction. You want your ML model to be as accurate as possible when predicting on new data (for which the target variable is unknown). Said differently, you want your model, which has been built from training data, to generalize well to new data. That way, when you deploy the model in production, you can be assured that the predictions generated are of high quality.

Therefore, when you evaluate the performance of a model, you want to determine *how well that model will perform on new data.* This seemingly simple task is wrought with complications and pitfalls that can befuddle even the most experienced ML users.

This section describes the difficulties that arise when evaluating ML models and proposes a simple workflow to overcome those menacing issues and achieve unbiased estimates of model performance.

4.1.1 The problem: overfitting and model optimism

To describe the challenges associated with estimating the predictive accuracy of a model, it's easiest to start with an example.

Imagine that you want to predict the production of bushels of corn per acre on a farm as a function of the proportion of that farm's planting area that was treated with a new pesticide. You have training data for 100 farms for this regression problem. As you plot the target (bushels of corn per acre) versus the feature (percent of the farm treated), it's clear that an increasing, nonlinear relationship exists, and that the data also has random fluctuations (see figure 4.2).

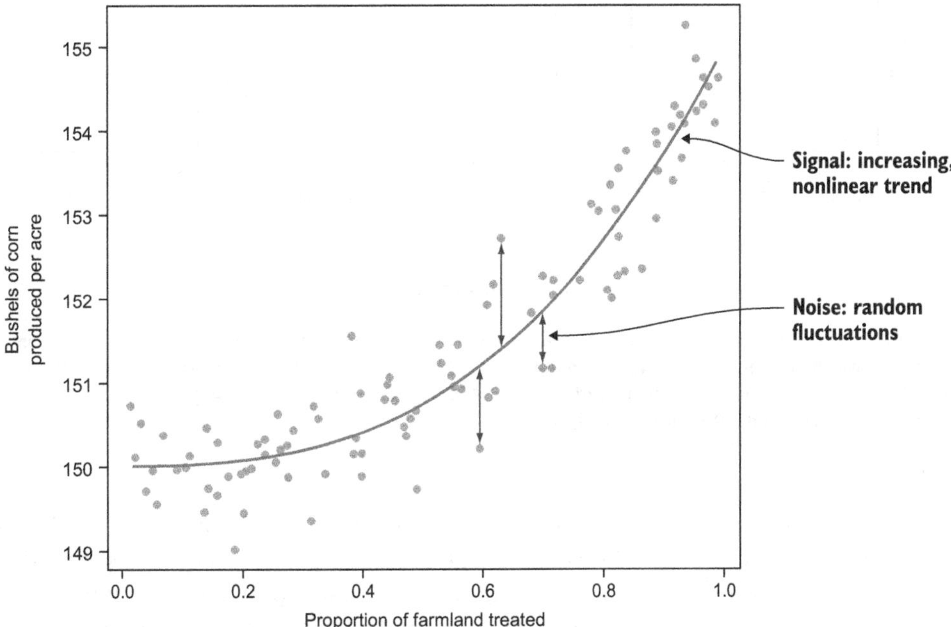

Figure 4.2 The training data for the corn production regression problem contains a clear signal and noise.

Now, suppose you want to use a simple nonparametric ML regression modeling technique to build a predictive model for corn production as a function of proportion of land treated. One of the simplest ML regression models is kernel smoothing. *Kernel smoothing* operates by taking local averages: for each new data point, the value of the target variable is modeled as the average of the target variable for only the training data whose feature value is close to the feature value of the new data point. A single parameter, called the *bandwidth parameter*, controls the size of the window for the local averaging.

Figure 4.3 demonstrates what happens for various values of the kernel-smoothing bandwidth parameters. For large values of the bandwidth, almost all of the training data is averaged together to predict the target, at each value of the input parameter. This causes the model to be flat and to underfit the obvious trend in the training data. Likewise, for small values of the bandwidth, only one or two training instances are used to determine the model output at each feature value. Therefore, the model effectively traces every bump and wiggle in the data. This susceptibility to model the intrinsic noise in the data instead of the true signal is called *overfitting*. Where you want to be is somewhere in the Goldilocks zone: not too underfit and not too overfit.

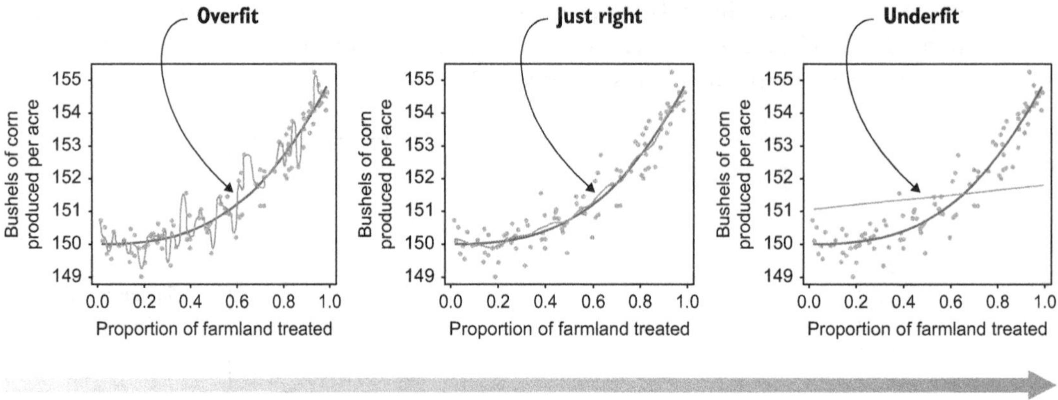

Figure 4.3 Three fits of a kernel-smoothing regression model to the corn production training set. For small values of the bandwidth parameter, the model is overfit, resulting in an overly bumpy model. For large values of the bandwidth parameter, the model is underfit, resulting in a model that's too flat. A good choice of the tuning parameter results in a fit that looks just right.

Now, let's get back to the problem at hand: determining how well your ML model will generalize to predict the corn output from data on different farms. The first step in this process is to select an evaluation metric that captures the quality of your predictions. For regression, the standard metric for evaluation is *mean squared error (MSE)*, which is the average squared difference between the true value of the target variable and the model-predicted value (later in this chapter, you'll learn about other evaluation metrics for regression and classification).

This is where things get tricky. Evaluated on the training set, the error (measured by MSE) of our model predictions gets ever smaller as the bandwidth parameter decreases. This is expected: the more flexibility that you allow the model, the better it'll do at tracing the patterns (both the signal and the noise) in the training data. But the models with smallest bandwidth are severely overfit to the training data because they trace every random fluctuation in the training set. Using these models to predict on new data will result in poor predictive accuracy, because the new data will have its own unique random noise signatures that are different from those in the training set.

Thus, a divergence occurs between the training set error and the generalization error of an ML model. This divergence is exemplified on the corn production data in figure 4.4. For small values of the bandwidth parameter, the MSE evaluated on the training set is extremely small, whereas the MSE evaluated on new data (in this case, 10,000 new instances) is much larger. Simply put, the performance of the predictions of a model evaluated on the training set isn't indicative of the performance of that model on new data. Therefore, it's dangerous to evaluate the performance of a model on the same data that was used to train the model.

> **CAUTION ABOUT DOUBLE-DIPPING THE TRAINING DATA** Using the training data for both model fitting and evaluation purposes can lead you to be overly optimistic about the performance of the model. This can cause you to ultimately choose a suboptimal model that performs poorly when predicting on new data.

As you see in the corn production data, choosing the model with the smallest training set MSE causes the selection of the model with the smallest bandwidth. On the training

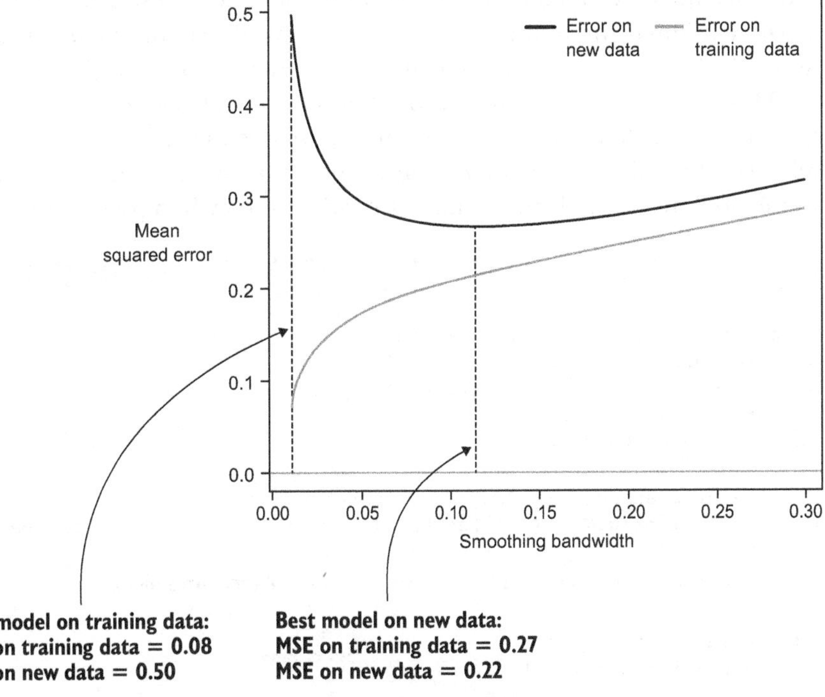

Figure 4.4 Comparison of the training set error to the error on new data for the corn production regression problem. The training set error is an overly optimistic measure of the performance of the model for new data, particularly for small values of the bandwidth parameter. Using the training set error as a surrogate for the prediction error on new data will get you into a lot of trouble.

set, this model yields an MSE of 0.08. But when applied to new data, the same model yields an MSE of 0.50, which is much worse than the optimal model (bandwidth = 0.12 and MSE = 0.27).

You need an evaluation metric that better approximates the performance of the model on new data. This way, you can be confident about the accuracy of your model when deployed to make predictions on new data. This is the topic of the next subsection.

4.1.2 The solution: cross-validation

We've diagnosed the challenge in model evaluation: the training set error isn't indicative of the model error when applied to new data. To get a good estimate of what your error rate will be for new data, you must use a more sophisticated methodology called *cross-validation* (often abbreviated *CV*) that rigorously employs the training set to evaluate what the accuracy will be on new data.

The two most commonly used methods for cross-validation are the holdout method and k-fold cross-validation.

THE HOLDOUT METHOD

Using the same training data to both fit and evaluate the accuracy of a model produces accuracy metrics that are overly optimistic. The easiest way around this is to use separate training and testing subsets. You use only the training subset to fit the model, and only the testing subset to evaluate the accuracy of the model.

This approach is referred to as the *holdout method*, because a random subset of the training data is held out from the training process. Practitioners typically leave out 20–40% of the data as the testing subset. Figure 4.5 depicts the basic algorithmic flow of the holdout method, and listing 4.1 provides the Python pseudocode.

Listing 4.1 Cross-validation with the holdout method

```
# assume that we begin with two inputs:
#    features - a matrix of input features
#    target - an array of target variables corresponding to those features
features = rand(100,5)
target = rand(100) > 0.5

N = features.shape[0] # The total number of instances
N_train = floor(0.7 * N) # The total number of training instances

idx = random.permutation(N)                     <-- Randomizes index

idx_train = idx[:N_train]                       | Splits index
idx_test = idx[N_train:]

features_train = features[idx_train,:]          | Breaks your data
target_train = target[idx_train]                | into training and
features_test = features[idx_test,:]            | testing subsets
target_test = target[idx_test]
```

```
# Build, predict, evaluate (to be filled out)
# model = train(features_train, target_train)
# preds_test = predict(model, features_test)
# accuracy = evaluate_acc(preds_test, target_test)
```

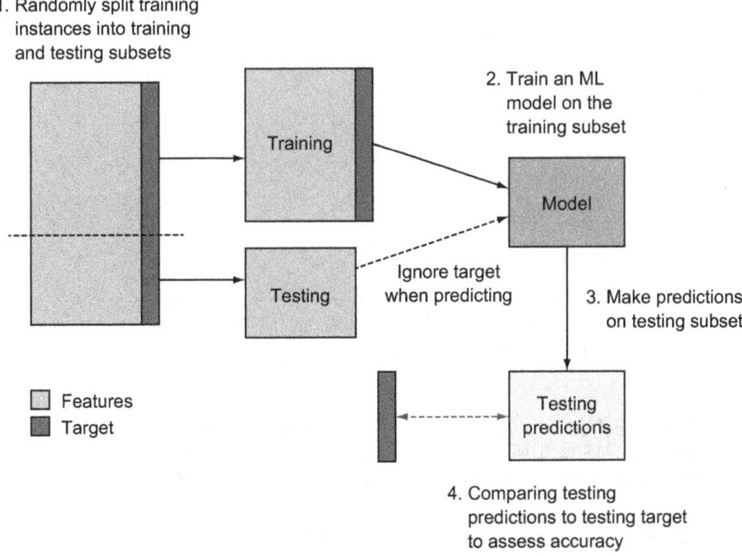

Figure 4.5 Flowchart of the holdout method of cross-validation.

Now, let's apply the holdout method to the corn production data. For each value of the bandwidth parameter, you apply the holdout method (using a 70/30 split) and compute the MSE on the predictions for the held-out 30% of data. Figure 4.6 demonstrates how the holdout method estimates of the MSE stack up to the MSE of the model when applied to new data. Two main things stand out:

- The error estimates computed by the holdout method are close to the new-data error of the model. They're certainly much closer than the training set error estimates (figure 4.4), particularly for small-bandwidth values.
- The holdout error estimates are noisy. They bounce around wildly compared to the smooth curve that represents the error on new data.

You could beat down the noise by doing repeated random training-testing splits and averaging the result. But over multiple iterations, each data point will be assigned to the testing set a different number of times, which could bias the result.

A better approach is to do k-fold cross-validation.

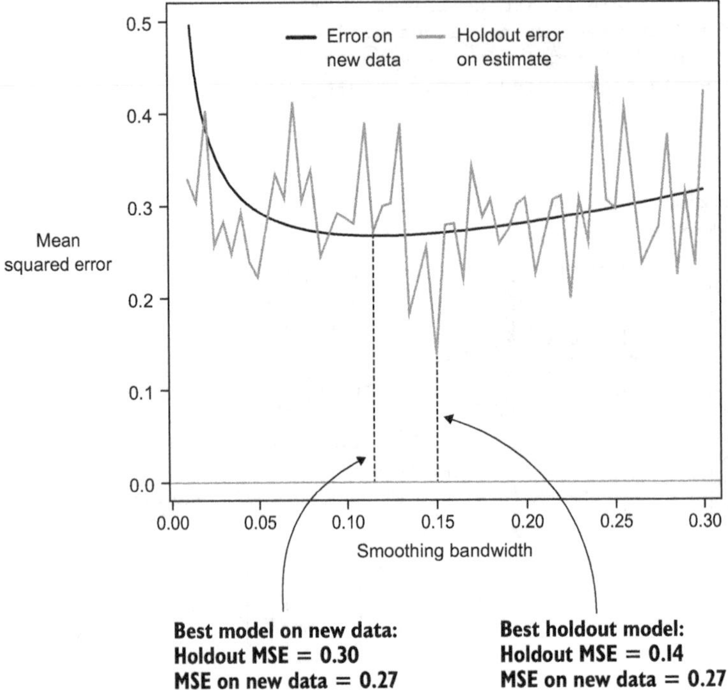

Figure 4.6 Comparison of the holdout error MSE to the MSE on new data, using the corn production dataset. The holdout error is an unbiased estimate of the error of each model on new data. But it's a noisy estimator that fluctuates wildly between 0.14 and 0.40 for bandwidths in the neighborhood of the optimal model (bandwidth = 0.12).

K-FOLD CROSS-VALIDATION

A better but more computationally intensive approach to cross-validation is *k-fold cross-validation*. Like the holdout method, k-fold cross-validation relies on quarantining subsets of the training data during the learning process. The primary difference is that k-fold CV begins by randomly splitting the data into *k* disjoint subsets, called *folds* (typical choices for k are 5, 10, or 20). For each fold, a model is trained on all the data *except* the data from that fold and is subsequently used to generate predictions for the data from that fold.

After all k-folds are cycled through, the predictions for each fold are aggregated and compared to the true target variable to assess accuracy. Figure 4.7 illustrates k-fold cross-validation, and listing 4.2 provides the pseudocode.

Finally, let's apply k-fold cross-validation to the corn production data. For each value of the bandwidth parameter, you apply k-fold cross-validation with k = 10 and compute the cross-validated MSE on the predictions. Figure 4.8 demonstrates how the k-fold cross-validation MSE estimates stack up to the MSE of the model when applied

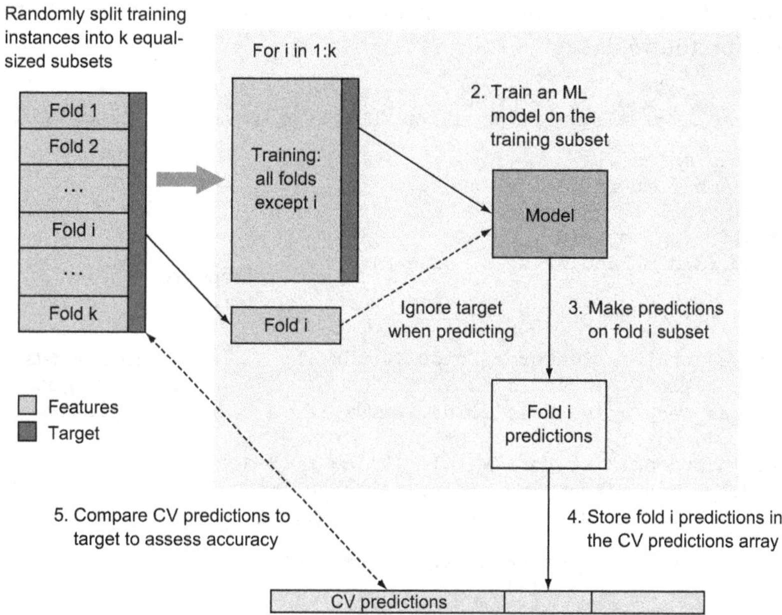

Figure 4.7 Flowchart of k-fold cross-validation

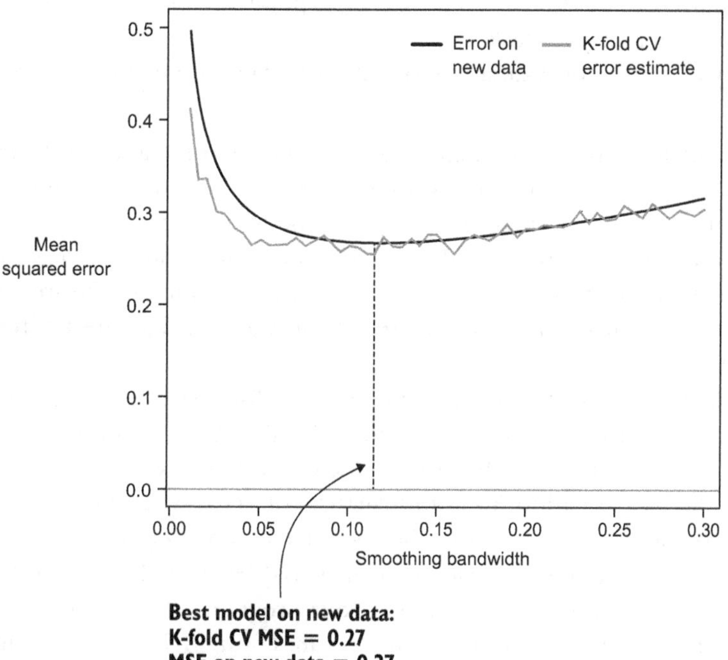

Figure 4.8 Comparison of the k-fold cross-validation error MSE to the MSE on new data, using the corn production dataset. The k-fold CV error is a good estimate for how the model will perform on new data, allowing you to use it confidently to forecast the error of the model and to select the best model.

to new data. Clearly, the k-fold cross-validation error estimate is close to the error of the model on future data.

Listing 4.2 Cross-validation with k-fold cross-validation

```
N = features.shape[0]
K = 10 # number of folds

preds_kfold = np.empty(N)
folds = np.random.randint(0, K, size=N)

for idx in np.arange(K):                          # Loops over the folds

    features_train = features[folds != idx,:]     # Breaks your data
    target_train = target[folds != idx]           # into training and
    features_test = features[folds == idx,:]      # testing subsets

    # Build and predict for CV fold (to be filled out)
    # model = train(features_train, target_train)
    # preds_kfold[folds == idx] = predict(model, features_test)

# accuracy = evaluate_acc(preds_kfold, target)
```

4.1.3 Some things to look out for when using cross-validation

Cross-validation gives you a way to estimate how accurately your ML models will predict when deployed in the wild. This is extremely powerful, because it enables you to select the best model for your task.

But when you apply cross-validation to real-world data, you need to watch out for a few things:

- Cross-validation methods (including both the holdout and k-fold methods) assume that the training data forms a representative sample from the population of interest. If you plan to deploy the model to predict on new data, that data should be well represented by the training data. If not, the cross-validation error estimates may be overly optimistic for the error rates on future data. Solution: Ensure that any potential biases in the training data are addressed and minimized.
- Some datasets use features that are temporal—for instance, using last month's revenue to forecast this month's revenue. If this is the case with your data, you must ensure that features that are available in the future can never be used to predict the past. Solution: You can structure your cross-validation holdout set or k-folds so that all the training set data is collected previous to the testing set.
- The larger the number of folds used in k-fold cross-validation, the better the error estimates will be, but the longer your program will take to run. Solution: Use at least 10 folds (or more) when you can. For models that train and predict quickly, you can use leave-one-out cross-validation (k = number of data instances).

Next, you'll build off of these cross-validation tools and take a deeper look at how to perform rigorous model evaluation for classification models.

4.2 Evaluation of classification models

We begin our discussion of evaluating classification models by presenting problems with only two classes, also known as *binary classification.* Chapter 3 introduced binary classification in machine learning as a powerful method for predicting a positive/negative outcome based on many factors or variables. A good example of binary classification is the detection of diseases or survival predictions.

Imagine that you want to predict whether a Titanic passenger would survive, based on personal, social, and economic factors. You'd gather everything you know about the passengers and train a classifier that could relate all this information to their survival probability. You first saw this example in chapter 2, but the first five rows of the Titanic Passengers dataset is shown again in figure 4.9.

Target column

	PassengerId	Survived	Pclass	Name	Gender	Age	SibSp	Parch	Ticket	Fare	Cabin	Embarked
0	1	0	3	Braund, Mr. Owen Harris	Male	22	1	0	A/5 21171	7.25	NaN	S
1	2	1	1	Cumings, Mrs. John Bradley (Florence Briggs Th...	Female	38	1	0	PC 17599	71.2833	C85	C
2	3	1	3	Helkkinen, Miss Laina	Female	26	0	0	STON/02. 3101282	7.925	NaN	S
3	4	1	1	Futrelle, Mrs. Jacques Heath (Lily May Peel)	Female	35	1	0	113803	53.1	C123	S
4	5	0	3	Allen, Mr. William Henry	Male	35	0	0	373450	8.05	NaN	S

Figure 4.9 The first five rows of the Titanic Passengers dataset. The target column indicates whether a passenger survived the sinking of the ship or died.

To build your classifier, you feed this dataset into a classification algorithm. Because the dataset consists of different types of data, you have to make sure the algorithm knows how to deal with these types. As discussed in the previous chapters, you might need to process the data prior to training the model, but for this chapter you'll view the classifier as a black box that has learned the mapping from the input variables to the target variable. The goal of this section is to evaluate the model in order to optimize the prediction accuracy and compare with other models.

With the data ready, you move to the next task: cross-validation. You'll divide the full dataset into training and testing sets and use the holdout method of cross-validation. The model will be built on a training set and evaluated on a held-out testing set. It's important to reiterate that your goal isn't necessarily to obtain the maximum model accuracy on the training data, but to obtain the highest predictive accuracy on unseen data. In the model-building phase, you're not yet in possession of this data, by definition, so you pretend that some of the training data is hidden for the learning algorithm.

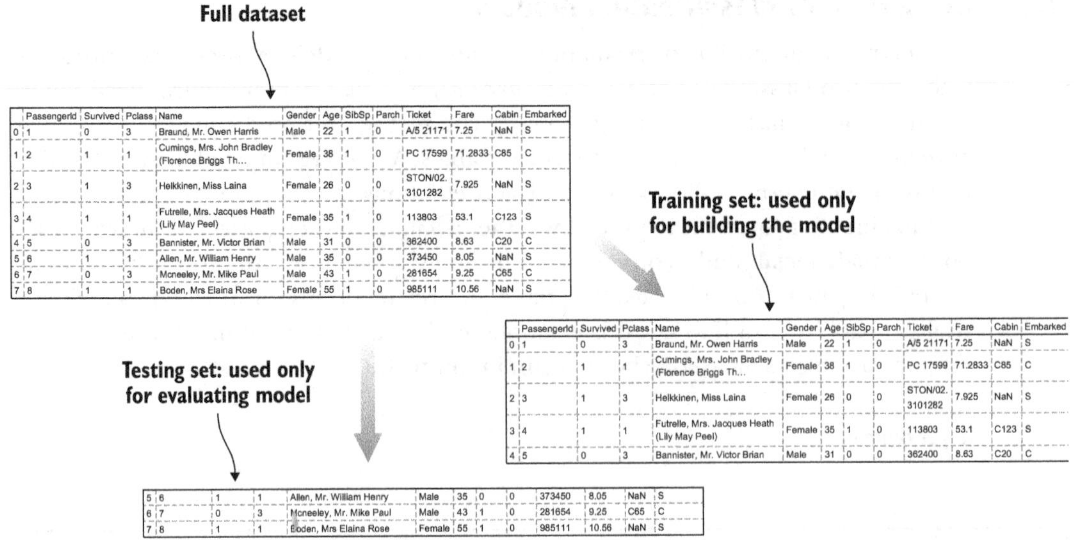

	PassengerId	Survived	Pclass	Name	Gender	Age	SibSp	Parch	Ticket	Fare	Cabin	Embarked
0	1	0	3	Braund, Mr. Owen Harris	Male	22	1	0	A/5 21171	7.25	NaN	S
1	2	1	1	Cumings, Mrs. John Bradley (Florence Briggs Th...	Female	38	1	0	PC 17599	71.2833	C85	C
2	3	1	3	Heikkinen, Miss Laina	Female	26	0	0	STON/O2. 3101282	7.925	NaN	S
3	4	1	1	Futrelle, Mrs. Jacques Heath (Lily May Peel)	Female	35	1	0	113803	53.1	C123	S
4	5	0	3	Bannister, Mr. Victor Brian	Male	31	0	0	362400	8.63	C20	C
5	6	1	1	Allen, Mr. William Henry	Male	35	0	0	373450	8.05	NaN	S
6	7	0	3	Mcneeley, Mr. Mike Paul	Male	43	1	0	281654	9.25	C65	C
7	8	1	1	Boden, Mrs Elaina Rose	Female	55	1	0	985111	10.56	NaN	S

	PassengerId	Survived	Pclass	Name	Gender	Age	SibSp	Parch	Ticket	Fare	Cabin	Embarked
0	1	0	3	Braund, Mr. Owen Harris	Male	22	1	0	A/5 21171	7.25	NaN	S
1	2	1	1	Cumings, Mrs. John Bradley (Florence Briggs Th...	Female	38	1	0	PC 17599	71.2833	C85	C
2	3	1	3	Heikkinen, Miss Laina	Female	26	0	0	STON/O2. 3101282	7.925	NaN	S
3	4	1	1	Futrelle, Mrs. Jacques Heath (Lily May Peel)	Female	35	1	0	113803	53.1	C123	S
4	5	0	3	Bannister, Mr. Victor Brian	Male	31	0	0	362400	8.63	C20	C

5	6	1	1	Allen, Mr. William Henry	Male	35	0	0	373450	8.05	NaN	S
6	7	0	3	Mcneeley, Mr. Mike Paul	Male	43	1	0	281654	9.25	C65	C
7	8	1	1	Boden, Mrs Elaina Rose	Female	55	1	0	985111	10.56	NaN	S

Figure 4.10 Splitting the full dataset into training and testing sets allows you to evaluate the model.

Figure 4.10 illustrates the dataset-splitting step in this particular example.

With the training set ready, you can build the classifier and make predictions on the testing set. Following the holdout method of figure 4.5, you obtain a list of prediction values: 0 (died) or 1 (survived) for all rows in the test set. You then go to step 3 of the evaluation workflow and compare these predictions to the actual survival values to obtain a performance metric that you can optimize.

The simplest performance measure of a classification model is to calculate the fraction of *correct* answers; if three out of four rows were correctly predicted, you'd say the *accuracy* of the model on this particular validation set is 3/4 = 0.75, or 75%. Figure 4.11 illustrates this result. The following sections introduce more-sophisticated ways of performing this comparison.

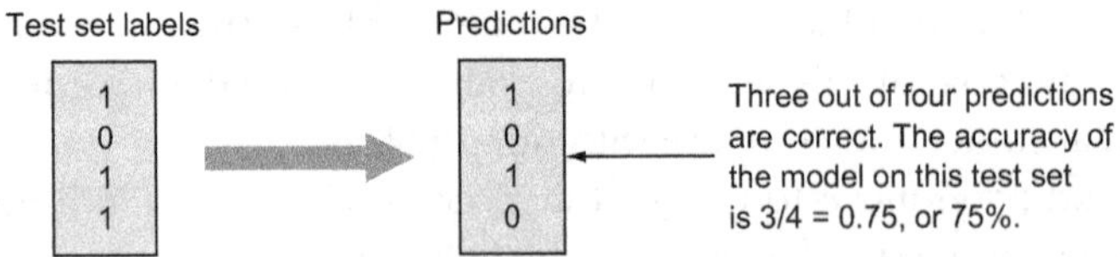

Figure 4.11 Comparing the testing set predictions with the actual values gives you the accuracy of the model.

4.2.1 Class-wise accuracy and the confusion matrix

The predictions provide more information than simply being correct or not. For example, you can analyze the accuracy per class (how many were predicted to survive but actually died or survived). For binary classification, you can be wrong in two ways: predicting 0 when the correct value is 1, or predicting 1 when the correct value is 0. In the same way, you can be correct in two ways. Figure 4.12 illustrates.

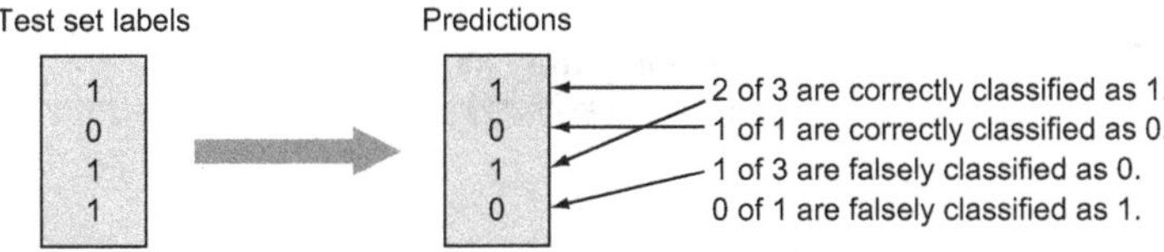

Figure 4.12 Counting the class-wise accuracy and error rate gives you more information on the model accuracy.

In many classification problems, it's useful to go beyond the simple counting accuracy and look at this class-wise accuracy, or class confusion. It turns out to be useful to display these four numbers in a two-by-two diagram called a *confusion matrix*, shown in figure 4.13.

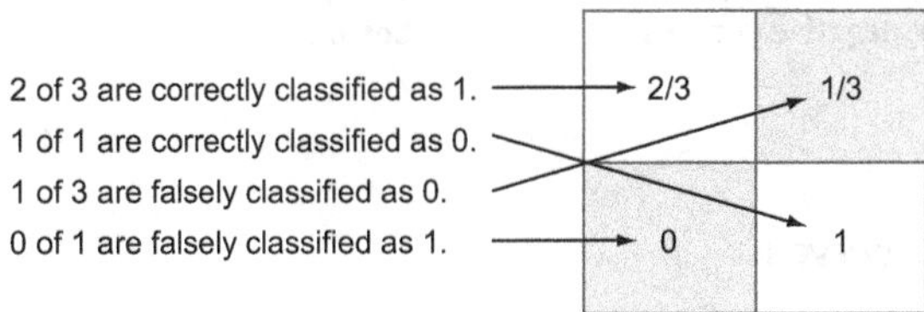

Figure 4.13 Organizing the class-wise accuracy into a confusion matrix

Each element in the matrix shows the class-wise accuracy or confusion between the positive and the negative class. Figure 4.14 relates the specific confusion matrix in figure 4.13 to the general concept of receiver operating characteristics (ROCs) that you'll employ widely throughout the rest of this book. Although these terms can be a bit confusing at first, they'll become important when talking to other people about the performance of your model.

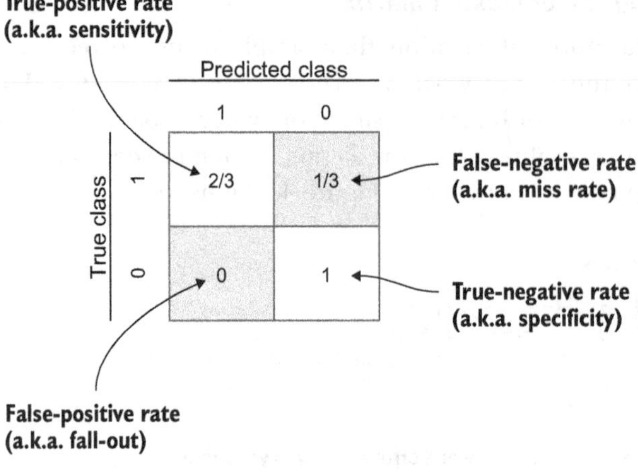

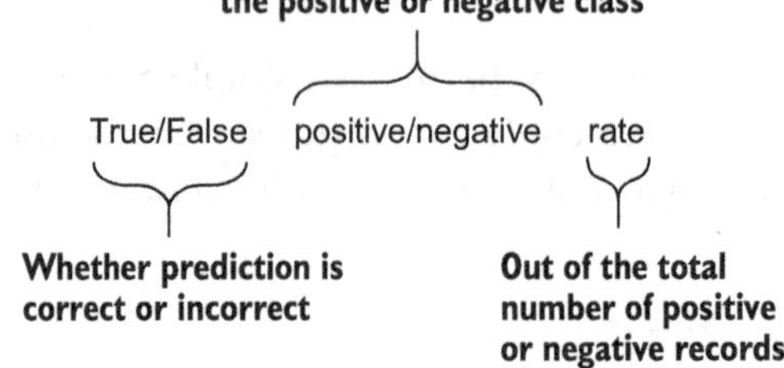

Figure 4.14 The confusion matrix for your binary classifier tested on only four rows. The ROC metrics pointed out in the figure are chopped up and explained in the bottom box.

4.2.2 Accuracy trade-offs and ROC curves

So far you've looked only at predictions for which the output is the predicted class; in our Titanic example, 1 for survival and 0 otherwise. Machine-learning predictions usually hold a degree of uncertainty, and many classification algorithms output not only the zero-one predictions, but the full prediction *probabilities*. For example, what was simply predicted as *survived* in our Titanic model may have had a probability of survival of 0.8, 0.99, or 0.5. It's clear that there's a big difference in the confidence of these answers, and in this section you'll take advantage of this information to evaluate your models in more detail.

The output of a *probabilistic classifier* is what we call the *probability vectors* or *class probabilities*. For every row in the test set, you get a real-valued number from 0 to 1 for every class in the classifier (summing to 1). Until now, you've made predictions by considering probabilities above 0.5 to determine the class predictions, from which you calculated all the performance metrics from the previous section. We say that the *threshold* that determines the class is 0.5. It's clear that you could choose any other threshold and would get different values for all of your metrics.

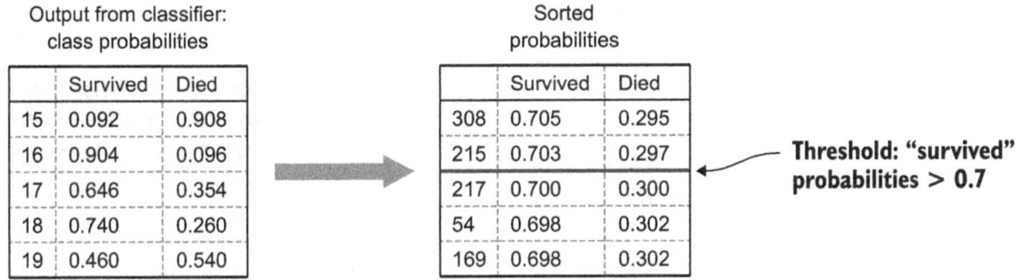

	Survived	Died
15	0.092	0.908
16	0.904	0.096
17	0.646	0.354
18	0.740	0.260
19	0.460	0.540

	Survived	Died
308	0.705	0.295
215	0.703	0.297
217	0.700	0.300
54	0.698	0.302
169	0.698	0.302

Figure 4.15 A subset of probabilistic predictions from the Titanic test set. After sorting the full table by decreasing survival probability, you can set a threshold and consider all rows above this threshold as survived. Note that the indices are maintained so you know which original row the instance refers to.

Figure 4.15 shows the process of sorting the probability vectors and setting a threshold of 0.7. All rows above the line are now predicted to survive, and you can compare these to the actual labels to get the confusion matrix and the ROC metrics at this particular threshold. If you follow this process for all thresholds from 0 to 1, you define the *ROC curve*, shown in figure 4.16.

From figure 4.16, you can read out the confusion matrix at all thresholds, making the ROC curve a powerful visualization tool when you're evaluating classifier performance. Given the true and predicted labels from any cross-validation process, the ROC curve is calculated as shown in listing 4.3.

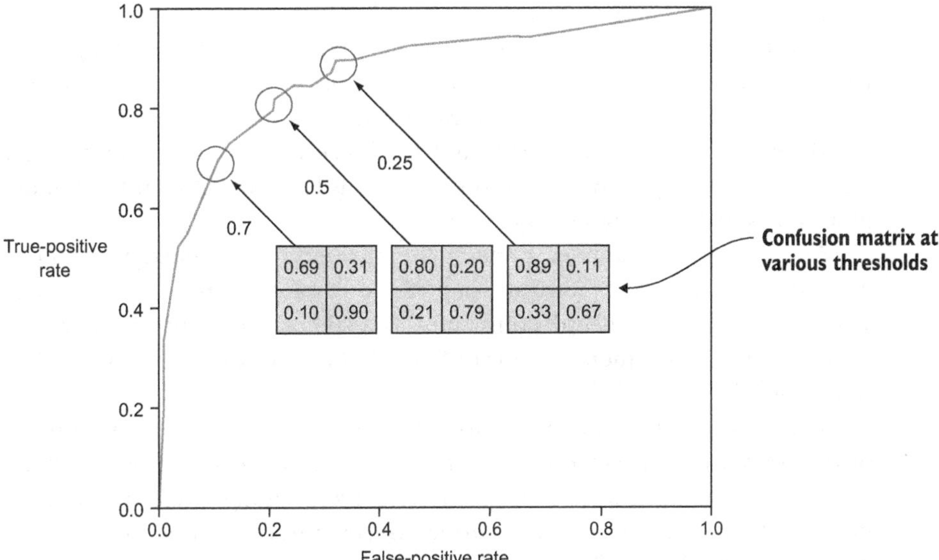

Figure 4.16 The ROC curve defined by calculating the confusion matrix and ROC metrics at 100 threshold points from 0 to 1. By convention, you plot the false-positive rate on the x-axis and the true-positive rate on the y-axis.

Listing 4.3 The ROC curve

```
import numpy as np

def roc_curve(true_labels, predicted_probs, n_points=100, pos_class=1):

  thr = np.linspace(0,1,n_points)
  tpr = np.zeros(n_points)
  fpr = np.zeros(n_points)

  pos = true_labels == pos_class
  neg = np.logical_not(pos)
  n_pos = np.count_nonzero(pos)
  n_neg = np.count_nonzero(neg)

  for i,t in enumerate(thr):
    tpr[i] = np.count_nonzero(np.logical_and(
             predicted_probs >= t, pos)) / n_pos
    fpr[i] = np.count_nonzero(np.logical_and(
             predicted_probs >= t, neg)) / n_neg
  return fpr, tpr, thr
```

Returns the false-positive and true-positive rates at n_points thresholds for the given true and predicted labels

Allocates the threshold and ROC lists

Precalculates values for the positive and negative cases, used in the loop

For each threshold, calculates the rate of true and false positives

If you follow the ROC curve, you see that when the false-positive rate increases, the true-positive rate decreases. This trade-off is the "no free lunch" of machine learning because you're able to sacrifice the fraction of instances that you classify correctly for more certainty that you're correct, and vice versa, depending on your choice of the probability threshold parameter.

In real-world scenarios, this trade-off can be extremely important to evaluate. If you're classifying whether a patient has cancer or not, it's much better to classify a few extra healthy patients as sick, and avoid classifying any sick patients as healthy. So you'd select the threshold that would minimize the false-negative rate, and hence maximize the true-positive rate and place you as far as possible in the top of the ROC plot while sacrificing the false-positive rate.

Another good example is spam filters, where you'll need to choose between unwanted emails being shown in your inbox or wanted emails being dumped in the spam folder. Or credit-card companies detecting fraudulent activities—would you rather call your customers often with false alarms or risk missing potential fraudulent transactions?

In addition to the trade-off information, the ROC curve itself also provides a view of the overall performance of the classifier. A perfect classifier would have no false positives and no missed detections, so the curve would be pushed to the top-left corner, as illustrated in figure 4.17. This leads us naturally to another evaluation metric: the area under the ROC curve (AUC). The larger this area, the better the classification performance. The AUC is a widely used choice for evaluating and comparing models, although in most cases it's important to inspect the full ROC curve in order to

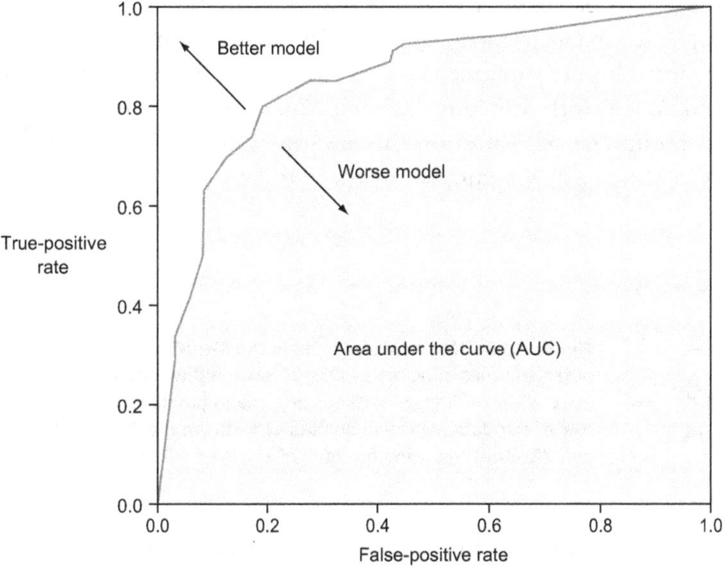
1.0
0.8
0.6
0.4
0.2
0.0
True-positive rate
Better model
Worse model
Area under the curve (AUC)
0.0
0.2
0.4
0.6
0.8
1.0
False-positive rate

Figure 4.17 The ROC curve illustrates the overall model performance. You can quantify this by defining the AUC metric: the area under the ROC curve.

understand the performance trade-offs. You'll use the ROC curve and the AUC evaluation metric to validate classification models throughout the rest of this book.

Listing 4.4 The area under the ROC curve

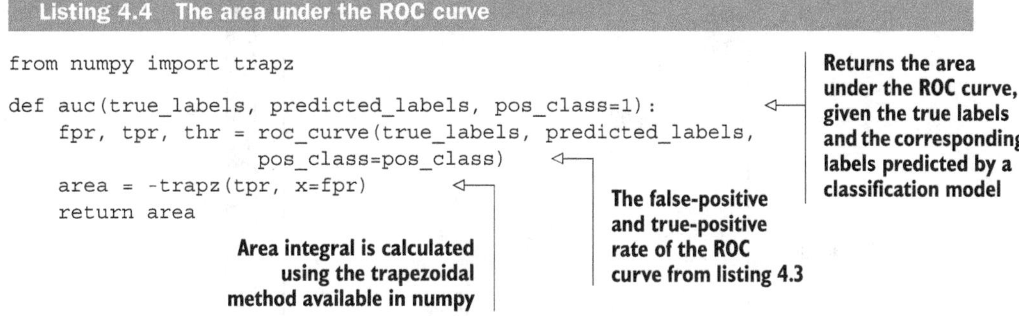

```
from numpy import trapz

def auc(true_labels, predicted_labels, pos_class=1):
    fpr, tpr, thr = roc_curve(true_labels, predicted_labels,
                              pos_class=pos_class)
    area = -trapz(tpr, x=fpr)
    return area
```

Returns the area under the ROC curve, given the true labels and the corresponding labels predicted by a classification model
The false-positive and true-positive rate of the ROC curve from listing 4.3
Area integral is calculated using the trapezoidal method available in numpy

4.2.3 Multiclass classification

So far you've looked only at binary, or two-class, classification problems, but luckily you can use many of the same tools for multiclass classifiers. A well-known multiclass classification problem is that of handwritten digit recognition. We all send physical mail from time to time, and there's a good chance that a machine-learning algorithm has been used in the process of determining the endpoint address of your letter. That sounds like a huge challenge if your handwriting is anything like ours, but such automated systems have nevertheless been in use by postal services for decades.

Because of the early success of machine learning on handwritten digit recognition, this example has been used throughout the ML literature as a benchmark of multiclass classification performance. The idea is to scan the handwritten digits and divide them into images with one letter in each. You then use image-processing algorithms or build a multiclass classifier on the raw grayscale pixels that can predict the digit. Figure 4.18 shows a few examples of the handwritten digit dataset known as MNIST.

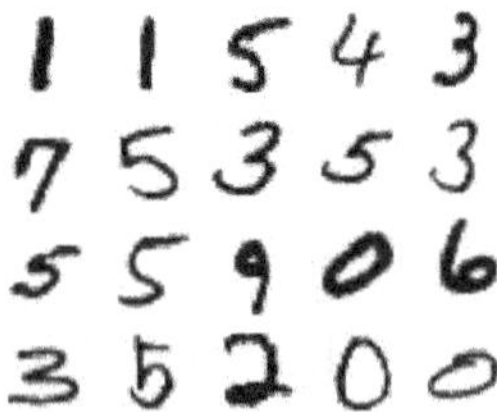

Figure 4.18 Handwritten digits in the MNIST dataset. The entire dataset consists of 80,000 such digits, each in a 28 x 28–pixel image. Without any image processing, each row of our dataset then consists of a known label (0 to 9) and 784 features (one for each of the 28 x 28 pixels).

You use the random forest algorithm (introduced in chapter 3) to build a classifier from the training set, and you generate the confusion matrix from the held-out testing set. Remember that you've worked with the confusion matrix for only binary classification. Luckily, you can easily define it for multiple classes, as every element in the matrix is the class on the row versus the class on the column. For the MNIST classifier, you can see in figure 4.19 that most of the power is located on the matrix diagonal, as

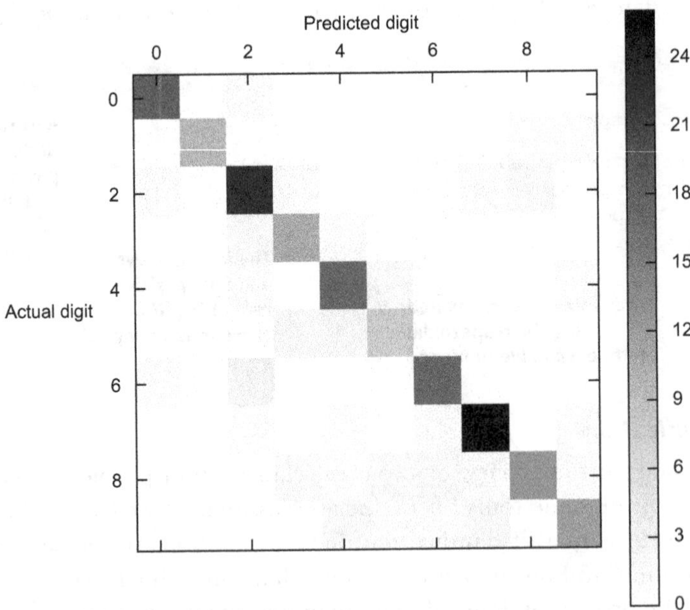

Figure 4.19 The confusion matrix for the 10-class MNIST handwritten digit classification problem

it should be, because it shows the number of instances that are *correctly* classified for each digit. The largest nondiagonal items show where the classifier is most confused. Inspecting the figure, you can see that the greatest confusion occurs between digits 4 and 9, 3 and 5, and 7 and 9, which makes sense, given what you know about the shape of the digits.

The reason for displaying the class-wise accuracy in the form of a matrix is to take advantage of our excellent visual abilities to process more information. In figure 4.19, you can clearly see how applying contrast to the confusion matrix can help take advantage of this ability.

So how do you generate the ROC curve for multiclass classifiers? The ROC curve is in principle applicable to only binary classification problems, because you divide the predictions into *positive* and *negative* classes in order to get ROC metrics such as the true-positive rate and false-positive rate commonly used on the ROC curve axis. To simulate binary classification in a multiclass problem, you use the *one-versus-all* trick. For each class, you denote the particular class as the *positive* class, and everything else as the *negative* class, and you draw the ROC curve as usual. The 10 ROC curves from running this process on the MNIST classifier are shown in figure 4.20. The most accurately classified digits are 0 and 1, consistent with the confusion matrix in figure 4.19. The confusion matrix, however, is generated from the most

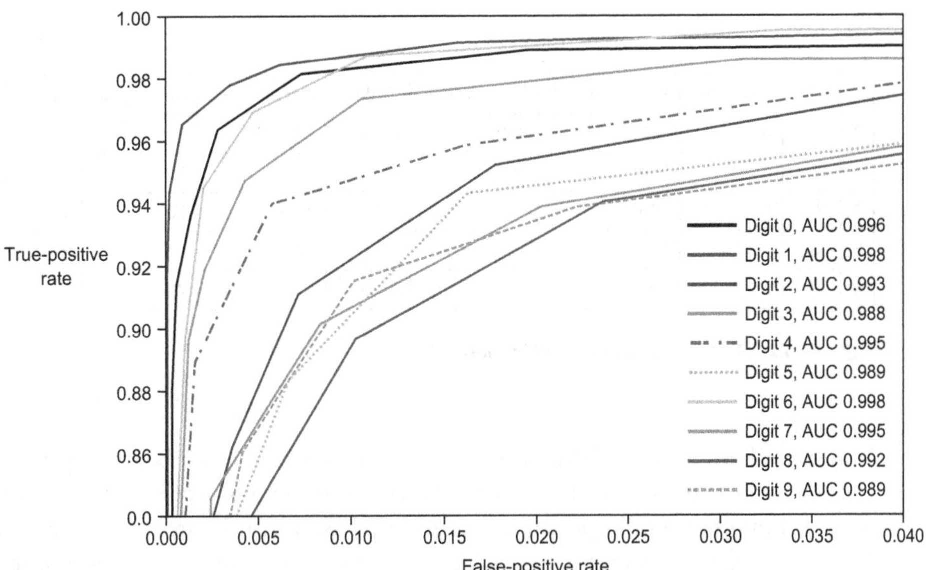

Figure 4.20 The ROC curves for each class of the MNIST 10-class classifier using the one-versus-all method for simulating a binary classification problem. Note that because the classifier is so good, we've zoomed closely into the top corner of the ROC curve in order to see any differences in the model performance between the classes. The AUC is calculated for each class and also shows a well-performing model overall.

probable class predictions, whereas the ROC curve shows the performance of the class at all probability thresholds.

Keep in mind, however, that the multiclass ROC curves don't show the entire confusion matrix on the curve. In principle, there's a full 10 x 10 confusion matrix at every point on the ROC curve, but we can't visualize this in a sufficiently simple way. In the multiclass case, it's therefore important to look at both the confusion matrix and the ROC curve.

4.3 Evaluation of regression models

You've already looked at regression models in previous chapters. Generally, *regression* is the term you use for models that predict a numeric outcome, such as an integer or floating-point value. For regression, you use a different set of performance metrics that we introduce in this section.

You'll use the Auto MPG dataset, first introduced in chapter 2, as the working example in this section. Figure 4.21 shows a small subset of this dataset. You run this dataset through all the necessary data transformations (see section 2.2 for more information about data transformations) and choose an appropriate model as discussed in chapters 2 and 3. In this case, you're interested in measuring the model performance.

Target variable (→ MPG)

	MPG	Cylinders	Displacement	Horsepower	Weight	Acceleration	Model/year	Origin
0	18	8	307	130	3504	12.0	70	1
1	15	8	350	165	3693	11.5	70	1
2	18	8	318	150	3436	11.0	70	1
3	16	8	304	150	3433	12.0	70	1
4	17	8	302	140	3449	10.5	70	1

Figure 4.21 A subset of the Auto MPG dataset

Using the basic model-evaluation workflow introduced at the beginning of this chapter, you use the data and your choice of algorithm to build a cross-validated regression model. Potential model performance metrics used in this process are introduced in the following sections, but figure 4.22 shows the most basic visualization of the regression performance on which those metrics are based: the scatter plot of predicted versus actual values.

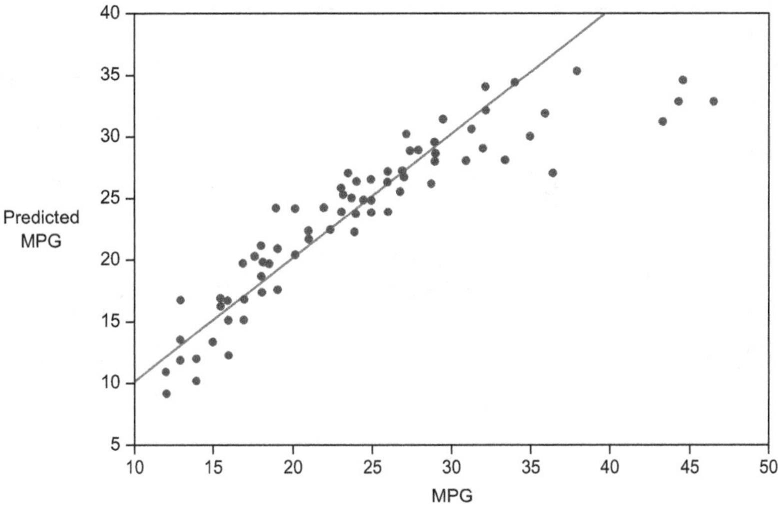

Figure 4.22 Scatter plot of the predicted MPG versus actual values from the testing set. The diagonal line shows the optimal model.

4.3.1 Using simple regression performance metrics

In contrast to classification models, regression carries no simple notion of a *correct* prediction. A numeric prediction is in general unlikely to be exactly right, but it can be *close to* or *far from* the correct value. This is also a consequence of the nature of what it means to be a *correct* value, because we usually consider numerical measurements to be drawn from a distribution with a degree of uncertainty known as the *error.* This section introduces two simple metrics to measure the regression performance: the root-mean-square error (the square root of the MSE) and the R-squared value.

The simplest form of performance measurement of a regression model is the *root-mean-square error,* or *RMSE.* This estimator looks at the difference from each of the predicted values to the known values, and calculates the mean in a way that's immune to the fact that predicted values can be both higher and lower than the actual values. Figure 4.23 illustrates RMSE calculation.

To encourage a better understanding of the details in the RMSE calculation, the following listing shows a code snippet.

Listing 4.5 The root-mean-square error

```
def rmse(true_values, predicted_values):
  n = len(true_values)
  residuals = 0
  for i in range(n):
    residuals += (true_values[i] - predicted_values[i])**2.
  return np.sqrt(residuals/n)
```

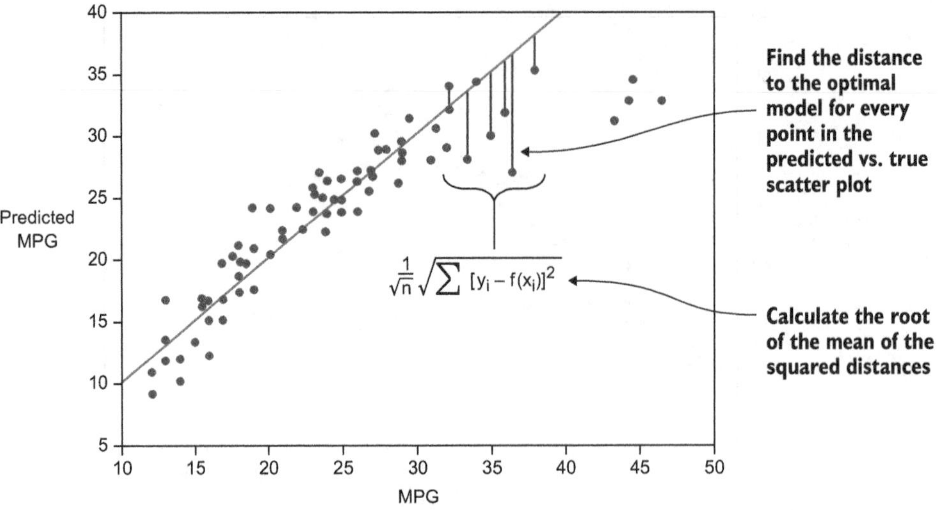

Figure 4.23 An RMSE calculation: in the equation, y_i and x_i are the ith target and feature vector, respectively, and f(x) denotes the application of the model to the feature vector, returning the predicted target value.

The advantage of RMSE is that the result is in the same units as the values themselves, but it's also a disadvantage in the sense that the RMSE value depends on the scale of the problem, and thus isn't easily comparable across datasets. If the predicted or actual values are larger numbers, the RMSE will be correspondingly higher. Although this isn't a problem when comparing models in the same project, it can be a challenge to understand the overall model performance and compare it to other models in general.

To overcome this, often it's worthwhile to also compute the R-squared, or R^2, metric, whose response is relative and always in the 0–1 range. If the model can predict the data better, the R-squared value is closer to 1. The following listing shows more details of the R-squared calculation.

Listing 4.6 The R-squared calculation

```
def r2(true_values, predicted_values):
  n = len(true_values)
  mean = np.mean(true_values)
  residuals = 0
  total = 0
  for i in range(n):
    residuals += (true_values[i] - predicted_values[i])**2.
    total += (true_values[i] - mean)**2.
  return 1.0 - residuals/total
```

Whether using MSE, RMSE, or R^2 as the evaluation metric, you should always keep the following in mind:

- Always use cross-validation to assess the model. If you don't, the metrics will always improve with increasing model complexity, causing overfitting.
- Wherever possible, the evaluation metric should align with the problem at hand. For instance, if predicting MPG from automobile features, an RMSE of 5 means that you expect the average prediction to differ from the true MPG by 5 miles per gallon.

In addition, regression uses lots of other evaluation metrics, many of which have built-in penalization for overfitting (and thus don't require cross-validation). Examples include the Akaikie information criterion (AIC) and Bayesian information criterion (BIC). Most textbooks on regression analysis cover these and more advanced topics.

4.3.2 Examining residuals

In the previous section, you saw how the residuals, the distance between the predicted and actual values, were used for both of the simple metrics introduced. These residuals can also be interesting to analyze visually themselves.

Figure 4.24 shows an example residual plot for our MPG dataset. This presents the same information as in the scatter plot in figure 4.23, but zoomed in on the scale of the residuals. In an ideal case, you expect the residuals to be distributed randomly around the 0-line. In the lower end of the figure, MPG values from 10 to 35, it looks like the residuals are randomly distributed around the 0-line, maybe with a slight bias toward overestimating the values. At values 35–45, however, you can see a clear bias

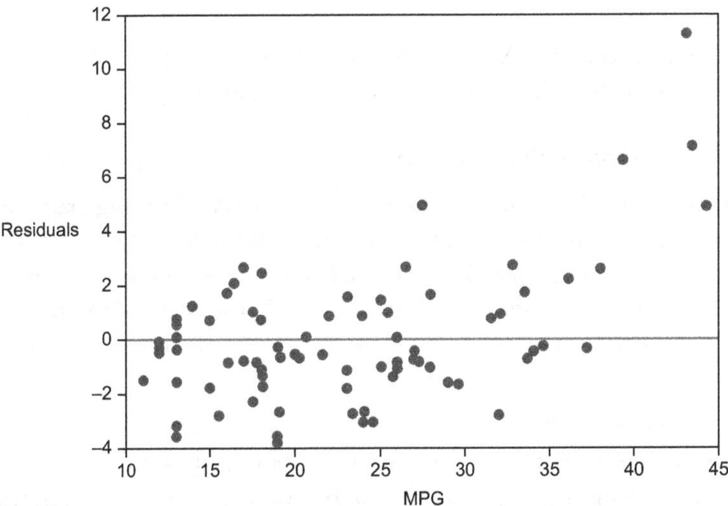

Figure 4.24 The residual plot from predictions on the MPG dataset. At the horizontal 0-line, the residual is 0.

toward underestimating the values, resulting in larger residual values. You can use this information to improve the model, either by tweaking model parameters, or by processing or amending the data. If you can acquire additional data, you could try to obtain labels for a few more high-MPG examples. In this case, you could find a few more high-MPG cars and add them to the dataset in order to improve the predictions in that part of the scale.

You've seen how cross-validation is used to test models and some of the performance metrics you can use to evaluate the results. For the simplest models, this is a matter of training, testing, and computing the appropriate performance metric(s). More-sophisticated algorithms have tuning parameters—knobs that can be turned by the user—that affect how they're trained and applied. Each combination of settings yields a different mode. In the next section, you'll see how sometimes a small adjustment can make a big difference in the results.

4.4 Model optimization through parameter tuning

Most machine-learning models come endowed with one or more *tuning parameters* that control the inner workings of the learning algorithm. These tuning parameters typically control the complexity of the relationship between the input features and target variable. As a result, the tuning parameters can have a strong influence on the fitted model and its predictive accuracy on new data.

For example, in section 4.1 you saw how a single turning parameter (the bandwidth in a kernel-smoothing regression algorithm) can cause wildly different model fits in the corn production dataset. For small values of the bandwidth parameter, the regression function was overly bumpy and overfit the data. Likewise, for large values of the bandwidth parameter, the regression function was too smooth and underfit the data.

This section introduces a rigorous methodology to optimize ML models with respect to the machine-learning algorithm tuning parameters.

4.4.1 ML algorithms and their tuning parameters

Each machine-learning algorithm contains a different set of tuning parameters that control how the algorithm uses training data to build a model. As the algorithms become more sophisticated, typically the tuning parameters become more numerous and esoteric. Here are the standard tuning parameters for some of the popular classification algorithms that you learned about in chapter 3, listed in order of increasing complexity:

- *Logistic regression*—None
- *K-nearest neighbors*—Number of nearest neighbors to average
- *Decision trees*—Splitting criterion, max depth of tree, minimum samples needed to make a split
- *Kernel SVM*—Kernel type, kernel coefficient, penalty parameter

- *Random forest*—Number of trees, number of features to split in each node, splitting criterion, minimum samples needed to make a split
- *Boosting*—Number of trees, learning rate, max depth of tree, splitting criterion, minimum samples needed to make a split

As an example, think back to chapter 3, where you applied a kernel SVM to the Titanic Passengers dataset. You saw that the model fit for two choices of the kernel coefficient parameter (called *gamma*) in figures 3.8 and 3.9. Note that the fits are different: setting gamma = 0.01 produces a complex, segmented decision boundary between the two classes, whereas setting gamma = 0.1 creates a smoother model. In this case, the fitted model is highly sensitive to the choice of the tuning parameter gamma.

What makes this difficult is that the appropriate choice for each tuning parameter for a given algorithm is entirely dependent on the problem and data at hand. What works well for one problem isn't necessarily appropriate for the next problem. Relying on heuristics and rule-of-thumb default tuning parameter settings may lead to poor predictive performance. Rigorous selection of tuning parameters is critical to ensure that your models are as accurate as they can be with the given data.

4.4.2 Grid search

The standard way to optimize the choice of tuning parameters for an ML model is via a brute-force *grid search*. As you map out the following basic grid-search algorithm, note that this strategy ties together the material on cross-validation and model evaluation from the previous sections of this chapter. The grid search algorithm is as follows:

1. Choose the evaluation metric that you want to maximize (for example, AUC for classification, R^2 for regression).
2. Choose which ML algorithm you want to use (for example, random forest).
3. Select which tuning parameters you want to optimize over (for example, number of trees and number of features per split) and the array of values to test for each parameter.
4. Define the grid as the Cartesian product between the arrays of each tuning parameter. For example, if the arrays are [50, 100, 1000] for number of trees and [10, 15] for number of features per split, then the grid is [(50,10), (50,15), (100,10), (100,15), (1000,10), (1000,15)].
5. For each combination of tuning parameters in the grid, use the training set to perform cross-validation (using either the hold-out or k-fold-CV method) and compute the evaluation metric on the cross-validated predictions.
6. Finally, select the set of tuning parameters corresponding to the largest value of the evaluation metric. This is the optimized model.

Why does this work? Grid search does an extensive search over the possible combinations of values for each of the tuning parameters. For each combination, it estimates the performance of that model on new data by comparing the cross-validated predictions to the true target variable. Then, the model with the best estimated accuracy (for new data) is chosen. This model has the highest likelihood of performing the best when applied to new data.

Let's apply grid search to the Titanic Passengers dataset. You'll use AUC as your optimization metric and SVM with a radial basis function (RBF) kernel as your classification algorithm. You can, in principle, also use grid search to select the best kernel. Indeed, you could use grid search to select between different algorithms!

Next, you select which tuning parameters to optimize over. For kernel SVM with an RBF kernel, you have two standard tuning parameters: the kernel coefficient, gamma; and the penalty parameter, C. The following listing shows how to run a grid search over those two parameters for this problem.

Listing 4.7 Grid search with kernel SVM

```
# Inputs: X - features, y - target

import numpy as np
from sklearn.metrics import roc_auc_score
from sklearn.svm import SVC

# grid of (gamma, C) values to try
gam_vec, cost_vec = np.meshgrid(np.linspace(0.01, 10., 11),
                     np.linspace(1., 10., 11))

AUC_all = []                                    <-- Initializes empty array to store AUC results

# set up cross-validation folds
N = len(y)
K = 10                                          <-- Number of cross-validation folds
folds = np.random.randint(0, K, size=N)

# search over every value of the grid
for param_ind in np.arange(len(gam_vec.ravel())):

    # initialize cross-validation predictions
    y_cv_pred = np.empty(N)

    # loop through the cross-validation folds
    for ii in np.arange(K):
        # break your data into training and testing subsets
        X_train = X.ix[folds != ii,:]
        y_train = y.ix[folds != ii]
        X_test = X.ix[folds == ii,:]

        # build a model on the training set
        model = SVC(gamma=gam_vec.ravel()[param_ind],
  C=cost_vec.ravel()[param_ind])
        model.fit(X_train, y_train)

        # generate and store model predictions on the testing set
        y_cv_pred[folds == ii] = model.predict(X_test)

    # evaluate the AUC of the predictions
    AUC_all.append(roc_auc_score(y, y_cv_pred))
```

```
indmax = np.argmax(AUC_all)
print "Maximum = %.3f" % (np.max(AUC_all))
print "Tuning Parameters: (gamma = %f, C = %f)" % (gam_vec.ravel()[indmax],
cost_vec.ravel()[indmax])
```

You find with the Titanic dataset that the maximum cross-validated AUC is 0.670, and it occurs at the tuning parameter vector (gamma = 0.01, C = 6). A contour plot showing the AUC evaluated over the grid as in figure 4.25 can be informative. A few factors jump out from this plot:

- The maximum occurs at the boundary of the grid (gamma = 0.01), meaning that you'd want to rerun the grid search on an expanded grid.
- A high amount of sensitivity exists in the accuracy of the predictions to the numerical value of the gamma parameter, meaning that you need to increase the granularity of sampling of that parameter.
- The maximum value occurs near gamma = 0, so expressing the grid on a log scale (for example, 10^{-4}, 10^{-3}, 10^{-2}, 10^{-1}) is sensible.
- There's not much sensitivity of the AUC as a function of C, so you can use a coarse sampling of that parameter.

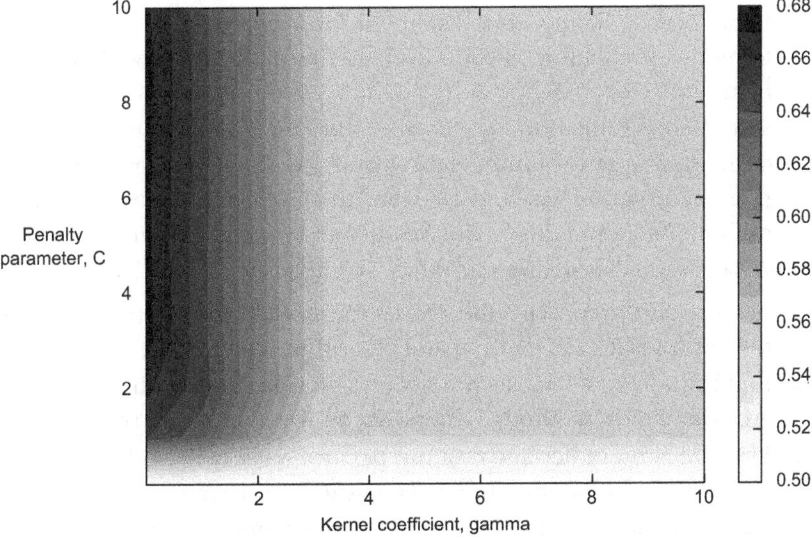

Figure 4.25 Contour plot showing the cross-validated AUC as a function of the two tuning parameters, gamma and C. The maximum occurs way off to the upper left, meaning that you need to expand the search and focus on that region.

Rerunning the grid search on a modified grid, you find that the maximum AUC is 0.690 and it occurs at (gamma = 0.08, C = 20). The value of optimizing over the tuning parameters is clear: a single model with arbitrary choice of tuning parameter could have attained a result as poor as AUC = 0.5 (no better than random guessing); the grid-search optimized model boosts the accuracy up to AUC = 0.69.

Note that grid search doesn't absolutely ensure that you've chosen the best set of tuning parameters. Because of the limitations caused by choosing a finite grid of possible values to try, the actual best value might have landed somewhere between the values of the grid. Readers who have some familiarity with optimization might be wondering why more-sophisticated optimization routines aren't traditionally used for tuning-parameter selection. The short answer is that the world of derivative-free, nonconvex optimization hasn't yet become part of the standard ML toolkit. The longer answer is that ML researchers on the cutting edge of the field are beginning to incorporate these methods into tuning-parameter optimization strategies.

4.5 Summary

In this chapter, you learned the basics of evaluating ML model performance. Here's a quick rundown of the main takeaways:

- When you evaluate models, you can't double-dip the training data and use it for evaluation as well as training.
- Cross-validation is a more robust method of model evaluation.
- Holdout cross-validation is the simplest form of cross-validation. A testing set is held out for prediction, in order to better estimate the model's capability to be generalized.
- In k-fold cross-validation, k-folds are held out one at a time, providing more-confident estimates of model performance. This improvement comes at a higher computational cost. If available, the best estimate is obtained if k = number of samples, also known as leave-one-out cross-validation.
- The basic model-evaluation workflow is as follows:
  1. Acquire and preprocess the dataset for modeling (chapter 2) and determine the appropriate ML method and algorithm (chapter 3).
  2. Build models and make predictions by using either the holdout or k-fold cross-validation methods, depending on the computing resources available.
  3. Evaluate the predictions with the performance metric of choice, depending on whether the ML method is classification or regression.
  4. Tweak the data and model until the desired model performance is obtained. In chapters 5–8, you'll see various methods for increasing the model performance in common real-world scenarios.
- For classification models, we introduced a few model-performance metrics to be used in step 3 of the workflow. These techniques include simple counting accuracy, the confusion matrix, receiver-operator characteristics, the ROC curve, and the area under the ROC curve.

- For regression models, we introduced the root-mean-square error and R-squared estimators. Simple visualizations, such as the prediction-versus-actual scatter plot and the residual plot, are useful.
- You can use a grid-search algorithm to optimize a model with respect to tuning parameters.

4.6 Terms from this chapter

Word	Definition
underfitting/overfitting	Using a model that's too simple or too complex, respectively, for the problem at hand.
evaluation metric	A number that characterizes the performance of the model.
mean squared error	A specific evaluation metric used in regression models.
cross-validation	The method of splitting the training set into two or more training/testing sets in order to better assess the accuracy.
holdout method	A form of cross-validation in which a single test set is held out of the model-fitting routine for testing purposes.
k-fold cross-validation	A kind of cross-validation in which data is split into k random disjoint sets (folds). The folds are held out one at a time, and cross-validated on models built on the remainder of the data.
confusion matrix	A matrix showing for each class the number of predicted values that were correctly classified or not.
receiver operating characteristic (ROC)	A number representing true positives, false positives, true negatives, or false negatives.
area under the ROC curve (AUC)	An evaluation metric for classification tasks defined from the area under the ROC curve of false positives versus true positives.
tuning parameter	An internal parameter to a machine-learning algorithm, such as the bandwidth parameter for kernel-smoothing regression.
grid search	A brute-force strategy for selecting the best values for the tuning parameters to optimize an ML model.

In the next chapter, you'll start looking at improving your models by focusing on their features. In addition to basic feature-engineering techniques, you'll learn advanced methods for extracting information out of text, images, and time-series data. You'll also see how to select the best features to optimize the performance of the model and avoid overfitting.

5 Basic feature engineering

This chapter covers

- Understanding the importance of feature engineering for your machine-learning project
- Using basic feature-engineering processes, including processing dates and times and simple texts
- Selecting optimal features and reducing the statistical and computational complexity of the model
- Using feature engineering at model-building and prediction time

The first four chapters have shown you how to fit, evaluate, and optimize a supervised machine-learning algorithm, given a set of input features and a target of interest. But where do those input features come from? How do you go about defining and calculating features? And how do practitioners know whether they're using the right set of features for their problem?

5.1 Motivation: why is feature engineering useful?

In this chapter, we explore how to create features from raw input data—a process referred to as *feature engineering*—and walk through a few examples of simple feature-engineering processes. This will set the groundwork for the more sophisticated feature-engineering algorithms covered in chapter 7.

5.1.1 What is feature engineering?

Feature engineering is the practice of using mathematical transformations of raw input data to create new features to be used in an ML model. The following are examples of such transformations:

- Dividing total dollar amount by total number of payments to get a ratio of dollars per payment
- Counting the occurrence of a particular word across a text document
- Computing statistical summaries (such as mean, median, standard deviation, and skew) of a distribution of user ping times to assess network health
- Joining two tables (for example, payments and support) on user ID
- Applying sophisticated signal-processing tools to an image and summarizing their output (for example, histogram of gradients)

Before diving into a few examples to demonstrate feature engineering in action, let's consider a simple question: why use feature engineering?

5.1.2 Five reasons to use feature engineering

This section describes a few ways that feature engineering provides value in a machine-learning application. This list isn't exhaustive, but rather introduces a few of the primary ways that feature engineering can boost the accuracy and computational efficiency of your ML models.

Transform original data to relate to the target

You can use feature engineering to produce transformations of your original data that are more closely related to the target variable. Take, for instance, a personal finance dataset that contains the current bank account balance and credit debt of each customer. If you're building a model to predict whether each customer will become delinquent in payments three months from now, then the engineered feature of

```
Ratio of debt-to-balance = amount of debt / amount of balance
```

would likely be highly predictive of the target.

In this case, although the raw inputs are present in the original dataset, the ML model will have an easier time of finding the relationship between debt-to-balance ratio and future delinquency if the engineered feature is directly used as an input. This will result in improved accuracy of predictions.

BRING IN EXTERNAL DATA SOURCES

Feature engineering enables practitioners to bring external data sources into their ML models. Imagine that you run an internet subscription service. The first time each customer logs in, you want to predict the lifetime value of that customer. Among a variety of metrics, you could capture the geographic location of each user. Although this data could be fed in directly as a categorical feature (for example, IP address or postal code), the model will likely have a difficult time determining the location-based signals that matter (in this case, those might be average income of each location, or urban versus rural).

You can do better by bringing in third-party demographic data. For example, this would allow you to compute the average income and population density of each user's location and to insert those factors directly into the training set. Now, instead of relying on the model to infer such subtle relationships from the raw location data, those predictive factors immediately become easier to deduce. Further, the feature engineering of location into income and population density enables you to assess which of these derivatives of location matter the most.

USE UNSTRUCTURED DATA SOURCES

Feature engineering enables you to use unstructured data sources in ML models. Many data sources aren't inherently structured into feature vectors that can be directly inserted into the ML framework presented in the first four chapters. Unstructured data such as text, time series, images, video, log data, and clickstreams account for the vast majority of data that's created. Feature engineering is what enables ML practitioners to produce ML feature vectors out of these kinds of raw data streams.

This chapter touches on some rather simple examples of feature engineering on text data. Subsequent chapters introduce the most commonly used types of feature engineering for text, images, and time-series data.

CREATE FEATURES THAT ARE MORE EASILY INTERPRETED

Feature engineering empowers ML practitioners to create features that are more interpretable and actionable. Often, using ML to find patterns in data can be useful for making accurate predictions, but you may face limitations in the interpretability of the model and the ultimate utility of the model to drive changes. In these cases, it may be more valuable to engineer new features that are more indicative of the processes that drive the data generation and the link between the raw data and the target variable.

Consider a simple example of machines that manufacture computer hardware. You could use the raw machine data, such as measurement of signal response and other processing signals, to build ML models to predict part failure. But features such as time since the last machine tune-up and volume of hardware produced can provide insight into the changeable aspects of the manufacturing process.

ENHANCE CREATIVITY BY USING LARGE SETS OF FEATURES

Feature engineering empowers you to throw in large sets of features to see what sticks. You can create as many features as you can dream up and see which of them carries predictive power when thrown in to train a model. This allows ML practitioners to escape from a rigid mindset when creating and testing features and could result in newly discovered trends and patterns.

Although overfitting becomes a concern when dozens or hundreds of features are used to train an ML model, rigorous feature-selection algorithms can be used to pare down the set of features to something more manageable. (For example, you can automatically determine that your predictions with the top 10 features are as good as or better than your predictions with all 1,000 features.) We describe these algorithms later this chapter, in section 5.3.

5.1.3 Feature engineering and domain expertise

Another way to conceptualize feature engineering is as a mechanism that imbues domain expertise into a machine-learning model. What we mean by this is simple: for each problem at hand, knowledge about the data and systems under study is accumulated over time. For some problems, these patterns will be straightforward enough to be easily learned by an ML model. But for more-challenging problems, the ML models stand to improve significantly from the codification of that domain expertise into the feature set. The following are examples of statements of domain expertise that could easily be coded into ML features:

- Web conversions are always higher on Tuesday (include the Boolean feature "Is it Tuesday?").
- Household power consumption increases with higher temperature (include temperature as a feature).
- Spam emails typically come from free email accounts (engineer the Boolean feature "Is from free email account?" or email domain).
- Loan applicants with recently opened credit cards default more often (use the feature "Days since last credit card opened").
- Customers often switch their cell-phone provider after others in their network also switch providers (engineer a feature that counts the number of people in a subscriber's network who recently switched).

Clearly, the list of potential domain expertise tidbits could go on and on. Indeed, the standard operating procedure for many companies is to use long lists of these ad hoc rules to make decisions and predictions. These business rules are a perfect set of engineered features on which to start building ML models!

Turned on its head, feature engineering can be a way to *test* the preconceived notions that are held by domain experts. If there's any question about whether a particular hypothesis holds any merit, it can be codified and used as a feature in an ML model. Then, the accuracy of the model can be tested with and without that feature to assess the conditional importance of the feature in predicting the target variable. If the gains in accuracy are negligible, this is evidence of the lack of added value of that idea.

Next, we present a few examples of simple feature engineering to show how these processes work in practice. We describe how feature engineering fits into the overall ML workflow and demonstrate how the predictive accuracy of ML models can be improved by employing some relatively straightforward feature-engineering processes.

5.2 Basic feature-engineering processes

Before diving into our example, let's revisit our basic ML workflow to show how feature engineering extends what you've seen so far. Figure 5.1 illustrates the workflow.

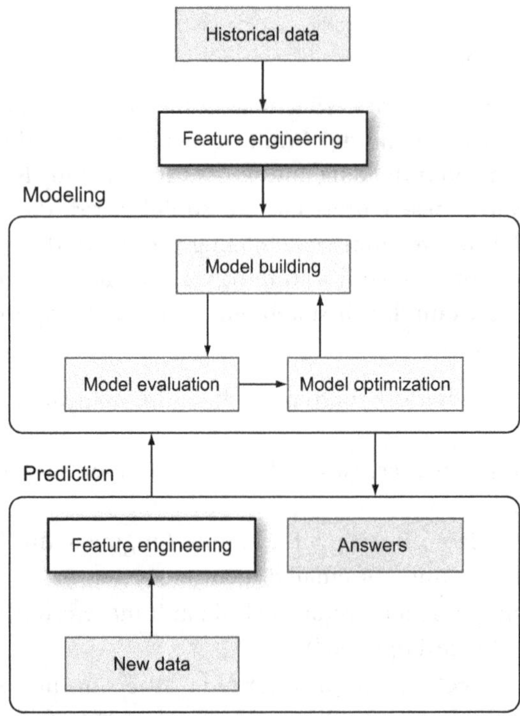

Figure 5.1 How feature engineering fits into the basic ML workflow. You extend the training data with features before building the model. When making predictions, you need to push new data through the same feature-engineering pipeline to ensure that the answers make sense.

The feature-engineering extension of the workflow allows you to expand on the training data to increase the accuracy of the ML algorithm. To ensure that feature engineering is used properly, you need to run the prediction data through the same feature-engineering pipeline that was applied to the training data. This ensures that predictions are generated by using exactly the same process as applied to the training data.

5.2.1 Example: event recommendation

To illustrate feature-engineering concepts, this section introduces an example from the real world: a challenge from the data science competition site Kaggle (www.kaggle.com).

Imagine that you're running an event-recommendation site and want to predict whether an event (such as a meeting, a happy hour, or a lecture) is interesting to a particular user. You have a set of training data describing which users have shown interest in which events in the past, and some information about the users and the events themselves. Your goal is to build an ML model to predict whether a particular event is interesting to a user—a binary classification model.

The data and information about the challenge are available at www.kaggle.com/c/event-recommendation-engine-challenge after you sign up on the Kaggle website (if you haven't already). The base datasets are the train.csv, events.csv, and users.csv files, which can be joined together on user and event identifiers. You limit the dataset to the events that have an explicit interested or not-interested selection and to the basic numerical and categorical features. Figure 5.2 shows a selection of this initial training dataset.

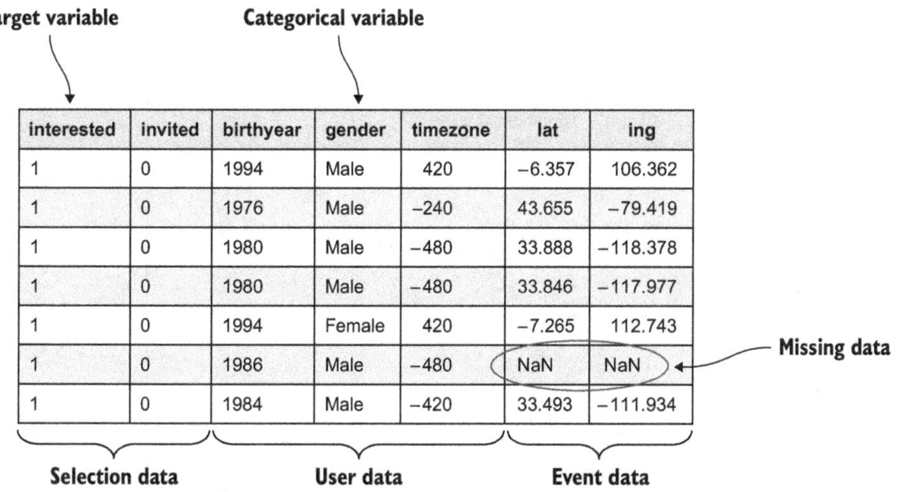

interested	invited	birthyear	gender	timezone	lat	lng
1	0	1994	Male	420	–6.357	106.362
1	0	1976	Male	–240	43.655	–79.419
1	0	1980	Male	–480	33.888	–118.378
1	0	1980	Male	–480	33.846	–117.977
1	0	1994	Female	420	–7.265	112.743
1	0	1986	Male	–480	NaN	NaN
1	0	1984	Male	–420	33.493	–111.934

Figure 5.2 A sample of the datasets used for training the event-recommendations model

Your sample training data contains the following features:

- `invited`—A Boolean indicating whether the individual was invited to the event
- `birthyear`—The year the person was born
- `gender`—The gender of the person
- `timezone`—The time zone of the current location of the individual
- `lat/lng`–The latitude/longitude of the event

To start, you'll build and evaluate a model based on only these six features. It's clear that this dataset is limited in terms of the patterns that can identify whether each user will be interested in the event. As you continue this section, you'll use a few straightforward feature-engineering transformations to extend the feature set and layer on new information.

You'll build an initial binary classification model to predict the target variable, `interested`, from the six input features. Following the ML workflow from chapters 1–4, you do the following:

1. Perform initial data-processing exercises (convert categorical columns to numerical, impute missing values).
2. Do the model training (using the random forest algorithm).
3. Evaluate the model (using 10-fold cross-validation and ROC curves). Figure 5.3 shows the cross-validated ROC curve. It attains an AUC score of 0.81.

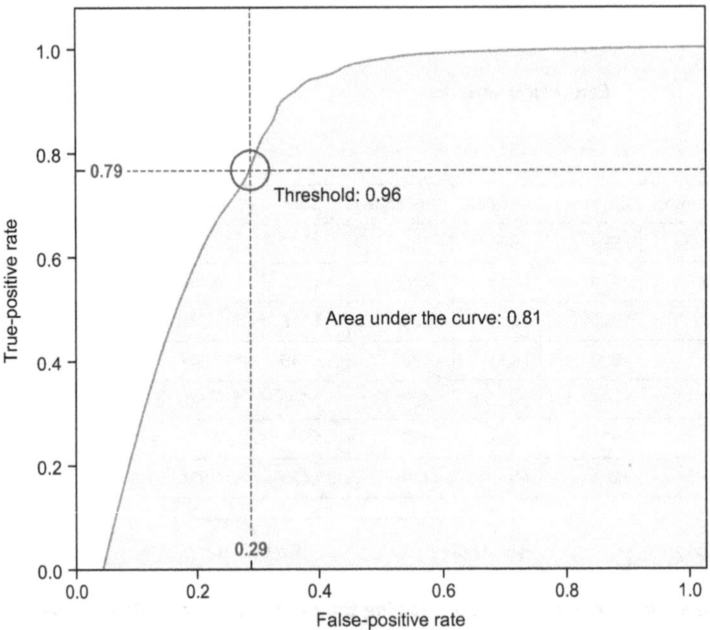

Figure 5.3 Cross-validated ROC curve and AUC metric for the simple event-recommendation model

5.2.2 *Handling date and time features*

Next, you'll use feature engineering to try to improve the results of your first model. In addition to the data shown in figure 5.2, each event in the dataset has an associated `start_time`. This data element is an ISO-8601 UTC string representing when the event is scheduled to begin. The data field has formatting like `2012-10-02 15:53:05.754000+00:00`, representing yyyy-mm-dd hh:mm:ss.mmmmmm_HH:MM.

The types of ML models described in chapter 3 can support numerical or categorical input features, of which a `datetime` string is neither. Therefore, you can't simply insert the column of strings directly into the model. What you can do, however, is perform transformations of the `datetime` elements into numerical features that capture the information encoded within the `datetime` string. This simple yet powerful concept of feature engineering can enable you to transform each `datetime` string into a smattering of features, such as these:

- Hour of the day
- Day of the week
- Month of the year
- Minute of the hour
- Quarter of the year

Figure 5.4 shows the first five rows of data that result from converting your single `start_time` feature into 10 `datetime` features.

datetime_hour_of_day	datetime_day_of_week	datetime_day_of_month	datetime_day_of_year	datetime_month_of_year
13	4	26	300	10
13	4	26	300	10
13	4	26	300	10
13	4	26	300	10
13	4	26	300	10

datetime_minute_of_hour	datetime_second_of_minute	datetime_year	datetime_quarter_of_year	datetime_week_of_year
30	0	2012	4	43
30	0	2012	4	43
30	0	2012	4	43
30	0	2012	4	43
30	0	2012	4	43

Figure 5.4 Additional date-time columns extracted from the timestamp column for the event-recommendation dataset

Next, you build a random forest model on this new, 16-feature dataset. Our cross-validated ROC curve is shown in figure 5.5.

The AUC of the model has increased from 0.81 to 0.85. Clearly, there was hidden value in the `start_time` information that, when imbued into the ML model via feature engineering, helped improve the model's accuracy. Most likely, events that occur on particular days of the week and at certain times of day are more popular than others.

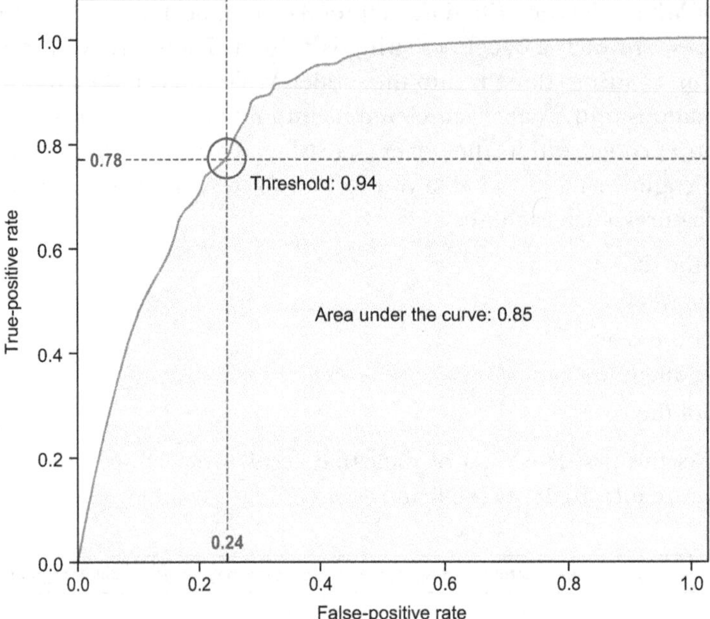

Figure 5.5 Cross-validated ROC curve for model including date-time features

5.2.3 Working with simple text features

In addition to the time of the event, the data includes basic text features from simple, natural language–processing routines. In the same way that `datetime` features can't be used directly by the model because they're neither numerical nor categorical, arbitrary text can't be fed into the ML algorithm without some kind of processing that turns the data into one of the two accepted types. To turn text into ML features, you employ a method called *bag of words*. The idea is simple in principle: count the number of occurrences of each word that appears in the text and insert a column in the dataset with the counts for that word. As always, though, you'll have a few complicating factors to deal with.

The features that you feed to your ML algorithm must be homogeneous: there must be the same number of features, and they must correspond to the same underlying concept, for all of the instances in your dataset. For example, if the first instance contains five occurrences of the word *family*, and the next instance doesn't, you must choose to either include a column for Family and set the count to 0 for the second instance, or leave it off both instances. Usually, you work with the entire text corpus of the dataset to decide which words get a column and which don't. In most cases, you build the bag of words for the entire dataset and include only the top-occurring words to get a column in your dataset. You can then have a catchall column for the rest of the words, which in principle determines the length of the text outside the selected top words.

Now, let's say you're selecting the top 100 words to get a Counts column in your dataset. You'll get a bunch of columns with counts for common but not useful words, such as *is*, *and*, and *the*. In the field of natural language processing, these words are known as *stop words* and are usually purged from the text before performing the bag-of-words counting.

We introduce more-advanced text feature concepts in the next chapter, but the last complicating factor to mention here is that the bag-of-words dataset quickly becomes large and sparse. We have a lot of features mostly filled with zeros, because a particular word usually isn't likely to appear in a random passage of text. The English dictionary is large (with more than 200 thousand words in use), and only a small fraction of those words are used in most texts. Some ML problems have a much narrower space, in which a class of words is more represented than in general. For example, figure 5.6 shows a few instances of the count features for the top words in our event-recommendation example; the sparsity of the data is clear. Some ML algorithms, such as naïve Bayes classifiers, handle sparse data well (by requiring no extra memory for the 0's), whereas most others don't.

2	0	2	0	0	0	0	0	0	0	0	0	0	0	1	0	0	0	0	0	0	0
2	0	2	0	0	0	0	0	0	0	0	0	0	0	1	0	0	0	0	0	0	0
0	0	0	0	0	0	0	0	0	0	0	0	0	0	0	0	0	0	0	0	0	0
1	0	2	1	0	0	0	0	0	0	0	0	0	0	2	0	0	0	0	0	0	0
1	1	0	0	0	0	0	2	0	0	0	0	0	0	1	0	0	0	1	2	0	0
0	0	0	0	0	0	0	0	0	0	0	0	0	0	0	0	0	0	0	0	0	0
0	0	0	1	0	0	0	0	0	0	0	0	0	0	0	0	0	0	0	0	0	0
0	0	2	0	0	33	0	3	1	0	0	0	1	1	1	1	0	0	0	0	0	3
0	0	0	0	0	0	0	0	0	0	0	0	0	0	0	0	0	0	0	0	0	0
1	0	1	0	1	0	0	0	0	0	0	0	0	0	2	0	0	0	0	0	0	0
0	0	0	3	0	0	0	0	0	0	0	0	0	0	0	0	0	0	0	0	0	0

Figure 5.6 A slice of the bag-of-words data for the event-recommendation example. These numbers are the counts of the top-occurring words in the event descriptions. A large fraction of the cells contain 0, so we call the dataset *sparse*.

In events.csv of our event-recommendation example, 100 features represent the bag of words for the 100 top-occurring words. You want to use these as features in the model, because particular events might be more popular than others. Figure 5.7 shows the resulting ROC curve after adding these features to the model.

The AUC metric in figure 5.7 doesn't increase from your previous model that included only basic and date-time features. This tells you that a particular event

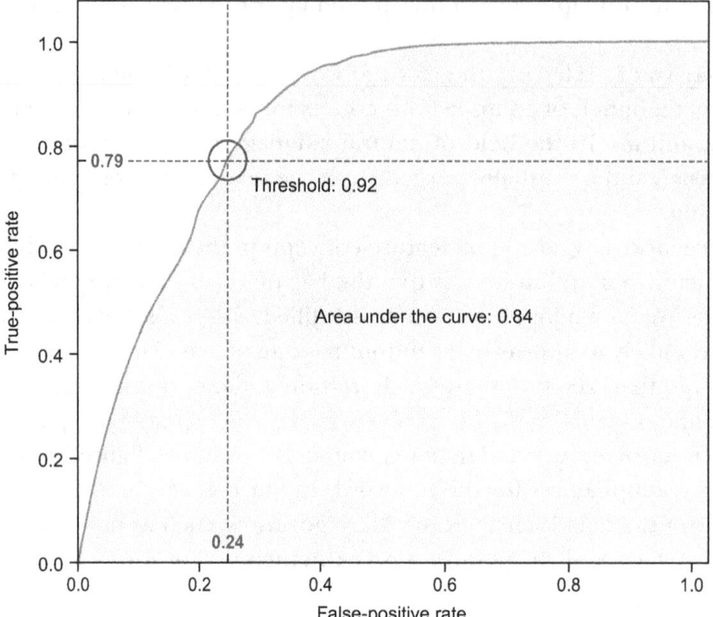

Figure 5.7 Cross-validated ROC curve for full model including date-time and text features

description isn't more likely to be interesting for users just because of the text. This model doesn't address the interests of individual users, but the user base in general. In a real recommendation engine, you could build a model for each user or each class of user. Other popular methods for recommendation engines use connections between events, users, and user friends to find recommendations.

5.3 Feature selection

Compared to basic statistical methods and human pattern-recognition abilities, one of the main advantages of machine-learning algorithms is the ability to handle a larger number of features. Most ML algorithms can handle thousands or millions of features. It's often a useful strategy to add more features in order to increase the accuracy of the model. But in machine learning, as in many other cases, more isn't always better.

Because more features enable the model to learn the mapping from features to the target in more detail, there's a risk that the model is overfitting the data. This increases the appeared accuracy of the model at training time, but might hurt the performance of predictions on new, unseen data. Figure 5.8 shows an example of overfitting (we first discussed overfitting in chapter 3).

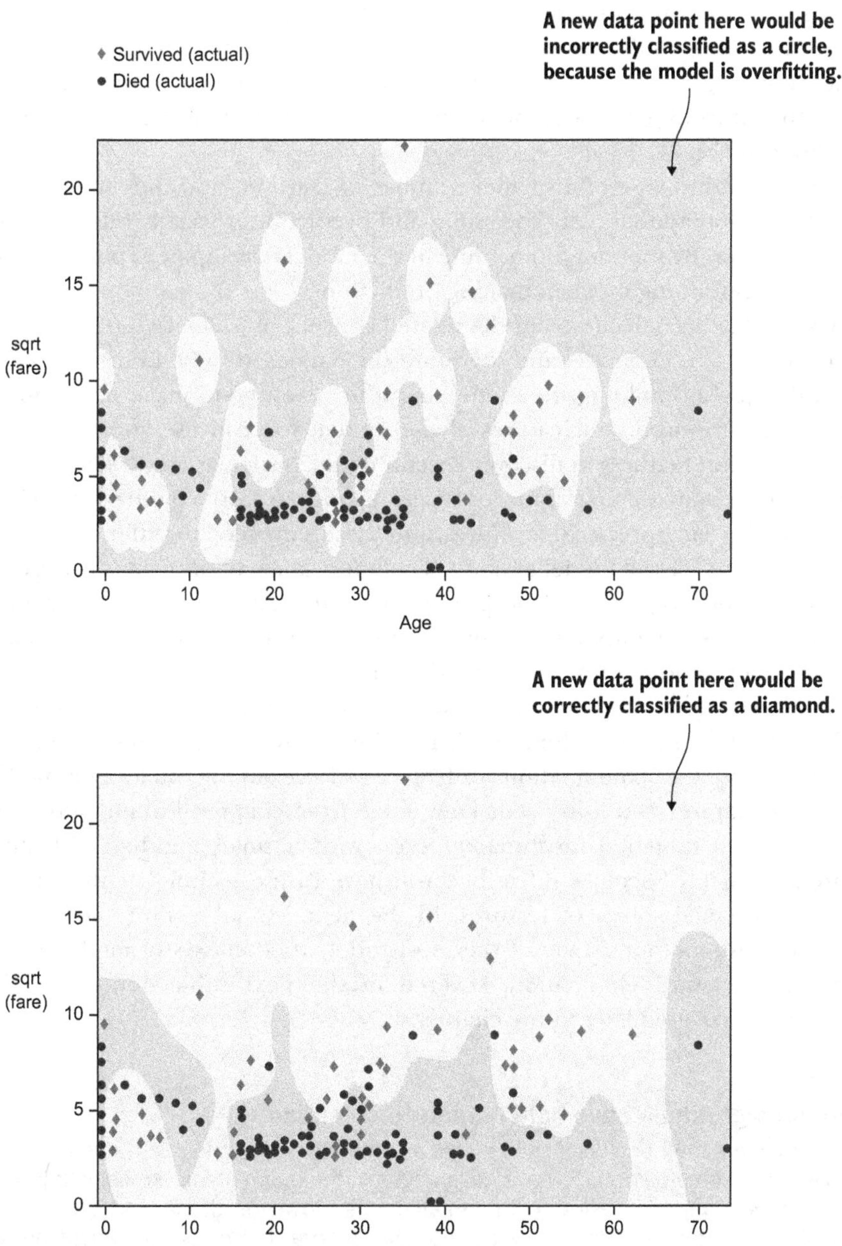

Figure 5.8 The decision boundary of two models fit on the same training data. In the model on the top, the decision boundary is too detailed, and the classification performance on new data can be affected.

In this section, you'll look at methods for selecting a subset of features in order to avoid overfitting, and thus increase the accuracy of the model when applied to new data. Some algorithms are more or less susceptible to overfitting, but it might be worth the effort to perform some of these optimizations if model accuracy is of particular importance.

Another advantage of a smaller number of features, and thus smaller models, is that the computational cost of training and prediction is usually related to the number of features. By spending some time in the model-development phase, you can save time when retraining or when making predictions.

Finally, feature selection and the related concept of *feature importance* can help you gain insight into the model and therefore the data used to build the model. In some cases, the goal of building the model might not even be to make predictions, but to get a view into important features of the model; you can use knowledge about the most significant features to discover certain patterns such as credit status being correlated with certain demographic or social factors. A cost could be associated with obtaining the data for specific features, and there's no need to suffer loss if the feature is unimportant for the model at hand. The importance of particular features can also reveal valuable insights into the predictions returned by the model. In many real-world use cases, it's important to understand something about *why* a certain prediction was made, and not just the particular answer.

With that, you should be well motivated to look more deeply into feature selection and the most common methods used. The simplest way to select the optimal subset of features is to try all combinations of features—for example, building a model for all subsets of features and using your knowledge from chapter 4 to measure the performance of the model. Unfortunately, even with a small number of features, this approach quickly becomes infeasible. You have to use techniques that can approximate the optimal subset of features. In the next few subsections, you'll investigate some of these methods. One of the most widely used classes of methods is forward selection/backward elimination, covered in the next subsection. Other heuristic methods are covered later in the chapter.

Some algorithms have built-in feature selection

Although the methods discussed in this section are applicable to any machine-learning algorithm, some algorithms have advantages in the realm of feature selection because they have similar behavior built in. In all cases, however, these built-in methods are unlikely to yield results comparable to the general methods, but might be significantly more efficient computationally. As a consequence, it might be useful to try the built-in methods before falling back on the more computationally intense general methods, or even use the built-in methods as a seed to save computation time on the general methods.

Examples of built-in feature-selection methods are the weights assigned to features in linear and logistic regression algorithms and the feature importances in decision trees and ensemble variants such as random forests, which capture (in a computationally efficient manner) the amount that predictive accuracy is expected to decrease if a feature were replaced with random noise. We can inspect the top feature importances of the random forest event-recommendation model from the previous section.

Feature	Importance
birthyear	
timezone	
datetime_week_of_year	
datetime_day_of_year	
lat	
datetime_hour_of_day	
lng	

The random forest feature importances for the top seven features in the event-recommendation model. By this measure, the birth year of a user and the time zone of the event are the two most important indicators of whether an event will be of interest to a user.

5.3.1 Forward selection and backward elimination

One of the most widely used sets of methods for approximating the best subset of features is the iterative selection methods that you'll look into here. The general concept is to start from no features and iteratively find the best features to add, or start from all features and iteratively remove the worst. The search is stopped when all features have been added or removed, when the increase in accuracy levels off, or at a predetermined size of the feature set.

These methods are referred to as *forward selection* and *backward elimination*, respectively. They don't guarantee finding the best subset of features, which is why we call it an *approximation.* One of the features that was left out, or removed, might have more predictive power when paired with a particular subset of features that hasn't yet been reached when the feature is removed. Remember that the power of machine learning comes from the ability to find patterns by combining many features. Or said differently, a weak feature may be strong in the presence of just the right set of other features.

In practice, however, forward selection or backward elimination works well to find a good subset of features with a much smaller computational complexity than the exhaustive search. When the number of features is particularly large, however, even this approach can be computationally infeasible. In those cases, it might be necessary to rely on built-in feature importance measures or other search heuristics, which we present in the next section.

The process of forward feature selection is shown in figure 5.9. Depending on the number of features, many models might need to be built. If the algorithm is run to the end, you'll need to build $N + (N - 1) + (N - 2)\ldots(N - N + 2) + (N - N + 1)$, or

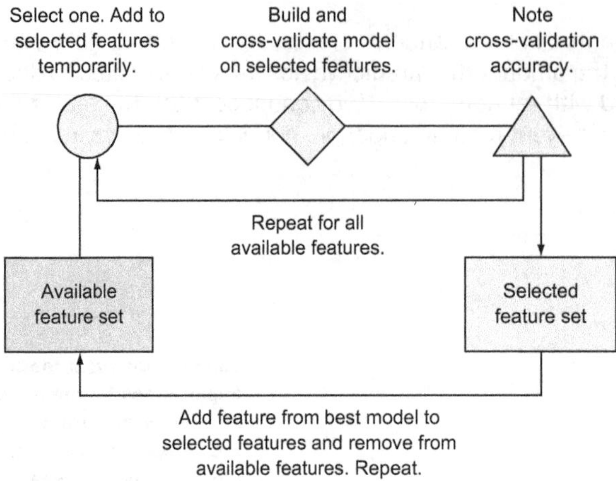

Figure 5.9 The process of forward feature selection. Beginning at the leftmost box, features are added iteratively until the best set of features–in terms of the cross-validated evaluation metric–is chosen.

$\Sigma_{i=0}^{N-1}(N-i)$. For 20, 100, 500, or 1,000 features, this is 210; 5,050; 125,250; and 500,500 model builds, respectively. In addition, each cross-validation iteration requires k models to be built, so if the model build takes any significant amount of time, this also becomes unmanageable. For smaller sets of features, or when running a smaller number of iterations (for example, because the increase in accuracy quickly levels off), this approach is effective in practice.

Figure 5.10 shows the equivalent process of backward elimination. The computational requirements are the same as forward selection, so the choice between forward and backward methods is usually a question of the problem at hand and the choice of algorithm. Some algorithms, for example, perform worse on a very small set of features, in which case backward elimination is the better approach.

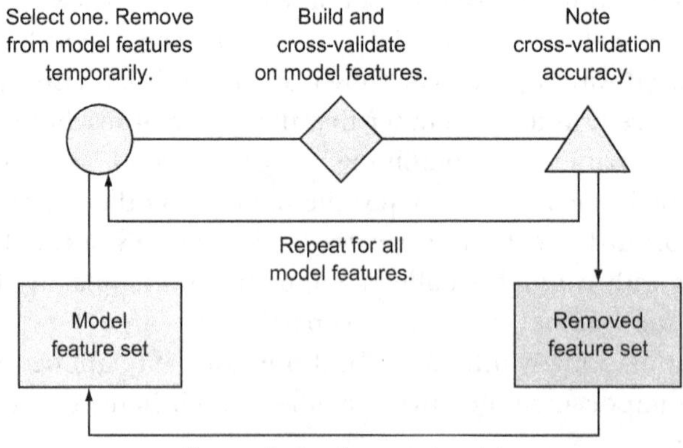

Figure 5.10 The process of backward feature elimination

A useful way to visualize an iterative feature-selection procedure is by plotting a vertical bar chart like the one in figure 5.11.

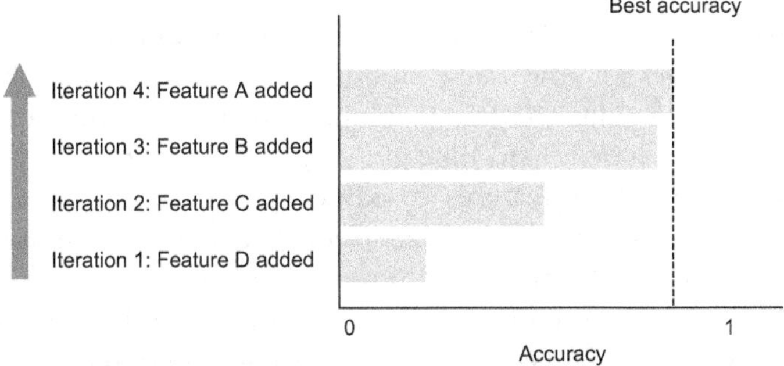

Figure 5.11 The iterative feature-selection bar chart, showing the evolution of accuracy in a feature-selection procedure—in this case, a forward selection algorithm. Any measure of accuracy (see chapter 4) that makes sense for the problem should be used here.

As we mentioned previously, some ML algorithms have built-in methods for feature selection. Instead of making feature selection based on built-in feature rankings, you can use a hybrid approach in which the built-in feature importance is used to find the best or worst feature in each iteration of the forward selection or backward elimination process. This can significantly reduce the computation time when you have many features, but will likely yield less-accurate approximations of the optimal feature subset.

5.3.2 Feature selection for data exploration

Feature selection can be used for more than avoiding overfitting or making the model leaner. A powerful use of feature selection is to gain insight into the model and the training data. In fact, in some cases, you might want to build a classifier only in order to run a feature-selection algorithm, and not for making predictions.

You can use feature selection to perform an exploratory analysis of the data that was used for building the model. From the feature-selection procedure, you know the most important features—the most informative set of features for predicting the target variable from all of the features. This tells you something about the data, which can be useful by itself. Imagine that your task is to predict whether a patient is likely to have cancer. Because you're not certain about the cause of the specific form of cancer, you add all the features you can get your hands on and use feature selection to find the top features. You're not only gaining a better cross-validated accuracy, but also using the data to indicate which factors are most likely to cause the disease or at least correlate with the probability of diagnosis. The discussed methods of feature selection don't tell you whether the features are powerful in the positive or negative direction (in the case of binary classification), but you can easily visualize the specific feature against the target variable to understand this (for example, using the visualizations in section 2.3).

Another unsupervised use case for feature selection is for *dimensionality reduction.* One of the great challenges when working with datasets with more than three variables is how to visualize the data. The human brain has been optimized for a three-dimensional world, and we have a hard time grasping more than that. In real-world data, however, having only three features is extremely unlikely, and you need to employ various techniques to visualize high-dimensional datasets. You can use feature selection as a way to show how the ML algorithms can divide the data into classes, for example, by simply plotting the two or three best features against the target variable. Figure 5.12 shows an example of a decision boundary shown in two dimensions, even though many more features were used to build the model.

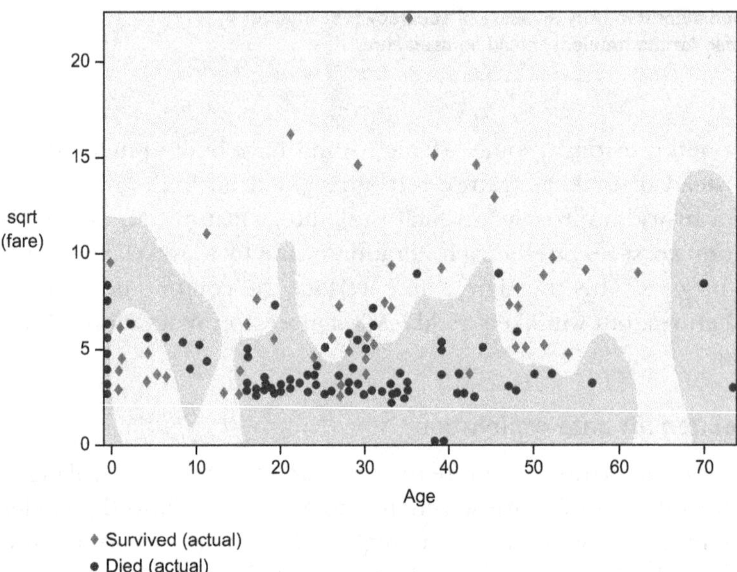

Figure 5.12 This decision boundary for classifying into circles and diamonds has only two features. The model was built on many more features, but the sqrt(Fare) and Age features were found by the feature-selection algorithm to be important in this particular problem (Titanic survival prediction). This plot was first introduced in chapter 3.

In the next section, you'll see an example of how feature selection can be useful in real-world problems.

5.3.3 Real-world feature selection example

For a great use case of feature engineering and feature selection in the real world, let's look at an example from science.

Your task is to find real supernova events from huge astronomical images among a large number of so-called bogus events (events that look real, but aren't). Figure 5.13 shows examples of real and bogus events.

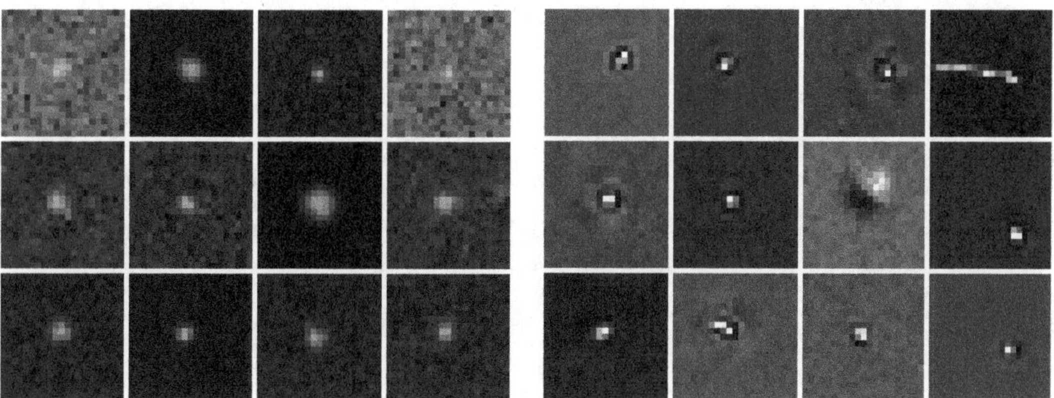

Figure 5.13 Real supernova images are shown in the panel on the left. Bogus candidate events are shown in the panel on the right.[1] The job of the classifier is to learn the difference between these two types of candidates from features extracted from the images. (These are obvious examples; many others are hard to classify, even for trained persons.)

The real/bogus classifier is built by first processing the raw image data into a set of features, some of which are discussed in the next chapter. You then run the featurized data through a random forest algorithm to build the classifier, and perform various model optimizations such as the ones outlined in chapters 3 and 4. The last part before putting this model into the live stream from the telescope is to determine the best features, avoid overfitting, and make the model as small as possible in order to support the real-time requirements of the project. The feature-selection plot, a slightly more advanced version of figure 5.11, is shown in figure 5.14.

[1] The supernova images and data graphs in this section originally appeared in the 2013 *Monthly Notices of the Royal Astronomical Society*, volume 435, issue 2, pages 1047-1060 (http://mnras.oxfordjournals.org/content/435/2/1047).

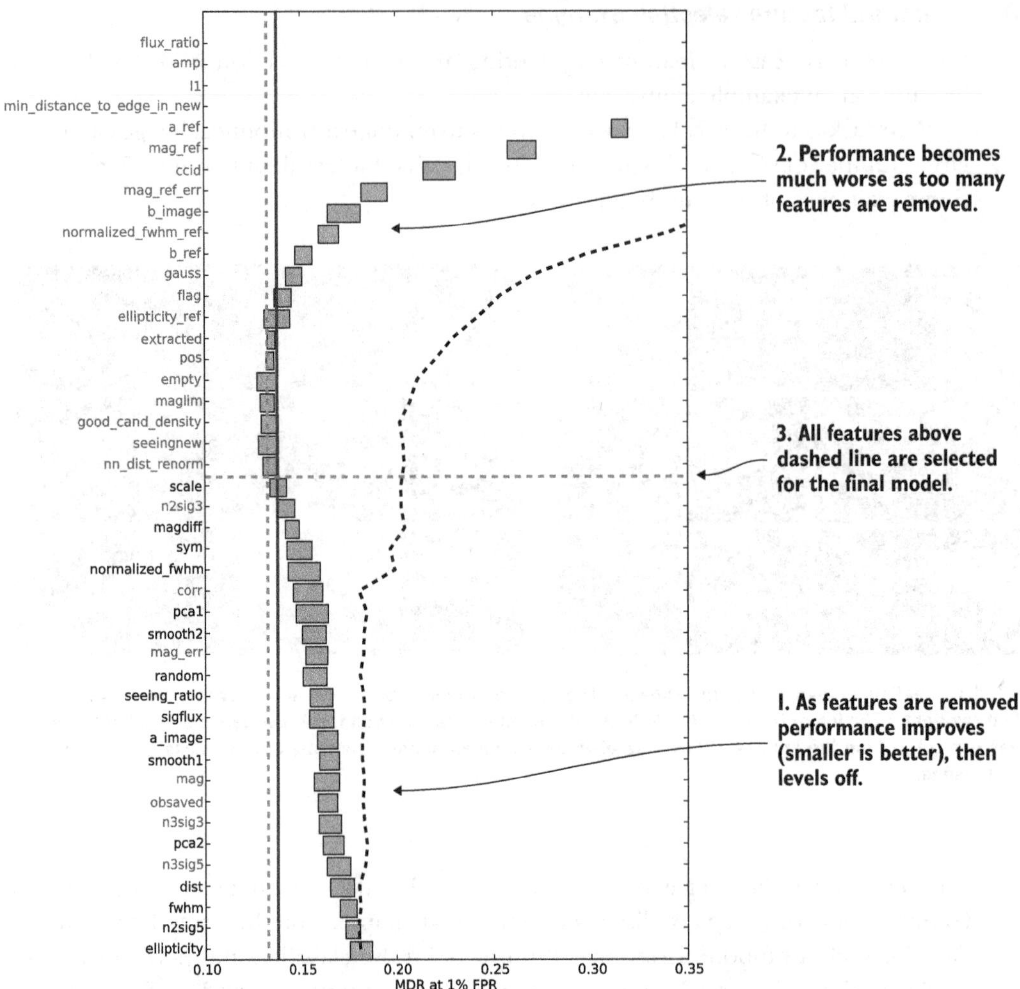

Figure 5.14 The feature-selection plot showing a backward elimination process. Each feature from the bottom up was selected for removal as the algorithm progressed, and in each step the customized evaluation metric of missed detection rate (MDR) at 1% false-positive rate (FPR) was computed. The bars show the performance metric obtained at each step (smaller is better in this case) by removing the feature (with standard deviation from cross-validation). After removing 23 features (out of 44), the cross-validated performance gain levels off and eventually becomes much worse when too many features have been removed. In the end, a significant 5 percentage points were gained in model performance by removing noisy features.

Now, by knowing which features are most important for the model, you can plot these features against real and bogus events in order to visualize how a particular feature helps solve the problem. Figure 5.15 shows the performance of four of the best features.

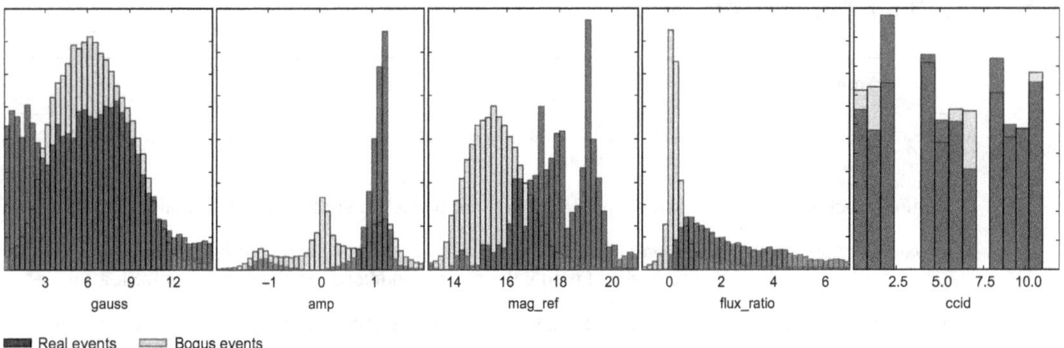

Figure 5.15 Visualization of the performance of four individual features chosen by our feature-selection algorithm to be among the best features for our model. The histograms show the number of real or bogus events that take on a particular value of the feature. You can see that the distributions of real versus bogus events are different in the *amp* and *flux_ratio* features, and they're selected as the top-performing features in our feature-selection procedure.

5.4 Summary

This chapter introduced feature engineering, which transforms raw data to improve the accuracy of ML models. The primary takeaways from this chapter are as follows:

- Feature engineering is the process of applying mathematical transformations to raw data to create new input features for ML modeling. The transformations can range from simple to extremely complex.
- Feature engineering is valuable for the following five reasons:
  - It can create features that are more closely related to the target variable.
  - It enables you to bring in external data sources.
  - It allows you to use unstructured data.
  - It can enable you to create features that are more interpretable.
  - It gives you the freedom to create lots of features and then choose the best subset via feature selection.
- There's an intricate link between feature engineering and domain knowledge.
- Feature engineering fits into the overall ML workflow in two places:
  - On the training dataset, prior to fitting a model
  - On the prediction dataset, prior to generating predictions
- Two types of simple feature engineering can be used on a problem of event recommendation:
  - Extraction of features from date-time information
  - Feature engineering on natural language text
- Feature selection is a rigorous way to select the most predictive subset of features from a dataset.

5.5 Terms from this chapter

Word	Definition
feature engineering	Transforming input data to extract more value and improve the predictive accuracy of ML models
feature selection	Process of choosing the most predictive subset of features out of a larger set
forward selection	A version of feature selection that iteratively adds the feature that increases the accuracy of model the most, conditional on the current active feature set
backward elimination	A version of feature selection that removes the feature that decreases the accuracy of model the most, conditional on the current active feature set
bag of words	A method for turning arbitrary text into numerical features for use by the ML algorithm

Chapter 7 expands on the simple feature-engineering approaches presented here so you can perform more-advanced feature engineering on data such as text, images, and time series. In the next chapter we'll use what we've learned in a full-chapter example.

Part 2

Practical application

In part 2, you'll go beyond a basic ML workflow to look at how to extract features from text, images, and time-series data to improve the accuracy of models even further, and to scale your ML system to larger data volumes. In addition, you'll go through three full example chapters to see everything in action.

In chapter 6, our first full example chapter, you'll try to predict the tipping behavior of NYC taxis.

In chapter 7, you'll look at advanced feature-engineering processes that allow you to extract value out of natural language text, images, and time series data. A lot of modern ML and artificial intelligence applications are based on these techniques.

In chapter 8, you'll use this advanced feature-engineering knowledge in another full example: predicting the sentiment of online movie reviews.

In chapter 9, you'll learn techniques for scaling ML systems to larger volumes of data, higher prediction throughput, and lower prediction latency. These are all important aspects of many modern ML deployments.

In chapter 10, you'll walk through a full example of building a model—on large amounts of data—that predicts online digital display advertisement clicks.

6 Example: NYC taxi data

This chapter covers

- Introducing, visualizing, and preparing a real-world dataset about NYC taxi trips
- Building a classification model to predict passenger tipping habits
- Optimizing an ML model by tuning model parameters and engineering features
- Building and optimizing a regression model to predict tip amount
- Using models to gain a deeper understanding of data and the behavior it describes

In the previous five chapters, you learned how to go from raw, messy data to building, validating, and optimizing models by tuning parameters and engineering features that capture the domain knowledge of the problem. Although we've used a variety of minor examples throughout these chapters to illustrate the points of the individual sections, it's time for you to use the knowledge you've acquired and work through a full, real-world example. This is the first of three chapters (along with chapters 8 and 10) entirely dedicated to a full, real-world example.

In the first section of this chapter, you'll take a closer look at the data and various useful visualizations that help you gain a better understanding of the possibilities of the data. We explain how the initial data preparation is performed, so the data will be ready for the modeling experiments in the subsequent sections. In the second section, you'll set up a classification problem and improve the performance of the model by tuning model parameters and engineering new features.

6.1 Data: NYC taxi trip and fare information

With companies and organizations producing more and more data, a large set of rich and interesting datasets has become available in recent years. In addition, some of these organizations are embracing the concept of *open data*, enabling the public dissemination and use of the data by any interested party.

Recently, the New York State Freedom of Information Law (FOIL) made available an extremely detailed dataset of New York City taxi trip records from every taxi trip of 2013.[1] This dataset collected various sets of information on each individual taxi trips including the pickup and drop-off location, time and duration of the trip, distance travelled, and fare amount. You'll see that this data qualifies as real-world data, not only because of the way it has been generated but also in the way that it's messy: there are missing data, spurious records, unimportant columns, baked-in biases, and so on.

And speaking of data, there's a lot of it! The full dataset is over 19 GB of CSV data, making it too large for many machine-learning implementations to handle on most systems. For simplicity, in this chapter you'll work with a smaller subset of the data. In chapters 9 and 10, you'll investigate methods that are able to scale to sizes like this and even larger, so by the end of the book you'll know how to analyze all 19 GB of data.

The data is available for download at www.andresmh.com/nyctaxitrips/. The dataset consists of 12 pairs of trip/fare compressed CSV files. Each file contains about 14 million records, and the trip/fare files are matched line by line.

You'll follow our basic ML workflow: analyzing the data; extracting features; building, evaluating, and optimizing models; and predicting on new data. In the next subsection, you'll look at the data by using some of the visualization methods from chapter 2.

6.1.1 Visualizing the data

As you get started with a new problem, the first step is to gain an understanding of what the dataset contains. We recommend that you start by loading the dataset and viewing it in tabular form. For this chapter, we've joined the trip/fare lines into a single dataset. Figure 6.1 shows the first six rows of data.

---

[1] Initially released in a blog post by Chris Wong: http://chriswhong.com/open-data/foil_nyc_taxi/.

medallion	hack_license	vendor_id	rate_code	store_and_fwd_flag
CD847FE5884F10A28217E9FBA11B275B	5FEFD00D9773268B72EE4E879852F190	CMT	1	N
20D9ECB2CA0767CF7A01564DF2844A3E	598CCE5B9C1918568DEE71F43CF26CD2	CMT	1	N
A954A71B6D44265AE756BF807E069396	D5CA7D478A14BA3BBFC20153C5C88B1A	CMT	1	N
F6F7D02179BE915B23EF2DB57836442D	088879B44B80CC9ED43724776C539370	VTS	1	0
BE386D8524FCD16B3727DCF0A32D9B25	4EB96EC9F3A42794DEE233EC8A2616CE	VTS	1	0
E9FF471F36A91031FE5B6D6228674089	72E0B04464AD6513F6A613AABB04E701	VTS	1	0
A5D125F5550BE7822FC6EE156E37733A	08DB3F9FCF01530D6F7E70EB88C3AE5B	VTS	1	0

pickup_datetime	dropoff_datetime	passenger_count	trip_time_in_secs	trip_distance
1/8/2013 10:44	1/8/2013 10:46	1	123	0.30
1/8/2013 7:51	1/8/2013 7:51	1	4	0.00
1/7/2013 10:05	1/7/2013 10:13	1	446	1.10
1/13/2013 4:36	1/13/2013 4:46	5	600	3.12
1/13/2013 4:37	1/13/2013 4:48	2	660	3.39
1/13/2013 4:41	1/13/2013 4:45	1	240	1.16
1/13/2013 4:37	1/13/2013 4:47	5	600	2.91

pickup_longitude	pickup_latitude	dropoff_longitude	dropoff_latitude	payment_type
-73.989296	40.756313	-73.987885	40.751122	DIS
-73.945396	40.802090	-73.945412	40.802025	NOC
-73.989090	40.748367	-73.974983	40.756035	DIS
-73.996933	40.720055	-73.993546	40.693043	CRD
-74.000313	40.730068	-73.987373	40.768406	CRD
-73.997292	40.720982	-74.000443	40.732376	CRD
-73.966843	40.756741	-73.987885	40.722713	CRD

fare_amount	surcharge	mta_tax	tip_amount	tolls_amount	tolls_amount	tipped
3.50	0.00	0.50	0.00	0.00	4.00	0
2.50	0.00	0.50	0.00	0.00	3.00	0
7.00	0.00	0.50	0.00	0.00	7.50	0
12.00	0.50	0.50	1.75	0.00	14.75	1
12.00	0.50	0.50	3.12	0.00	16.12	1
5.50	0.50	0.50	1.20	0.00	7.70	1
11.00	0.50	0.50	2.00	0.00	14.00	1

Figure 6.1 The first six rows of the NYC taxi trip and fare record data. Most of the columns are self-explanatory, but we introduce some of them in more detail in the text that follows.

The `medallion` and `hack_license` columns look like simple ID columns that are useful for bookkeeping but less interesting from an ML perspective. From their column names, a few of the columns look like categorical data, like `vendor_id`, `rate_code`, `store_and_fwd_flag`, and `payment_type`. For individual categorical variables, we recommend visualizing their distributions either in tabular form or as bar plots. Figure 6.2 uses bar plots to show the distribution of values in each of these categorical columns.

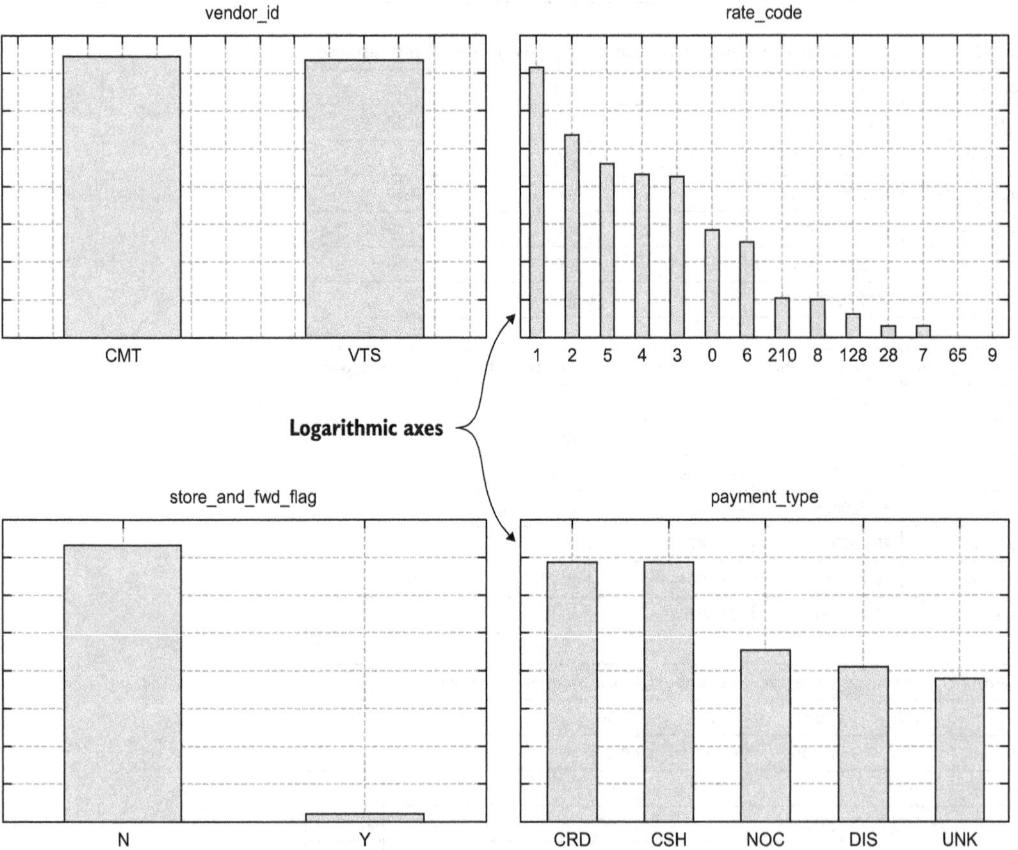

Figure 6.2 The distribution of values across some of the categorical-looking columns in our dataset

Next, let's look at some of the numerical columns in the dataset. It's interesting to validate, for example, that correlations exist between things like trip duration (`trip_time_in_secs`), distance, and total cost of a trip. Figure 6.3 shows scatter plots of some of these factors plotted against each other.

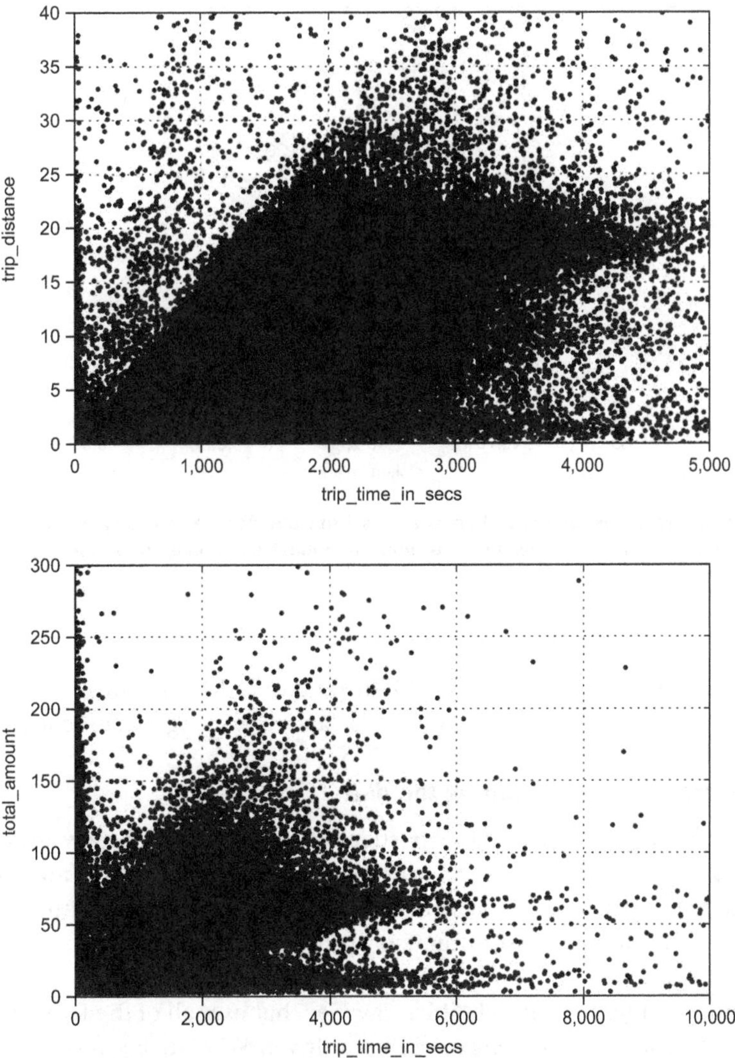

Figure 6.3 Scatter plots of taxi trips for the time in seconds versus the trip distance, and the time in seconds versus the trip amount (USD), respectively. A certain amount of correlation exists, as expected, but the scatter is still relatively high. Some less-logical clusters also appear, such as a lot of zero-time trips, even expensive ones, which may indicate corrupted data entries.

Finally, in figure 6.4, you can visualize the pickup locations in the latitude/longitude space, defining a map of NYC taxi trips. The distribution looks reasonable, with most pickup locations occurring in downtown Manhattan, many occurring in the other boroughs, and surprisingly a few happening in the middle of the East River!

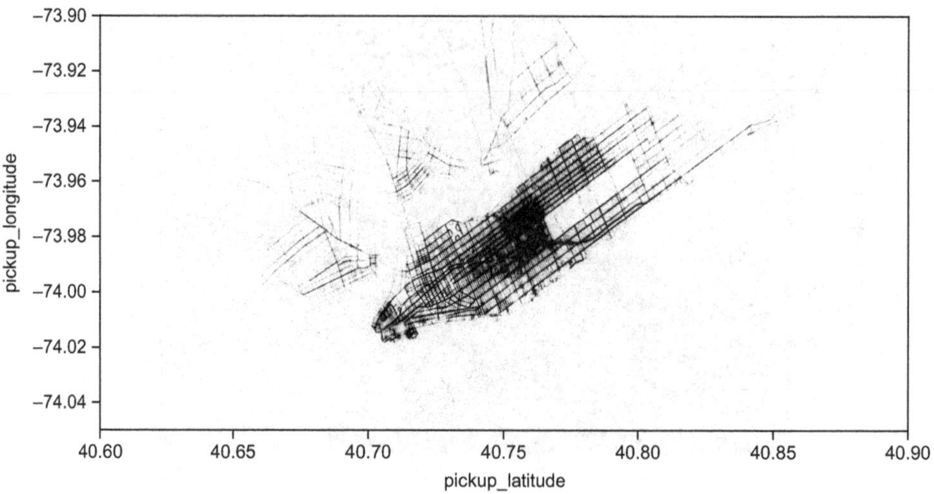

Figure 6.4 The latitude/longitude of pickup locations. Note that the x-axis is flipped, compared to a regular map. You can see a huge number of pickups in Manhattan, falling off as you move away from the city center.

With a fresh perspective on the data you're dealing with, let's go ahead and dream up a realistic problem that you can solve with this dataset by using machine learning.

6.1.2 *Defining the problem and preparing the data*

When we first looked at this data, a particular column immediately grabbed our attention: `tip_amount`. This column stores the information about the amount of the tip (in US dollars) given for each ride. It would be interesting to understand, in greater detail, what factors most influence the amount of the tip for any given NYC taxi trip.

To this end, you might want to build a classifier that uses all of the trip information to try to predict whether a passenger will tip a driver. With such a model, you could predict tip versus no tip at the end of each trip. A taxi driver could have this model installed on a mobile device and would get no-tip alerts and be able to alter the situation before it was too late. While you wait for approval for having your app installed in all NYC taxis, you can use the model to give you insight into which parameters are most important, or predictive, of tip versus no tip in order to attempt to boost overall tipping on a macro level. Figure 6.5 shows a histogram of the tip amount across all taxi trips.

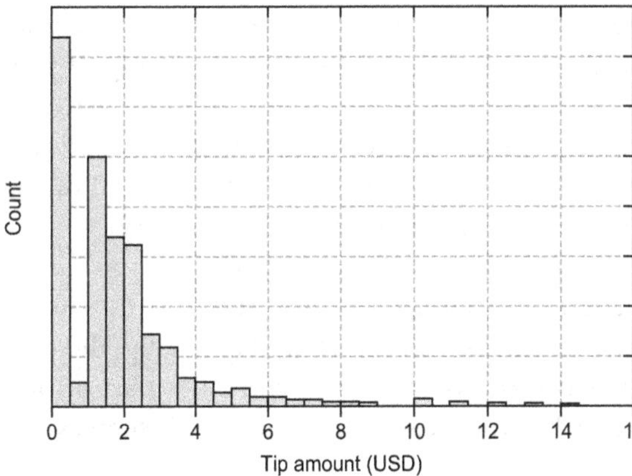

Figure 6.5 The distribution of tip amount. Around half the trips yielded $0 tips, which is more than we'd expect intuitively.

So the plan for our model is to predict which trips will result in no tip, and which will result in a tip. This is a job for a binary classifier. With such a classifier, you'll to be able to do the following:

- Assist the taxi driver by providing an alert to predicted no-tip situations
- Gain understanding of how and why such a situation might arise by using the dataset to uncover the driving factors (pun intended!) behind incidence of tipping in NYC taxi rides

A STORY FROM THE REAL WORLD

Before you start building this model, we'll tell you the real story of how our first attempt at tackling this problem was quite unsuccessful, disguised as very successful—the worst kind of unsuccessful—and how we fixed it. This type of detour is extremely common when working with real data, so it's helpful to include the lessons learned here. When working with machine learning, it's critical to watch out for two pitfalls: *too-good-to-be-true scenarios* and making *premature assumptions* that aren't rooted in the data.

As a general rule in ML, if the cross-validated accuracy is higher than you'd have expected, chances are your model is cheating somewhere. The real world is creative when trying to make your life as a data scientist difficult. When building initial tip/no-tip classification models, we quickly obtained a very high cross-validated predictive accuracy of the model. Because we were so excited about the model performance on this newly acquired dataset—we nailed it—we temporarily ignored the warnings of a cheating model. But having been bitten by such things many times before, the overly optimistic results caused us to investigate further.

One of the things we looked at was the importance of the input features (as you'll see in more detail in later sections). In our case, a certain feature totally dominated in terms of feature importance in the model: *payment type*.

From our own taxi experience, this could make sense. People paying with credit cards (in the pre-Square era) may have a lower probability of tipping. If you pay with cash, you almost always round up to whatever you have the bills for. So we started segmenting the number of tips versus no tips for people paying with a credit card rather than cash. Alas, it turned out that the vast majority (more than 95%) of the millions of passengers paying with a credit card did tip. So much for that theory.

So how many people paying with cash tipped? *All* of them?

In actuality, *none* of the passengers paying with cash had tipped! Then it quickly became obvious. Whenever a passenger paid with cash and gave a tip, the driver didn't register it in whatever way was necessary for it to be included as part of our data. By going through our ML sanity checks, we unearthed millions of instances of potential fraud in the NYC taxi system!

Returning to the implications for our ML model: in a situation like this, when there's a problem in the generation of the data, there's simply no way to trust that part of the data for building an ML model. If the answers are incorrect in nefarious ways, then what the ML model learns may be completely incorrect and detached from reality.

Ultimately, to sidestep the problem, we opted to remove from the dataset all trips paid for with cash. This modified the objective: to predict the incidence of tipping for only noncash payers. It always feels wrong to throw away data, but in this case we decided that under the new data-supported assumption that all cash-payment data was untrustworthy, the best option was to use the noncash data to answer a slightly different problem. Of course, there's no guarantee that other tip records aren't wrong as well, but we can at least check the new distribution of tip amounts. Figure 6.6 shows the histogram of tip amounts after filtering out any cash-paid trips.

With the bad data removed, the distribution is looking much better: only about 5% of trips result in no tip. Our job in the next section is to find out why.

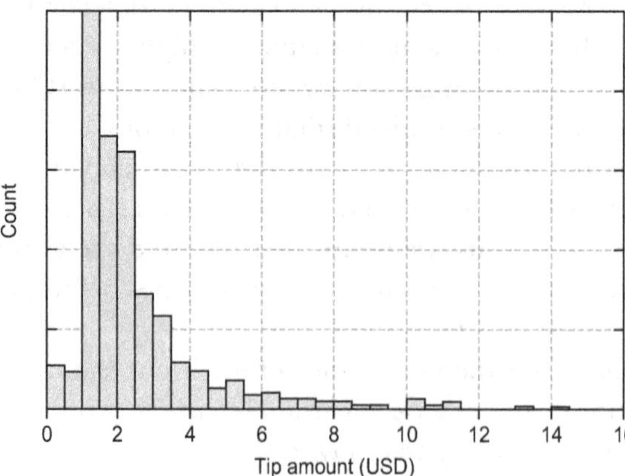

Figure 6.6 The distribution of tip amounts when omitting cash payments (after discovering that cash tips are never recorded in the system)

6.2 Modeling

With the data prepared for modeling, you can easily use your knowledge from chapter 3 to set up and evaluate models. In the following subsections, you'll build different versions of models, trying to improve the performance with each iteration.

6.2.1 Basic linear model

You'll start this modeling endeavor as simply as possible. You'll work with a simple, logistic regression algorithm. You'll also restrict yourself initially to the numerical values in the dataset, because those are handled by the logistic regression algorithm naturally, without any data preprocessing.

You'll use the scikit-learn and pandas libraries in Python to develop the model. Before building the models, we shuffled the instances randomly and split them into 80% training and 20% holdout testing sets. You also need to scale the data so no column is considered more important than others a priori. If the data has been loaded into a pandas `DataFrame`, the code to build and validate this model looks something like the following listing.

Listing 6.1 Logistic regression tip-prediction model

```
from sklearn.preprocessing import StandardScaler
from sklearn.linear_model import SGDClassifier
from sklearn.metrics import roc_curve, roc_auc_score
from pylab import *

sc = StandardScaler()
data_scaled = sc.fit_transform(data[feats])

sgd = SGDClassifier(loss="modified_huber")

sgd.fit(
    data.ix[train_idx,feats],
    data['tipped'].ix[train_idx]
)

preds = sgd.predict_proba(
    data.ix[test_idx,feats]
)

fpr, tpr, thr = roc_curve(
    data['tipped'].ix[test_idx],
    preds[:,1]
)
auc = roc_auc_score(data['tipped'].ix[test_idx], preds[:,1])

plot(fpr,tpr)
plot(fpr,fpr)
xlabel("False positive rate")
ylabel("True positive rate")
```

Annotations:
- Scales the data to be between –1 and 1
- Uses loss-function that handles outliers well
- Fits the classifier on the training features and target data
- Makes predictions on the held-out test set
- Calculates ROC curve and AUC statistics
- Plots ROC curve

The last part of listing 6.1 plots the ROC curve for this first, simple classifier. The holdout ROC curve is shown in figure 6.7.

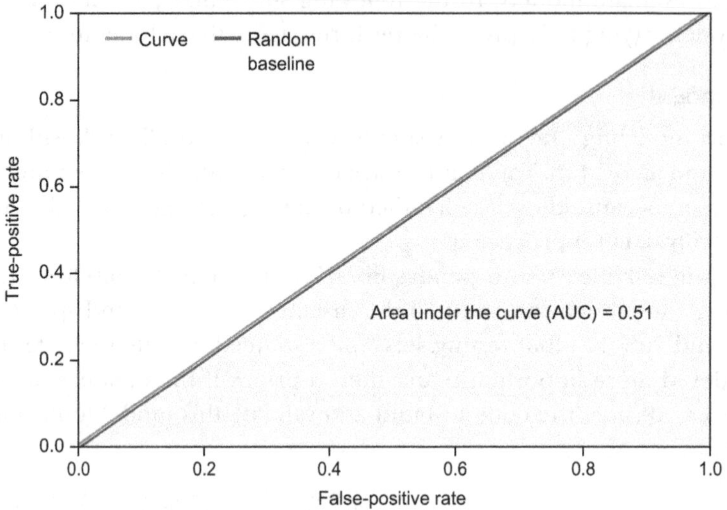

Figure 6.7 The receiver operating characteristic (ROC) curve of the logistic regression tip/no-tip classifier. With an area under the curve (AUC) of 0.5, the model seems to perform no better than random guessing. Not a good sign for our model.

There's no way around it: the performance of this classifier isn't good! With a holdout AUC of 0.51, the model is no better than random guessing (flipping a coin weighted 95% "tip" and 5% "no tip" to predict each trip), which is, for obvious reasons, not useful. Luckily, we started out simply and have a few ways of trying to improve the performance of this model.

6.2.2 Nonlinear classifier

The first thing you'll try is to switch to a different algorithm—one that's nonlinear. Considering how poor the first attempt was, it seems that a linear model won't cut it for this dataset; simply put, tipping is a complicated process! Instead, you'll use a nonlinear algorithm called *random forest*, well known for its high level of accuracy on real-world datasets. You could choose any of a number of other algorithms (see the appendix), but we'll leave it as an exercise for you to evaluate and compare different algorithms. Here's the code (relative to the previous model) for building this model.

Listing 6.2 Random forest tip-prediction model

```
from sklearn.ensemble import RandomForestClassifier
from sklearn.metrics import roc_curve, roc_auc_score
from pylab import *

rf = RandomForestClassifier(n_estimators=100)
rf.fit(data.ix[train_idx,feats], data['tipped'].ix[train_idx])
preds = rf.predict_proba(data.ix[test_idx,feats])

fpr, tpr, thr = roc_curve(data['tipped'].ix[test_idx], preds[:,1])
auc = roc_auc_score(data['tipped'].ix[test_idx], preds[:,1])

plot(fpr,tpr)
plot(fpr,fpr)
xlabel("False positive rate")
ylabel("True positive rate")

fi = zip(feats, rf.feature_importances_)
fi.sort(key=lambda x: -x[1])
fi = pandas.DataFrame(fi, columns=["Feature","Importance"])
```

Plots ROC curve

Features importance

The results of running the code in listing 6.2 are shown in figure 6.8. You can see a significant increase in holdout accuracy—the holdout AUC is now 0.64—showing clearly that there's a predictive signal in the dataset. Some combinations of the input features are capable of predicting whether a taxi trip will yield any tips from the passenger. If you're lucky, further feature engineering and optimization will be able to boost the accuracy levels even higher.

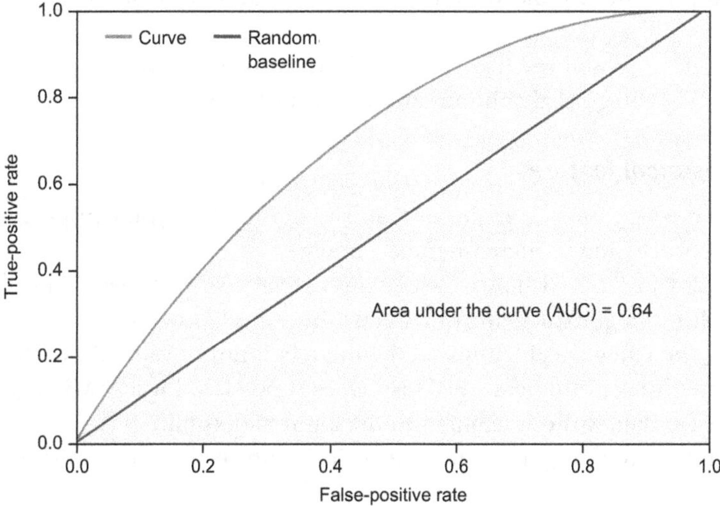

Figure 6.8 The ROC curve of the nonlinear random forest model. The AUC is significantly better: at 0.64, it's likely that there's a real signal in the dataset.

You can also use the model to gain insight into what features are most important in this moderately predictive model. This exercise is a crucial step for a couple of reasons:

- It enables you to identify any cheating features (for example, the problem with noncash payers) and to use that as insight to rectify any issues.
- It serves as a launching point for further feature engineering. If, for instance, you identify latitude and longitude as the most important features, you can consider deriving other features from those metrics, such as distance from Times Square. Likewise, if there's a feature that you thought would be important but it *doesn't* appear on the top feature list, then you'll want to analyze, visualize, and potentially clean up or transform that feature.

	Feature	Importance
0	dropoff_latitude	0.165411
1	dropoff_longitude	0.163337
2	pickup_latitude	0.163068
3	pickup_longitude	0.160285
4	trip_time_in_secs	0.122214
5	trip_distance	0.112020
6	fare_amount	0.067795
7	passenger_count	0.017850
8	surcharge	0.014259
9	rate_code	0.006974
10	tolls_amount	0.004067
11	mta_tax	0.002720

Figure 6.9 The important features of the random forest model. The drop-off and pickup location features seem to dominate the model.

Figure 6.9 (also generated by the code in listing 6.2) shows the list of features and their relative importance for the random forest model. From this figure, you can see that the location features are the most important, along with time, trip distance, and fare amount. It may be that riders in some parts of the city are less patient with slow, expensive rides, for example. You'll look more closely at the potential insights gained in section 6.2.5.

Now that you've chosen the algorithm, let's make sure you're using all of the raw features, including categorical columns and not just plain numerical columns.

6.2.3 *Including categorical features*

Without going deeper into the realm of feature engineering, you can perform some simple data preprocessing to increase the accuracy.

In chapter 2, you learned how to work with categorical features. Some ML algorithms work with categorical features directly, but you'll use the common trick of "Booleanizing" the categorical features: creating a column of value 0 or 1 for each of the possible categories in the feature. This makes it possible for any ML algorithm to handle categorical data without changes to the algorithm itself.

The code for converting all of the categorical features is shown in the following listing.

Listing 6.3 Converting categorical columns to numerical features

```
def cat_to_num(data):
    categories = unique(data)
    features = {}
    for cat in categories:
        binary = (data == cat)
        features["%s:%s"%(data.name, cat)] = binary.astype("int")
    return pandas.DataFrame(features)
```

Function for converting a categorical column to a set of numerical columns

```
payment_type_cats = cat_to_num(data['payment_type'])
vendor_id_cats = cat_to_num(data['vendor_id'])
store_and_fwd_flag_cats = cat_to_num(data['store_and_fwd_flag'])
rate_code_cats = cat_to_num(data['rate_code'])
```

Converts four categorical features in the dataset to numerical

```
data = data.join(payment_type_cats)
data = data.join(vendor_id_cats)
data = data.join(store_and_fwd_flag_cats)
data = data.join(rate_code_cats)
```

Adds the converted data to the full dataset used for training and testing

After creating the Booleanized columns, you run the data through listing 6.2 again and obtain the ROC curve and feature importance list shown in figure 6.10. Note that your holdout AUC has risen slightly, from 0.64 to 0.656.

As model performance increases, you can consider additional factors. You haven't done any real feature engineering, of course, because the data transformations applied so far are considered basic data preprocessing.

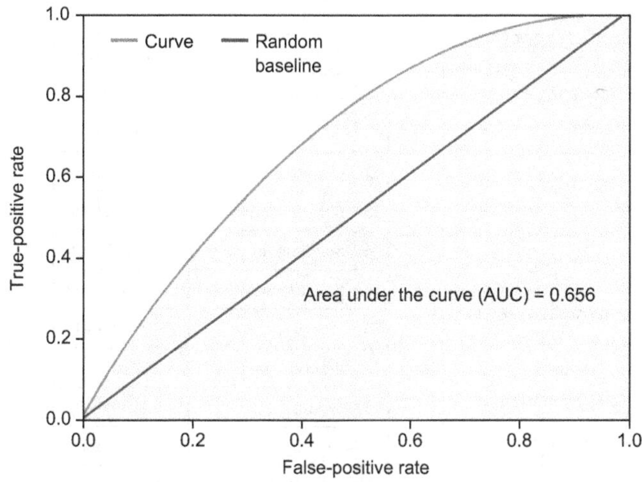

	Feature	Importance
0	dropoff_latitude	0.163023
1	pickup_latitude	0.161114
2	dropoff_longitude	0.160988
3	pickup_longitude	0.158672
4	trip_time_in_secs	0.111172
5	trip_distance	0.106693
6	fare_amount	0.067567
7	passenger_count	0.019286
8	surcharge	0.010330
9	payment_type:NOC	0.008361
10	payment_type:CRD	0.008247

New features

Figure 6.10 The ROC curve and feature importance list of the random forest model with all categorical variables converted to Boolean (0/1) columns, one per category per feature. The new features are bringing new useful information to the table, because the AUC is seen to increase from the previous model without categorical features.

6.2.4 Including date-time features

At this point, it's time to start working with the data to produce new features, what you've previously known as *feature engineering*. In chapter 5, we introduced a set of date-time features transforming date and timestamps into numerical columns. You can easily imagine the time of the day or day of the week to have some kind of influence on how a passenger will tip.

The code for calculating these features is presented in the following listing.

Listing 6.4 Date-time features

```
# Datetime features (hour of day, day of week, week of year)

pickup = pandas.to_datetime(data['pickup_datetime'])
dropoff = pandas.to_datetime(data['dropoff_datetime'])
data['pickup_hour'] = pickup.apply(lambda e: e.hour)
data['pickup_day'] = pickup.apply(lambda e: e.dayofweek)
data['pickup_week'] = pickup.apply(lambda e: e.week)
data['dropoff_hour'] = dropoff.apply(lambda e: e.hour)
data['dropoff_day'] = dropoff.apply(lambda e: e.dayofweek)
data['dropoff_week'] = dropoff.apply(lambda e: e.week)
```

Converts date-time columns (text) to real dates and times

Adds hour, day, and week features to pickup times

Adds hour, day, and week features to drop-off times

With these date-time features, you can build a new model. You run the data through the code in listing 6.2 once again and obtain the ROC curve and feature importance shown in figure 6.11.

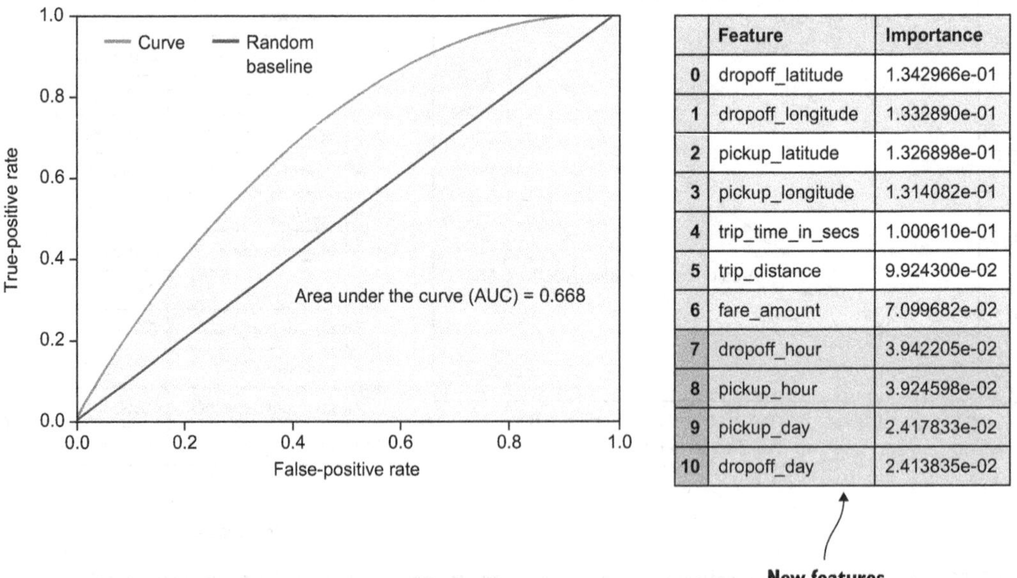

	Feature	Importance
0	dropoff_latitude	1.342966e-01
1	dropoff_longitude	1.332890e-01
2	pickup_latitude	1.326898e-01
3	pickup_longitude	1.314082e-01
4	trip_time_in_secs	1.000610e-01
5	trip_distance	9.924300e-02
6	fare_amount	7.099682e-02
7	dropoff_hour	3.942205e-02
8	pickup_hour	3.924598e-02
9	pickup_day	2.417833e-02
10	dropoff_day	2.413835e-02

Figure 6.11 The ROC curve and feature importance list for the random forest model, including all categorical features and additional date-time features

You can see an evolution in the accuracy of the model with additional data preprocessing and feature engineering. At this point, you're able to predict whether a passenger will tip the driver with an accuracy significantly above random. Up to now, you've looked only at improving the data in order to improve the model, but you can try to improve this model in two other ways:

- Vary the model parameters to see whether the default values aren't necessarily the most optimal
- Increase the dataset size

In this chapter, we've been heavily subsampling the dataset in order for the algorithms to handle the dataset, even on a 16 GB–memory machine. We'll talk more about scalability of methods in chapters 9 and 10, but in the meantime we'll leave it to you to work with this data to increase the cross-validated accuracy even further!

6.2.5 Model insights

It's interesting to gain insight about the data through the act of building a model to predict a certain answer. From the feature importance list, you can understand which parameters have the most predictive power, and you use that to look at the data in new ways. In our initial unsuccessful attempt, it was because of inspection of the feature importance list that we discovered the problem with the data. In the current working model, you can also use the list to inspire some new visualizations.

At every iteration of our model in this section, the most important features have been the pickup and drop-off location features. Figure 6.12 plots the geographical distribution of drop-offs that yield tips from the passenger, as well as drop-offs from trips that don't.

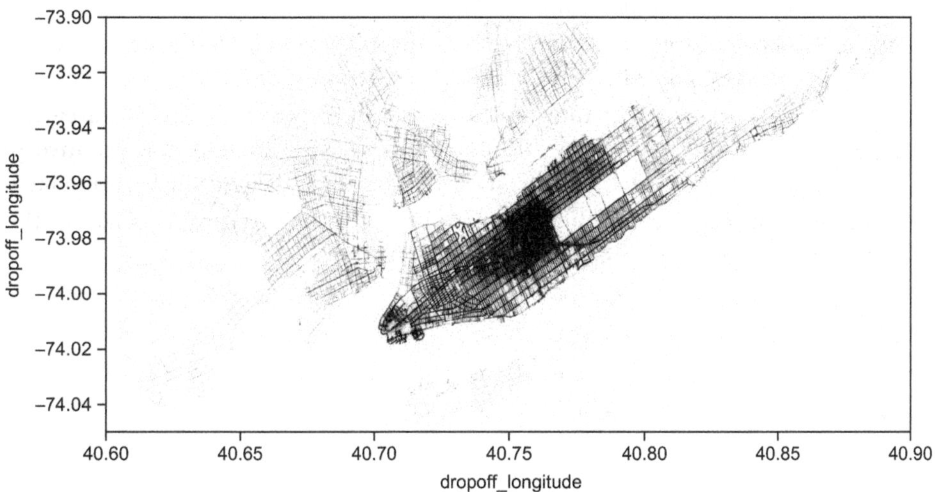

Figure 6.12 The geographical distribution of drop-offs

Figure 6.12 shows an interesting trend of not tipping when being dropped off closer to the center of the city. Why is that? One possibility is that the traffic situation creates many slow trips, and the passenger isn't necessarily happy with the driver's behavior. As a non–US-citizen, I have another theory. This particular area of the city has a high volume of both financial workers and tourists. We'd expect the financial group to be distributed farther south on Manhattan. There's another reason that tourists are the most likely cause of this discrepancy, in my mind: many countries have vastly different rules for tipping than in the United States. Some Asian countries almost never tip, and many northern European countries tip much less, and rarely in taxis. You can make many other interesting investigations based on this dataset. The point is, of course, that real-world data can often be used to say something interesting about the real world and the people generating the data.

6.3 Summary

This chapter introduced a dataset from the real world and defined a problem suitable for the machine-learning knowledge that you've built up over the previous five chapters. You went through the entire ML workflow, including initial data preparation, feature engineering, and multiple iterations of model building, evaluation, optimization, and prediction. The main takeaways from the chapter are these:

- With more organizations producing vast amounts of data, increasing amounts of data are becoming available within organizations, if not publicly.
- Records of all taxi trips from NYC in 2013 have been released publicly. A lot of taxi trips occur in NYC in one year!
- Real-world data can be messy. Visualization and knowledge about the domain helps. Don't get caught in too-good-to-be-true scenarios and don't make premature assumptions about the data.
- Start iterating from the simplest possible model. Don't spend time on premature optimization. Gradually increase complexity.
- Make choices and move on; for example, choose an algorithm early on. In an ideal world, you'd try all combinations at all steps in the iterative process of building a model, but you'd have to fix some things in order to make progress.
- Gain insights into the model and the data in order to learn about the domain and potentially improve the model further.

6.4 Terms from this chapter

Word	Definition
open data	Data made available publicly by institutions and organizations.
FOIL	Freedom of Information Law. (The federal version is known as the Freedom of Information Act, or FOIA.)
too-good-to-be-true scenario	If a model is extremely accurate compared to what you would have thought, chances are that some features in the model, or some data peculiarities, are causing the model to "cheat."
premature assumptions	Assuming something about the data without validation, risking biasing your views of the results.

7 Advanced feature engineering

This chapter covers

- Using advanced feature-engineering concepts to increase the accuracy of your machine-learning system
- Extracting valuable features from text by using natural-language-processing techniques
- Extracting meaning from images and using them as features in your machine-learning project

You explored the basic concepts behind feature engineering in chapter 5 and applied simple feature-engineering techniques to real-world data in chapter 6. In this chapter, you'll look at more-sophisticated techniques that you can use when faced with types of data that have become common in today's world. The two most important of these are text and images. This chapter presents advanced techniques for extracting features from text and image data, in order to use this data in your machine-learning pipelines.

7.1 Advanced text features

You already looked at simple feature engineering for text data in chapter 5. This section provides more details about the ideas behind these techniques, and presents more-advanced concepts that can improve the accuracy of your models even further.

Recall that your mission in extracting features from text is to somehow convert texts of various lengths and words into a common set of features. In chapter 5, you learned about the bag-of-words representation, in which you count the occurrences of words across all texts and use the counts of the top-N words as N new features. This work of transforming natural-language text into machine-usable data is commonly referred to as *natural language processing*, or NLP.

7.1.1 Bag-of-words model

Bag of words is one of the simplest but also most widely used techniques in NLP. It's a great approach to start with for any text-based problem. It's also the basis of many other more advanced methods that you'll look at later in this chapter. You'll learn about this model in two parts: first, tokenization and transformation, and then vectorization.

TOKENIZATION AND TRANSFORMATION

The splitting of a text into pieces is known as *tokenization*. The most common way to split is on words, but in some cases (for example, in character-based languages), you may want to split on characters or split on pairs or groups of words or even something more advanced. Groups of words in a split are known as *n-grams*. Two- or three-word combinations are known as *bigrams* and *trigrams*, respectively (and they're the most common after one-word *unigrams*). Bigrams in the example in figure 7.1 include

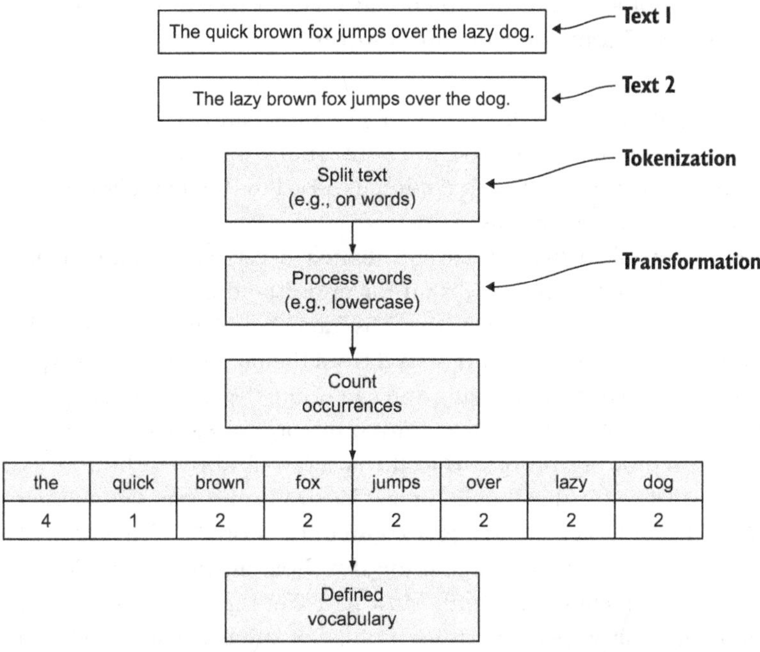

Figure 7.1 The initial steps in the bag-of-words extraction algorithm

"the lazy," "brown fox," and so forth. Trigrams include "brown fox jumps" and "jumps over the."

Expanding to multiple words may help your models in some cases, by offering more contextualization of the text. But using multiple words also typically inflates the number of features quite dramatically. In practice, you usually start with only unigram representations. If you want to move to higher-grade grams, you have to make sure to use an ML algorithm that handles sparse data. You'll learn more about that in the following subsection.

The next step in our bag-of-words algorithm is to make any *transformations* necessary to the tokens extracted from the text. A good example of a transformation is converting all words to lowercase, such that you don't produce features for both "fox" and "Fox," which may add to the noise of the model. In some cases, however, you may want to preserve the case, if it makes sense in your project (for example, if proper names are common in the text and highly predictive, or if ALL CAPS is meaningful). *Stemming*—which strips word suffixes—can also be a powerful transformation for extracting more signals out of different words with similar meanings. Using stemming, for instance, causes the words "jump," "jumping," "jumps," and "jumped" to all be expressed as the token "jump" in your dictionary. Other transformations such as custom handling of numbers, punctuation, and special characters can also be useful, depending on the text at hand.

Next, you can define the dictionary that you'll generate your text features from. For machine-learning projects, it's common to set a limit on the number of features, hence the number of words, in your dictionary. This is usually done by sorting by the word occurrences and using only the top-N words.

VECTORIZATION

You can use your bag-of-words dictionary to generate features to use in your ML models. After defining the dictionary, you can convert any text to a set of numbers corresponding to the occurrences of each dictionary word in the text. Figure 7.2 shows this process, which is called *vectorization.*

But there's a problem that we haven't discussed yet. Most natural-language texts include many words that aren't important for understanding the topic, but are simply "filling." These include words such as "the," "is," and "and." In NLP research, these are called *stop words,* and they're usually removed from the dictionary as they typically aren't highly predictive of anything interesting and can dilute the more meaningful words that are important from an ML perspective. With our words already sorted by occurrences, the usual way to remove stop words is to throw away all words with more occurrences than a certain word-count threshold. Figure 7.2 shows an example; a larger text (the third row in the figure) has a much larger count of the word "the" than any of the other words. The challenge, then, is to define the threshold at which a particular word is a stop word and not a meaningful word. Most NLP libraries, such as the NLTK Python library, include prebuilt stop-word lists for a range of languages so you don't have to do this every time. In some cases, though, the list of stop words will be different for your

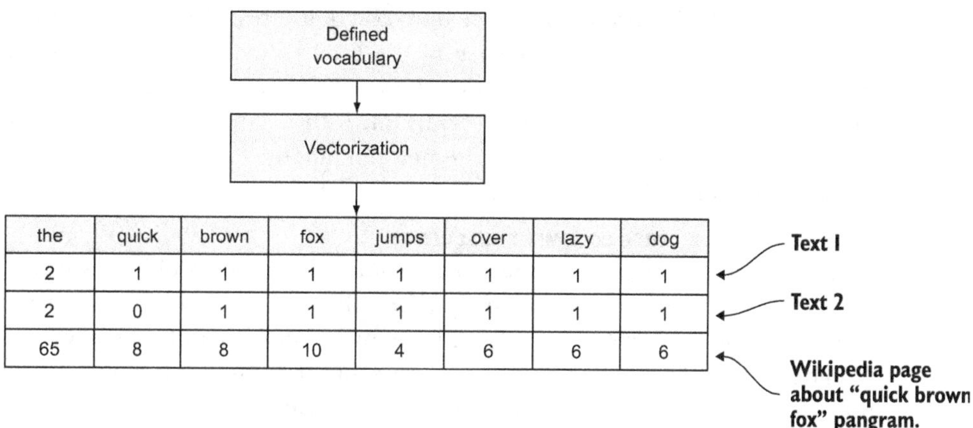

Defined
vocabulary
Vectorization
the
quick
brown
fox
jumps
over
lazy
dog
2
1
1
1
1
1
1
1
2
0
1
1
1
1
1
1
65
8
8
10
4
6
6
6
Text I
Text 2
Wikipedia page
about "quick brown
fox" pangram.

Figure 7.2 Using the vocabulary, you can now represent each text as a list of numbers. The rows show the count for the two small texts in figure 7.1 and the count for the Wikipedia page about the sentence "The quick brown fox jumps over the lazy dog," which is an English pangram (it includes all letters in the English alphabet).

specific project, and you'll need to choose a stop-word threshold (a standard choice is to exclude any words that appear in more than 90% of all documents).

Although not apparent in figure 7.2, any realistic dictionary will have many words, and usually only a small subset of those will be present in the texts that you're generating features for. This combination usually makes text features include lots of zeros. Only a small number of the dictionary words will be found in a given text, so we call the bag-of-words features *sparse*. If you have many sparse features (it's common to have 1,000 features with only a small percent nonzero elements), it's a good idea to choose an ML algorithm that can handle sparse features natively, or an algorithm that can deal with many low-significance features without sacrificing accuracy. The naïve Bayes algorithms in the scikit-learn Python library handle sparse data natively, and are therefore well suited for text-classification problems. Algorithms such as random forest are known to handle lots of low-significance features well, although your mileage may vary. You should always test the efficacy of different methods by using the evaluation and optimization techniques discussed in chapter 4.

7.1.2 Topic modeling

The bag-of-words method is simple to understand and implement. But other, more-advanced methods could lead to big increases in ML model accuracy. This section introduces three of those methods.

One problem with the bag-of-words model is the nature of simple word counts. If a certain word (not a stop word) is common in a corpus—for example, the word "data" in a corpus of ML papers—it's not necessarily informative to know that the word also appears in a new text. Instead, you'd do better by focusing on relatively rare words that are more highly predictive of the outcome of interest. To this end, it's common to scale the word counts by the inverse of the total count of that word in the corpus. Because you want to describe a text the best you can using only numbers, and a word that isn't abundant in the training corpus but *is* abundant in a new document is likely more indicative of the meaning of the new document, you're better off giving preferential treatment to that rare word.

TERM FREQUENCY-INVERSE DOCUMENT FREQUENCY

A commonly used algorithm that tries to solve this exact problem is called *term frequency–inverse document frequency*, or *tf-idf* for short. This algorithm is calculated as a product of the term frequency (tf) and the inverse document frequency (idf).

The tf can be calculated in different ways, but the simplest is to use the number of times a word occurs in a particular document. It's also common to use other versions of the tf factor, such as binary (1 if the word is in a document, and 0 otherwise) and logarithmic (1 + log[tf]).

The inverse document frequency is calculated as the logarithm of the total number of documents, divided by the number of documents that contain the term, so that relatively uncommon words attain higher values. In its simplest form, the tf-idf equation looks like this:

$$tf-idf(term, doc, docs) = count(term\ in\ doc) \frac{count(docs)}{count(docs\ with\ term)}$$

Tf-idf can be powerful for generating good ML features from any corpus of text. It can also be useful in other areas, such as search. Because you're generating a vector of numbers for any document, you can also find "distances" between documents, as distances between their tf-idf vector representations. If the user search query is a document, you can find the distances between any other documents in your dataset in this way, and hence return a ranked list of documents to the user based on the query. Listing 7.1 in the next section shows how to use the scikit-learn Python library to generate tf-idf vectors from documents, along with a more advanced technique called *latent semantic indexing*.

LATENT SEMANTIC ANALYSIS

Latent semantic analysis, or LSA (also commonly called *latent semantic indexing*, or LSI) is a more sophisticated method of topic modeling. It's also more advanced both conceptually and computationally. The idea is to use the bag-of-word counts to build a term-document matrix, with a row for each term and a column for each document. The elements of this matrix are then normalized similarly to the tf-idf process in order to avoid frequent terms dominating the power of the matrix.

The main trick of the LSA algorithm is in its notion of a concept. A *concept* is a pattern of similar terms in the document corpus. For example, the concept of "dog" may have related terms (words, in this case) of "barking," "leash," and "kennel." The algorithm doesn't label the concept "dog" but instead figures out which words are related by their co-occurrence in documents and then ascertains that these words are connected through a certain abstract concept. The word "dog" may itself be an important term related to the "dog" concept. These topics are considered *hidden* or *latent* in the data, hence the name *latent* semantic analysis.

LSA uses *singular value decomposition* (SVD)[1]—a well-known mathematical tool—to split the term-document matrix (A) into three matrices (T,S,D). T is the term-concept matrix that relates the terms (for example, "barking" and "kennel") to concepts (for example, "dog"), and D is the concept-document matrix that relates individual documents to concepts that you'll later use to extract the features from the LSA model. The S matrix holds the singular values. In LSA, these denote the relative importance that a term has to a document. In the same way as you restricted the number of features in the bag-of-words and tf-idf algorithms, you can now select the top singular values and restrict the feature space to something more manageable; recall that the term-document matrix (A) can be extremely large and sparse.

Using the top-N components of the SVD, you generate N features for your ML model by taking the corresponding rows from the concept-document matrix (D). When new documents come in for prediction, you can generate a new set of features from the previously learned LSA model by performing the matrix multiplication: $D = A^T T S^{-1}$. Here A^T is the word count (or tf-idf), using the defined dictionary, for the new document, and T and S are the term-concept and singular-value matrices from the SVD.

Although it's useful to understand the principles of LSA, not everyone knows linear algebra well enough to do these calculations. Luckily, plenty of implementations can readily be used in your ML project. The scikit-learn Python library includes the functionality needed to run LSA by (1) using tf-idf to generate the term-document matrix, (2) performing the matrix decomposition, and (3) transforming the documents to vectors, as shown in the following listing.

Listing 7.1 Latent semantic analysis using scikit-learn

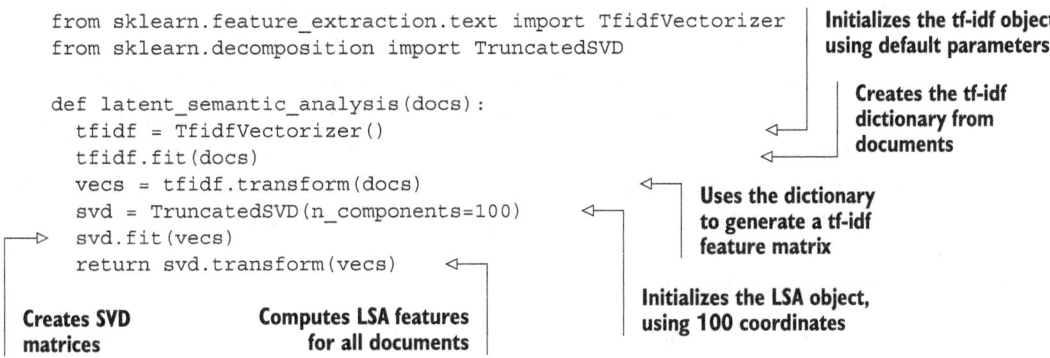

```
from sklearn.feature_extraction.text import TfidfVectorizer
from sklearn.decomposition import TruncatedSVD

def latent_semantic_analysis(docs):
  tfidf = TfidfVectorizer()
  tfidf.fit(docs)
  vecs = tfidf.transform(docs)
  svd = TruncatedSVD(n_components=100)
  svd.fit(vecs)
  return svd.transform(vecs)
```


---

1 For readers familiar with principal component analysis (which is presented later in this chapter), SVD is the same technique that enables you to compute PCA coordinates from a dataset. You can think of LSA as "PCA for bag of words."

Next, you'll look at a few advanced extensions to LSA that have recently become popular in the field of topic modeling.

PROBABILISTIC METHODS

LSA is based on linear algebra (math with vectors and matrices), but an equivalent analysis can be done using probabilistic methods that model each document as a statistical mixture of topic distributions. These concepts are all relatively advanced, and we won't go into the mathematical details here, but the probabilistic approach can perform better in terms of model accuracy for some datasets.

The probabilistic analogue to LSA is known as pLSA (for probabilistic). A more widely used version of this is called *latent Dirichlet analysis* (LDA), in which specific assumptions are made on the distribution of topics. You build in the assumption that a document can be described by a small set of topics and that any term (word) can be attributed to a topic. In practice, LDA can perform well on diverse datasets. The following code listing highlights how LDA can be used in Python using the Gensim library.

Listing 7.2 Latent Dirichlet analysis in Python using Gensim

```
import gensim.models.ldamodel.LdaModel

def lda_model(docs):
  return LdaModel(docs, num_topics=20)

def lda_vector(lda_model, doc):
  return lda_model[doc]
```

- Must install Gensim first, by running "pip install gensim" (annotation for the import line)
- Builds LDA model, setting the number of topics to extract (annotation for def lda_model)
- Generates features for a new document (annotation for def lda_vector)

The number of topics used in the LDA model is a parameter that needs to be tuned to the data and problem at hand. We encourage you to define your performance metric and use the techniques in chapter 4 to optimize your model. It's also worth noting that the LDA in Gensim can be updated on the fly with new documents if new training data is coming in continuously. We encourage you to check out the many other interesting natural-language and topic-modeling algorithms in Gensim. In chapter 10, you'll use some of these advanced text-feature-extraction techniques to solve a real-world machine-learning problem. The next section introduces a completely different method for text-feature extraction: expanding the content of the text.

7.1.3 Content expansion

We now turn to a completely different concept for extracting features from text. The methods of this section don't represent the text with numbers, but rather expand the text content to include more text (which can then be featurized) or to introduce other useful information for the specific ML problem. The following are some common content-expansion methods.

FOLLOW LINKS

If you're looking to build an ML classifier by extracting text features from tweets (for instance, for a Twitter sentiment analysis that classifies a post as positive or negative in sentiment), you'll often find the 140-character limit problematic. You might not have enough information to obtain the desired accuracy of the model.

Many tweets contain links to external web pages that can hold much more text, and that you could *expand* the tweet with the text from the link in order to improve the quality of the data. You could even follow links deeper on the web page to build a larger corpus of text.

KNOWLEDGE-BASE EXPANSION

A more advanced text-extension method is to detect named entities in the text and extend the original text with information about each named entity in an online knowledge base, such as Wikipedia. In this situation, named entities would be anything that you could look up on Wikipedia. You'd then grab the text from the Wikipedia entry for that named entity and perform any of the text-extraction algorithms from section 7.1.2.

Extracting named entities isn't a trivial task, and has been the subject of several research groups. One of the issues stems from ambiguous names. If one word could have multiple meanings, you risk expanding your feature set with completely wrong information. One possible solution is to disambiguate the named entities again by using a knowledge base like Wikipedia. First of all, you could assume that any other words in the tweet, for example, would also be common in the knowledge-base text. You could also use the Wikipedia link graph to find how close two named entities fall in the knowledge base. An example is a tweet that includes the named entity "Tesla." Some tweets will relate to the electronic car company, whereas others will be about inventor Nikola Tesla. If the tweet contains the word "car" or "model," it's most likely about Tesla, the company. If it contains the related entity of "Edison," it might be about the person (Tesla and Edison worked together in NYC in 1884).

TEXT META-FEATURES

Another technique for extending the text features with valuable data is to analyze the text for *meta-features.* Unlike the previously discussed techniques, these types of features are problem-dependent.

Let's take the example of tweets again. A tweet contains all sorts of valuable data that's particular to tweets and can be extracted, such as hashtags and mentions, as well as meta-information from Twitter, such as counts of retweets and favorites. As another example for web-based text, you could extract basic information from link text, such as the top-level domain. In general text, you could extract the count of words or characters or the number of special characters in different languages. Extracting the language could be an ML classifier itself that provides the answer as a feature to another classifier.

To choose the right text meta-features, you should use your imagination and knowledge of the problem at hand. Remember that the ML workflow is an iterative process; you can develop a new feature, go back through the pipeline, and analyze how the accuracy is improved over time.

You can use the text to get at other types of data as well. The text might include dates and times that could be useful for the ML model to understand, or there may be time information in the metadata of the text. Chapter 5 presented date-time feature extractions, which can be used in this context as well.

If you're analyzing a web page, or there's a URL in the text, you may have access to images or videos that are important for understanding the context of the text. Extracting features from images and videos requires even more-advanced techniques, which you'll investigate next.

7.2 Image features

One of the strongholds of human intelligence is our visual and spatial sense and our ability to recognize patterns and objects in images and the 3D scenes we navigate every day. Much of the way we think is based on these abilities. Computers, on the other hand, think in bits and their visual analogue, pixels. Historically, this fact has severely limited computers' ability to match human levels of cognition when it comes to visual pattern recognition. Only with the advent of sophisticated algorithms in computer vision and artificial intelligence—from which machine learning has arguably sprung—are researchers and practitioners getting closer to reaching human levels, although most often in narrowly specified areas. On the other hand, if you can get close to matching human-level pattern recognition accuracy with computer vision and machine-learning techniques, you can reap some of the benefits of most computational systems: scalability, availability, and reproducibility.

This section presents a few ways to extract features from images that can be used in your ML workflows. First, you'll look at simple image features including raw pixels, colors, and image metadata.

7.2.1 Simple image features

The simplest way to deal with images is worth mentioning, not only because it may sometimes be enough, but also because it shows the true power of the machine-learning approach, as compared to manual or conventional statistical approaches. You treat the values of pixels in the image as the features that go into your ML model.

In practice, you make a single row with all the pixels, converting the two-dimensional image into one dimension. If it's a color image, you have basically three images in one (red, blue, green channels). Normal pixel values are 0.0 to 1.0, or 0 to 255 (for 8-bit images). You may have guessed that for any modern image, this creates thousands or millions of features that will increase the computational requirements and potentially lead to overfitting, hence affecting the accuracy. That's why this approach isn't often used in practice. Still, you'd probably be surprised how well this can work without any sophisticated feature engineering for some ML problems, such as classifying indoor versus outdoor images.

In principle, all the information is encoded in the pixels. If you're not going to use the raw pixels for performance reasons (computationally or accuracy-wise), you have to find a way to represent the image with fewer features that works well enough for your specific problem. This is exactly the same problem you were solving in the previous section on text features and many other feature-engineering techniques. Toward the end of section 7.2.2, we introduce some new methods for automatic feature extraction, but most current practical ML projects on images use some of the techniques described in this section.

COLOR FEATURES

Let's say you're trying to classify images into categories based on the landscape of the images. Categories could be *sky*, *mountain*, or *grass*, for example. In this case, it sounds useful to represent the images by the constituent colors. You can calculate simple color statistics of each color channel of the image, such as *mean*, *median*, *mode*, *standard deviation*, *skewness*, and *kurtosis*. This leads to 6 x 3 = 18 features for common RGB (red-green-blue channel) images.

Another set of features representing colors in the images are the color ranges of the image. Table 7.1 shows a list of possible color ranges that will cover much of the color space.

Table 7.1 Examples of color-range features. You add 1 to the divisors to avoid producing missing values from dividing by 0.

Color range	Definition
Red range	Max value in red channel minus min value in red channel
Red-to-blue range	Red range / (max value in blue channel minus min value in blue channel plus 1)
Blue-to-green range	(Min value in blue channel minus max value in blue channel) / (min value in green channel minus max value in green channel plus 1)
Red-to-green range	Red range / (max value in green channel minus min value in green channel plus 1)

IMAGE METADATA FEATURES

In addition to color information, the image may contain metadata that's helpful for your problem. Most photographs, for example, include EXIF data that's recorded by the camera at the time the picture was taken. If you're building a model to predict whether an image is considered interesting or beautiful to a user, the algorithm could use the brand of the camera and the lens, the value of the aperture, and the zoom level. Table 7.2 outlines image metadata features that may be useful.

Table 7.2 Image metadata features that can be included in the ML pipeline

Feature	Definition
Manufacturer	The company that made the camera
Orientation	The orientation of the camera (landscape or portrait)

Table 7.2 Image metadata features that can be included in the ML pipeline *(continued)*

Feature	Definition
Date-time	Time of the shooting (use the date-time features introduced in chapter 5)
Compression	How the image is compressed (usually JPEG or RAW)
Resolution	The number of pixels in the width and height dimensions
Aspect ratio	A measurement indicated by dividing the height and width resolutions
Exposure time	The number or fraction of seconds of exposure
Aperture	The f-number representing the aperture (for example, 2.8 or 4.0)
Flash	Whether the flash was on
Focal length	The distance from the lens to the point of focus

With these simple features, you might be able to solve quite a few machine-learning problems that have images as part of the data. Of course, you haven't represented any of the shapes or objects in the image, which will, for obvious reasons, be important for many image-classification problems! The next section introduces more-advanced computer-vision techniques commonly used to represent objects and shapes.

7.2.2 *Extracting objects and shapes*

So far, you haven't considered objects or shapes when extracting information from images. In this subsection, you'll look at a few ways to represent shapes with numerical features that can be automatically extracted via statistical and computational methods.

EDGE DETECTION

Probably the simplest way to represent shapes in images is to find their edges and build features on those. Figure 7.3 shows an example of *edge detection* in an image.

Figure 7.3 Applying the Canny edge-detection algorithm to a photo of a girl (input on left) produces a new binary image (on right) with only the edges traced. (Image by JonMcLoone at English Wikipedia, CC BY-SA 3.0, https://commons.wikimedia.org/w/index.php?curid=44894482.)

Several well-known algorithms can find edges in an image. Some of the most commonly used are the *Sobel* and *Canny* edge-detection algorithms. Figure 7.3 shows the Canny algorithm.

> **Image processing in Python with scikit-image**
>
> We've mentioned the scikit-learn Python library a few times in this book already, as it provides an easy way to try many machine-learning algorithms. The analogue to this in the computer-vision and image-processing world is scikit-image. This is an equally useful way to try algorithms that we talk about in this section.
>
> If you're using Pip, scikit-image can easily be installed with the following:
>
> ```
> $ pip install scikit-image
> ```
>
> Here's a simple example of using this library for edge detection:
>
> ```
> >>> import skimage
> >>> image = skimage.data.camera()
> >>> edges = skimage.filter.sobel(image)
> ```

Now that you've extracted edges from images, you can extract features from those edges. The simplest way is to calculate a number that represents the total number of edges in an image. If `edges` is your edge images and `res` is the resolution of the image, the equation is as follows:

$$edge\_score = \frac{\Sigma edges}{res_x \times res_y}$$

Together with other features, this may be useful in determining objects of interest. You can define other edge-based features depending on your use case. For example, you could choose to calculate the preceding edge score for multiple parts of the image in a grid.

ADVANCED SHAPE FEATURES

More-sophisticated feature-extraction algorithms that can be used to detect particular shapes and objects exist. One of these is the *histogram of oriented gradients* (HOG). In machine learning, these algorithms can be used to detect human faces or particular animals in images, for example.

The HOG algorithm is a multistep process of various image-processing techniques. The goal of the algorithm is to describe shapes and objects in image regions that aren't too sensitive to small changes in scale and orientation. This is achieved as follows:

1. Calculate the gradient image (which direction the edges of the image are "moving")
2. Divide the image into small blocks called *cells*

3. Calculate the orientation of the gradients inside those cells
4. Calculate the histogram of those orientations in the individual cells

Usually, larger blocks of the image are defined from the smaller cells and used for normalization of the gradient values in the cells. In this way, you can avoid being too sensitive to changes in lighting or shadows. Each cell can then be flattened into a list of features that describe the shapes in the image and can be used in the ML pipeline.

As usual, you're concerned with understanding the usefulness of the algorithms from a practical perspective, and so you can go ahead and use an already implemented library for HOG features. The scikit-image Python library has an easy-to-use version of HOG. The following listing shows how to calculate HOG features for an image. Figure 7.4 shows the result of the HOG transformation applied to a photograph of American astronaut Eileen Collins, the first female commander of a Space Shuttle.

Listing 7.3 Histogram of oriented gradients in Python with scikit-image

```
import skimage

image = skimage.color.rgb2gray(skimage.data.astronaut())
hog = skimage.feature.hog(image, orientations=9, pixels_per_cell=(8,8),
      cells_per_block=(3,3), normalise=True, visualise=True)
```

Figure 7.4 Applying the HOG transformation. This image is from the HOG example page on scikit-image documentation (http://scikit-image.org/docs/dev/auto_examples/features_detection/plot_hog.html#sphx-glr-auto-examples-features-detection-plot-hog-py).

Here you see how to calculate HOG features easily while defining the number of orientations to consider, the size of the cells in pixels, the size of the blocks in cells, and whether to normalize and visualize the result.

With HOG features, you have a powerful way to find objects in images. As with everything, in certain cases, HOG doesn't work well—for instance, when the object changes orientation significantly. You should make proper tests of the ML system as usual to determine usefulness for the problem at hand.

DIMENSIONALITY REDUCTION

We're almost always in the game of dimensionality reduction when performing feature extraction, except perhaps for the content-expansion methods in the previous section. But a few techniques are commonly used for dimensionality reduction in general, and the most widely used is called *principal component analysis* (PCA).

PCA allows you to take a set of images and find "typical" images that can be used as building blocks to represent the original images. Combining the first couple of principal components enables you to rebuild a large portion of the training images, whereas subsequent components will cover less-frequent patterns in the images. Features for a new image are generated by finding the "distance" from a principal image, thus representing the new image by a single number per principal image. You can use as many principal components as make sense in your ML problem.

PCAs are known to be linear algorithms; they can't represent inherently nonlinear data. There are several extensions to PCA or other types of nonlinear dimensionality reduction. An example that we've had good experiences with is *diffusion maps.*

AUTOMATIC FEATURE EXTRACTION

A renaissance has occurred in the world of artificial neural networks. Invented in the '80s and inspired by the biology of the brain, these networks were at the center of the artificial intelligence field that has evolved into the machine-learning field we know today. For a few decades, they were considered useful methods for some ML problems. But because they were hard to configure and interpret, had problems with overfitting, and were less computationally scalable, they ended up as a last resort when real-world problems needed solving. Now, several breakthroughs in machine-learning research have mostly taken care of these issues. *Deep neural nets* (DNNs) are now considered state of the art for many ML problems, but especially those that deal with images, video, or voice. Figure 7.5 shows the layout of a neural net.

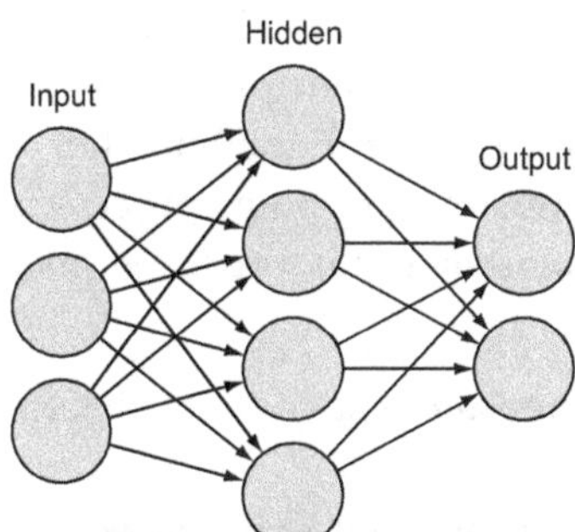

Figure 7.5 A simple artificial neural network. Deep neural nets are made of many layers of these simple networks. (Image from Wikipedia.)

In DNNs, each layer is capable of defining a set of new features that are useful for the problem at hand. The weights between nodes then define the importance of those features for the next layer, and so forth. This approach was traditionally prone to overfitting, but recently developed techniques allow for the removal of node connections in a way that the accuracy is maintained while decreasing the risk of overfitting.

The use of DNNs, also known as *deep belief networks* or *deep learning*, is still a relatively new field. We encourage you to follow its development.

7.3 Time-series features

Many datasets that are amassed by modern data-collection systems come in the form of *time series*, measurements of a process or set of processes across time. Time-series data is valuable because it provides a window into the time-varying characteristics of the subjects at hand and enables ML practitioners to move beyond employing static snapshots of these subjects to make predictions. But fully extracting the value out of time-series data can be difficult. This section describes two common types of time-series data—classical time series and point processes (event data)—and details some of the most widely used time-series features.

7.3.1 Types of time-series data

There are two main types of time-series data: classical time series and point processes. *Classical time series* consist of numerical measurements that are taken over time. Typically, these measurements are evenly spaced over time (hourly, daily, weekly, and so forth) but can also consist of irregularly sampled data. These are examples of classical time-series data:

- The value of the stock market, in billions of dollars (for example, measured hourly, daily, or weekly)
- The day-to-day energy consumption of a commercial building or residential home
- The value, in dollars, of a client's bank account over time
- Sets of diagnostics monitored in an industrial manufacturing plant (for example, physical performance measurements of different parts or measurements of plant output over time)

Point processes, on the other hand, are collections of events that occur over time. As opposed to measuring numerical quantities over time, point processes consist of a timestamp for each discrete event that happens, plus (optionally) other metadata about the event such as category or value. For this reason, point processes are also commonly referred to as *event streams*. Examples of point processes include the following:

- The activity of a web user, measuring the time and type of each click (this is also called *clickstream data*)
- Worldwide occurrences of earthquakes, hurricanes, disease outbreak, and so forth

- The individual purchases made by a customer throughout the history of their account
- Event logs in a manufacturing plant, recording every time an employee touches the system and every time a step in the manufacturing process is completed

An astute reader may note that for some time series, a one-to-one mapping exists between the classical time-series representation and the underlying point process. For example, a customer's bank account can easily be viewed either as the value of the account over time (classical time series) or as a list of the individual transactions (point process). This correspondence can be useful in creating various types of time-series features on a single dataset. But the conversion isn't always possible. (For example, it's difficult to imagine what a classical time-series related to simple web clicks would be.)

To make this more concrete, let's look at time-series data that can be just as easily viewed as a point process or a time series. Table 7.3 shows the first few rows of a crime dataset from San Francisco, collected between 2003 and 2014 (dataset publicly available at https://data.sfgov.org). In all, the dataset consists of more than 1.5 million crimes that occurred in the city. For each crime, the data includes the exact date and time of the crime, type of crime, and location.

Table 7.3 San Francisco crime data in its raw form, as a sequence of events

Incident number	Date	Time	District	Category
80384498	04/13/2008	00:54	NORTHERN	DRUNKENNESS
80384147	04/13/2008	00:55	CENTRAL	NONCRIMINAL
80384169	04/13/2008	00:56	BAYVIEW	ASSAULT
80384169	04/13/2008	00:56	BAYVIEW	DRUG/NARCOTIC
80384153	04/13/2008	00:57	BAYVIEW	OTHER
80384175	04/13/2008	01:00	CENTRAL	ASSAULT
80384943	04/13/2008	01:00	CENTRAL	LARCENY/THEFT
80392532	04/13/2008	01:00	INGLESIDE	LARCENY/THEFT
80384943	04/13/2008	01:00	CENTRAL	FRAUD
80384012	04/13/2008	01:15	NORTHERN	SUSPICIOUS OCC

You can aggregate this raw data into classical time-series data in a multitude of ways: by year, by month, by day of week, and so on, potentially with a different time series for each district or category. Listing 7.4 demonstrates how to aggregate the raw event data into a time series of the monthly number of crimes in San Francisco. The resulting time series of integer crime count by month is plotted in figure 7.6. The data shows a

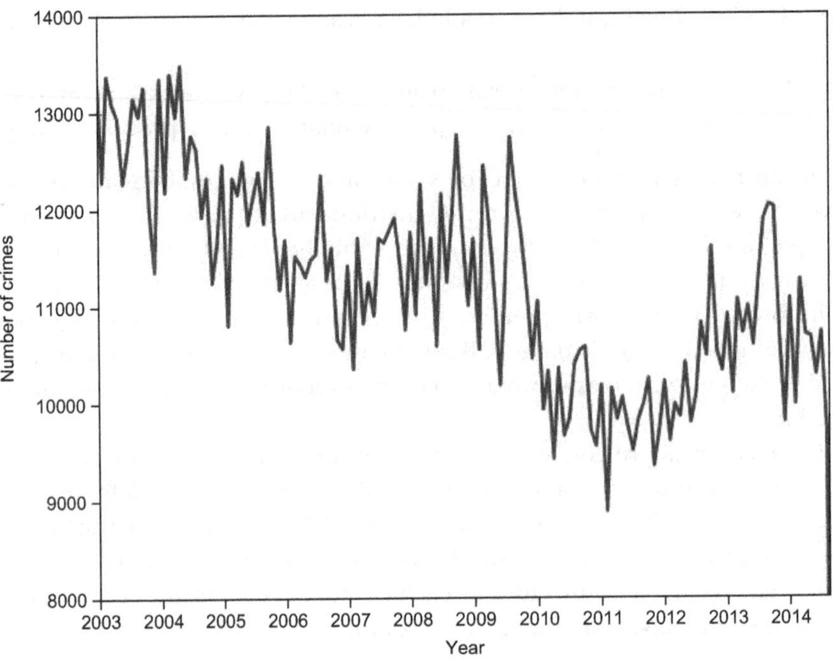

Figure 7.6 Classical time series of monthly crime count in San Francisco. This data was processed from the raw event data. For ML modeling, you can derive features from the event data, the classical time series, or both.

marked decline from the rate of 13,000 crimes per month in 2003, and a recent uptick in crime activity.

Listing 7.4 Converting SF crime event data to classical time series

```
import pandas as pd
from datetime import datetime
from matplotlib import pyplot as plt

df = pd.read_csv("sfpd_incident_all.csv")

df['Month'] = map(lambda x: datetime.strptime("/".join(x.split("/")[0::2]),
     "%m/%Y"),df['Date'])

df_ts = df.groupby('Month').aggregate(len)["IncidntNum"]        <-- Creates classical time series

plt.plot(df_ts.index,df_ts.values,'-k',lw=2)        <-- Plots time series
plt.xlabel("Month")
plt.ylabel("Number of Crimes")
```

7.3.2 *Prediction on time-series data*

Just as there are two common types of time-series data, there are also two common types of predictions that you can make from time-series data. The first is *time-series forecasting*, which attempts to predict future values of the time series (or times of future events) based on past measurements. Time-series forecasting problems include the following:

- Predicting tomorrow's price of a stock
- Predicting tomorrow's temperature in Phoenix, Arizona
- Forecasting next year's energy consumption in Denmark
- Forecasting the date of the next major hurricane in North America

The first three of these tasks involve predicting future values of a classical time series, whereas the fourth is a prediction on a point-process dataset. The common thread is that each task involves analyzing the values of a single time series to make predictions about the future. Note that the vast majority of literature on time-series forecasting falls under the branch of time-series analysis, whereas comparatively little attention has been focused here by ML practitioners (though that is changing). For further details, any Google or Amazon search will reveal an abundance of results!

The second common type of time-series prediction is *time-series classification or regression.* Instead of predicting future values of a single time series, the aim here is to classify (or predict a real-valued output on) hundreds or thousands of time series. Examples of this type of problem include the following:

- Using each user's online clickstream to predict whether each user will click a specific ad
- Employing a time series of QA measurements to determine which of a set of manufactured goods (for example, lightbulbs) are most likely to fail in the next month
- Predicting the lifetime value of each user of an online app based on each user's in-app activity stream from the first week after sign-up
- Predicting which patients are most likely to suffer post-op complications based on their medical records

Unlike time-series forecasting, ML has had a large influence on time-series classification and regression. The following section focuses primarily on creating time-series features for classification/regression purposes, but many of those methods can also be applied for time-series forecasting.

7.3.3 *Classical time-series features*

This section describes several of the most common feature-engineering approaches for classical time series. We start with the simplest time-series metrics and describe progressively more complicated and sophisticated approaches.

SIMPLE TIME-SERIES FEATURES

It may sound absurd, but the simplest time-series metrics involve ignoring the time axis altogether! Analyzing the distribution of measurements without considering the timestamps can often provide useful information for classification, regression, or forecasting. For discussion purposes, we outline four simple (yet powerful) metrics that involve only the marginal distribution of time-series measurements:

- *Average*—The mean or median of the measurements can uncover tendencies in the average value of a time series.
- *Spread*—Measurements of the spread of a distribution, such as standard deviation, median absolute deviation, or interquartile range, can reveal trends in the overall variability of the measurements.
- *Outliers*—The frequency of time-series measurements that fall outside the range of the typical distribution (for example, larger than two, three, or four standard deviations from the mean) can carry predictive power in many use cases, such as prediction of process-line interruptions or failures.
- *Distribution*—Estimating the higher-order characteristics of the marginal distribution of the time-series measurements (for example, skew or kurtosis), or going a step further and running a statistical test for a named distribution (for example, normal or uniform), can be predictive in some scenarios.

You can make things more sophisticated by computing *windowed statistics*, which entails calculating the preceding summary metrics within a specified time window. For instance, the mean or standard deviation of only the last week of measurements may be highly predictive. From there, you can also compute *windowed differences*, which would be the difference in those metrics from one time window to the next. The following listing presents a code example of computing those features.

Listing 7.5 Windowed statistics and differences

```
import pandas as pd
from datetime import datetime
import numpy as np

window1 = (datetime(2014,3,22),datetime(2014,6,21))

idx_window = np.where(map(lambda x: x>=window1[0] and x<=window1[1],
    df_ts.index))[0]

mean_window = np.mean(df_ts.values[idx_window])
std_window = np.std(df_ts.values[idx_window])

window2 = (datetime(2013,3,22),datetime(2013,6,21))

idx_window2 = np.where(map(lambda x: x>=window2[0] and x<=window2[1],
    df_ts.index))[0]
   mean_wdiff = mean_window - np.mean(df_ts.values[idx_window2])
std_wdiff = std_window - np.std(df_ts.values[idx_window2])
```

window = spring 2014

Finds which data points fall within the window

Computes the windowed mean and standard deviation

Computes the windowed difference from spring 2013

Computes the windowed difference in mean and standard deviation

ADVANCED TIME-SERIES FEATURES

Next, you move to more-sophisticated classical time-series features. *Autocorrelation* features measure the statistical correlation of a time series with a *lagged* version of itself. For example, the one-autocorrelation feature of a time series takes the original time series and correlates it with the same time series shifted over by one time bin to the left (with nonoverlapping portions removed). By shifting the time series like this, you can capture the presence of periodicity and other statistical structure in the time series. The shape of the autocorrelation function (autocorrelation computed over a grid of time lags) captures the essence of the structure of the time series. In Python, the `statsmodels` module contains an easy-to-use autocorrelation function. Figure 7.7 shows how the autocorrelation is computed and plots an autocorrelation function for the SF crime data.

Fourier analysis is one of the most commonly used tools for time-series feature engineering. The goal of Fourier analysis is to decompose a time series into a sum of sine and cosine functions on a range of frequencies, which are naturally occurring in many real-world datasets. Performing this decomposition enables you to quickly identify periodic structure in the time series. The Fourier decomposition is achieved by using the discrete Fourier transform, which computes the *spectral density* of the time series—how well it correlates to a sinusoidal function at each given frequency—as a function of frequency. The resulting decomposition of a time series into its component spectral densities is called a *periodogram*. Figure 7.8 shows the periodogram of the San Francisco crime data, computed using the `scipy.signal.periodogram` function (several Python modules have methods for periodogram estimation). From the periodogram, various ML features can be computed, such as the spectral density at specified frequencies, the sum of the spectral densities within frequency bands, or the location of the highest spectral density (which describes the fundamental frequency of oscillation of the time series). The following listing provides example code for periodogram computation and features.

Listing 7.6 Periodogram features

```
import pandas as pd
import numpy as np
import scipy.signal

f, psd = scipy.signal.periodogram(df_ts, detrend='linear')

plt.plot(f, psd,'-ob')
plt.xlabel('frequency [1/month]')
plt.ylabel('Spectral Density')
plt.show()

# Features:
period_psd1 = 1./f[np.argmax(psd)]

sdens_gt_12m = np.sum(psd[f > 1./12])

sdens_ratio_12m = float(sdens_gt_12m) / np.sum(psd[f <= 1./12])
```

Computes the periodogram

Feature 1: period of highest psd peak; for this data, should be = 47.0 months

Feature 2: sum of spectral density higher than 1/12 months

Feature 3: ratio of spectral density higher than to less than 1/12 months

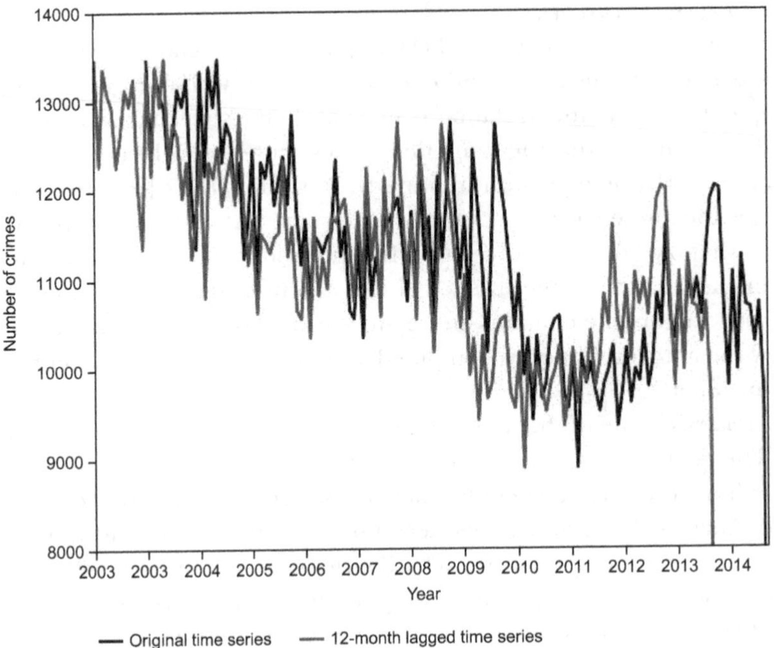

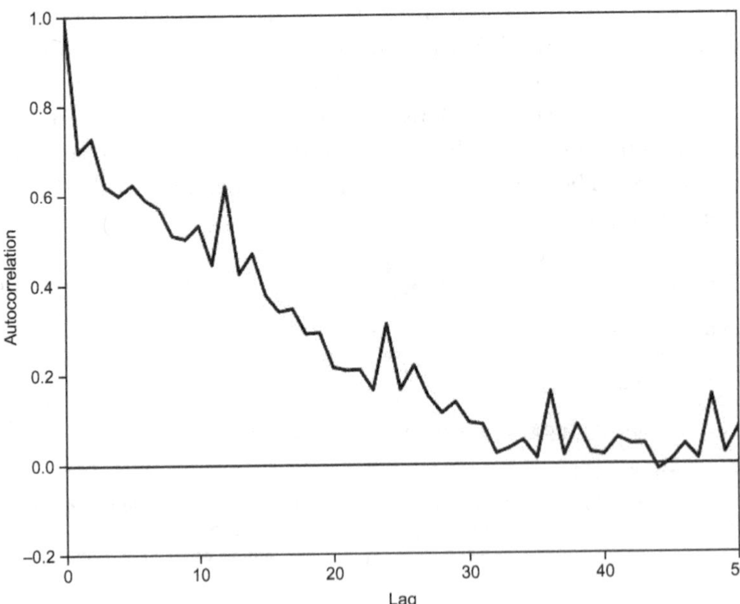

Figure 7.7 Top: Correlation of the original time series and 12-month lagged time series defines the 12-month autocorrelation. Bottom: The autocorrelation function for the SF crime data. The autocorrelation is high for short time scales, showing high dependence of any month's crime on the previous months' values.

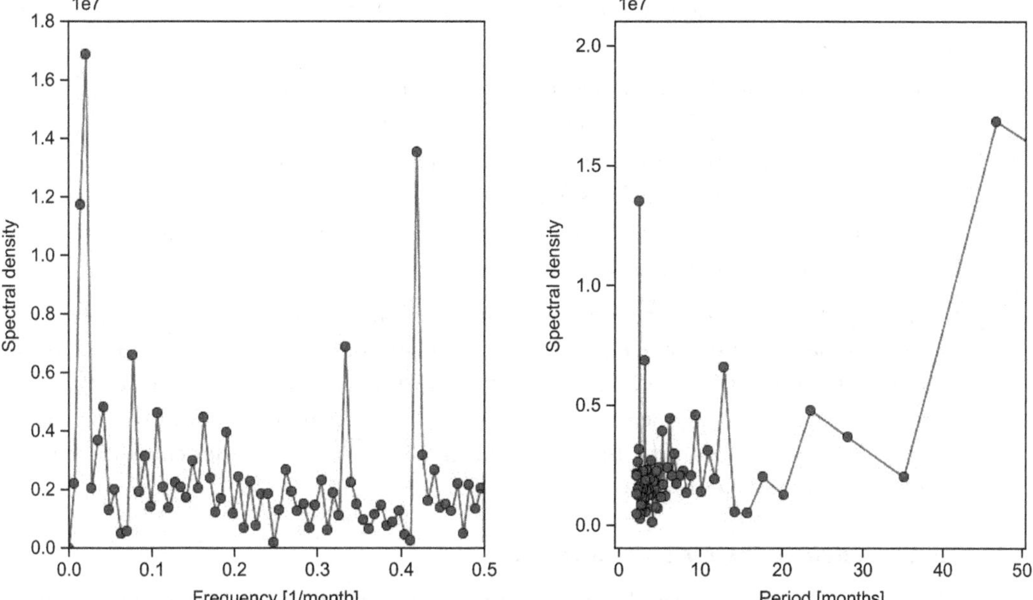

Figure 7.8 Left: Periodogram of the San Francisco crime data, showing the spectral density as a function of frequency. Right: The same periodogram with the x-axis transformed from frequency to period.

Several classical time-series models are commonly used in the time series analysis literature. The purpose of these models is to describe each value of the time series as a function of the past values of the time series. The models themselves have been widely used for time-series forecasting for decades. Now, as machine learning has become a mainstay in time-series data analysis, they're often used for prediction in conjunction with more-sophisticated ML models such as SVMs, neural nets, and random forests. Examples of time-series models include the following:

- *Autoregressive (AR) model*—Each value in the time series is modeled as a linear combination of the last p values, where p is a free parameter to be estimated.
- *Autoregressive–moving average (ARMA) model*—Each value is modeled as the sum of two polynomial functions: the AR model and a moving-average (MA) model that's a linear combination of the previous q error terms.
- *GARCH model*—A model commonly used in financial analysis that describes the random noise terms of a time series using an ARMA model.
- *Hidden Markov model (HMM)*—A probabilistic model that describes the observed values of the time series as being drawn from a series of hidden states, which themselves follow a Markov process.

You can use these models to compute time-series features in various ways, including these:

- Using the predicted values from each of the models (and the differences between the predictions) as features themselves
- Using the best-fit parameters of the models (for example, the values of p and q in an ARMA(p,q) model) as features
- Calculating the statistical goodness-of-fit (for example, mean-square error) of a model and using it as a feature

In this way, a blend of classical time-series models and state-of-the-art machine-learning methodologies can be achieved. You can attain the best of both worlds: if an ARMA model is already highly predictive for a certain time series, the ML model that uses those predictions will also be successful; but if the ARMA model doesn't fit well (as for most real-world datasets), the flexibility that the ML model provides can still produce highly accurate predictions.

7.3.4 Feature engineering for event streams

This section presents a brief look at feature engineering for event streams. As shown previously in listing 7.4, event data can be converted to a classical time series. This enables you to employ all the feature-engineering processes described in the preceding two sections to extract classical time-series data on point-process data. But a number of additional features can be computed on event data because of its finer granularity.

Analogous to the windowed statistics described in section 7.1.3, you can compute simple windowed and difference statistics on event data. But because point-process data allows an individual timestamp of each and every event, you can compute these statistics on any time window that you want, down to an extremely fine granularity. Further, statistics such as "time since last event," "number of events in the past 48 hours," and "average length of time between events" suddenly become possible.

Finally, just as classical time series are often modeled with statistical models like ARMA and HMM, point-process data is often described with models such as Poisson processes and nonhomogeneous Poisson processes. In a nutshell, these models describe the rate of incoming events as a function of time and enable you to predict the expected time until the next event. Feel free to explore these methods more on your own! Just as with the classical time-series models, machine-learning features can be derived from point-process models in three ways: using the predictions from the model, the parameters of the model, and the statistical goodness-of-fit of the model.

7.4 Summary

In this chapter, you looked at methods for generating features from text and images. You can use these features in your ML algorithms to build models that are capable of "reading" or "seeing" with human-level perception. The main takeaways are as follows:

- For text-based datasets, you need to transform variable-length documents to a fixed-length number of features. Methods for this include the following:
  - Simple bag-of-words methods, in which particular words are counted for each document.
  - The tf-idf algorithm, which takes into account the frequency of words in the entire corpus to avoid biasing the dictionary toward unimportant-but-common words.
  - More-advanced algorithms for topic modeling, such as latent semantic analysis and latent Dirichlet analysis.
  - Topic-modeling techniques can describe documents as a set of topics, and topics as a set of words. This allows sophisticated semantic understanding of documents and can help build advanced search engines, for example, in addition to the usefulness in the ML world.
  - You can use the scikit-learn and Gensim Python libraries for many interesting experiments in the field of text extraction.
- For images, you need to be able to represent characteristics of the image with numeric features:
  - You can extract information about the colors in the image by defining color ranges and color statistics.
  - You can extract potentially valuable image metadata from the image file itself; for example, by tapping into the EXIF metadata available in most image files.
  - In some cases, you need to be able to extract shapes and objects from images. You can use the following methods:
    - Simple edge-detection-based algorithms using Sobel or Canny edge-detection filters
    - Sophisticated shape-extraction algorithms such as histogram of oriented gradients (HOG)
    - Dimensionality reduction techniques such as PCA
    - Automated feature extraction by using deep neural nets
- Time-series data comes in two flavors: classical time series and point processes. A plethora of ML features can be estimated from this data.
  - Two principal machine-learning tasks are performed on time-series data:
    - Forecasting the value of a single time series
    - Classifying a set of time series
  - For classical time series, the simplest features involve computing time-windowed summary statistics and windowed differences.
  - More-sophisticated features involve the statistical characterization of the time series, using tools such as autocorrelation and Fourier analysis.

- Various classical time-series models can be used to derive features. These include AR, ARMA, GARCH, and HMM.
- From point-process data, you can compute all these features and more, because of the finer granularity of the data.
- Common models for point-process data include Poisson processes and non-homogeneous Poisson processes.

7.5 Terms from this chapter

Word	Definition
feature engineering	Transforming input data to extract more value and improve the predictive accuracy of ML models.
natural language processing	The field that aims to make computers understand natural language.
bag of words	A method for transforming text into numbers; counting the number of occurrences of a particular word in a document.
stop words	Words that are common but not useful as a feature (for example, "the," "is," "and").
sparse data	When data consists of mostly 0s and few data cells, we call the data sparse. Most NLP algorithms produce sparse data, which you need to use or transform for your ML algorithms.
tf-idf	Term-frequency, inverse-document frequency. A bag-of-words method that's normalized by text from the entire corpus.
latent semantic analysis	A method for finding topics of interest in documents and connecting them to a set of words.
latent Dirichlet analysis	An extension of the idea from LSA that works well with many text problems in practice.
content expansion	The process of expanding the original content into more data (for example, by following links in a document).
meta-features	A set of features that aren't extracted from the content itself, but some connected metadata.
EXIF data	A standard for defining metadata on images. Includes information about the photo (for example, manufacturer of the camera, resolution, aperture).
edge detection	The process of detecting edges in images to remove the noise of most images.
HOG	Histogram of oriented gradients. An approach to image features that understands particular shapes and objects.
PCA	Principal component analysis. A way to represent images by simpler, typical images, thus reducing the number of dimensions in images. Instead of 100 pixels, an image can be approximated by two numbers: the distance to the two most principal components.

Word	Definition
deep neural nets	An extension to artificial neural nets that has recently shown to perform well for machine learning on audiovisual data.
classical time series	Series of numerical measurements over time.
point process	Series of events collected over time, each with a precise timestamp known.
time-series forecasting	Predicting future values of an individual time series.
periodogram	Plot of the Fourier power spectral density of a time series as a function of frequency of oscillation. This technique can reveal the fundamental modes of oscillation and is a useful feature-engineering tool for time-series data.

8 Advanced NLP example: movie review sentiment

This chapter covers

- Using a real-world dataset for predicting sentiment from movie reviews
- Exploring possible use cases for this data and the appropriate modeling strategy
- Building an initial model using basic NLP features and optimizing the parameters
- Improving the accuracy of the model by extracting more-advanced NLP features
- Scaling and other deployment aspects of using this model in production

In this chapter, you'll use some of the advanced feature-engineering knowledge acquired in the previous chapter to solve a real-world problem. Specifically, you'll use advanced text and NLP feature-engineering processes to build and optimize a model based on user-submitted reviews of movies.

As always, you'll start by investigating and analyzing the dataset at hand to understand the feature and target columns so you can make the best decisions about which feature-extraction and ML algorithms to use. You'll then build the initial model from the simplest feature-extraction algorithms to see how you can quickly get a useful model with only a few lines of code. Next, you'll dig a little deeper into the library of feature-extraction and ML modeling algorithms to improve the accuracy of the model even further. You'll conclude by exploring various deployment and scalability aspects of putting the model into production.

8.1 Exploring the data and use case

In this chapter, you'll use data from a competition on *Kaggle*—a data-science challenge site where data scientists from around the world work on solving well-defined problems posed by companies to win prizes. You'll work with this data as you learn to use the tools developed in the previous chapters to solve a real-world problem via machine learning.

The data used in this chapter is from the Bag of Words Meets Bags of Popcorn competition (www.kaggle.com/c/word2vec-nlp-tutorial). You need to create an account on the Kaggle platform to download the data, but that's probably a good thing because you might want to try your newly acquired ML skills on a big-prize competition anyway!

In the following sections, we begin by describing the dataset, what the individual columns mean, and how the data was generated. Next, we dive a level deeper, present the data attributes, and make some initial observations about the data that we have. From here, we brainstorm possible use cases that we could solve with the dataset at hand and review the data requirements and real-world implications of each potential use case. Finally, we use this discussion to select a single use case that we'll solve in the remainder of the chapter.

Note that although we structure this section to first describe and explore the data and then to figure out a use case to solve, typically the steps are taken in reverse order. Usually an ML practitioner will start with a use case, hypothesis, or set of questions to answer and then search for and explore data to appropriately solve the problem at hand. This is the preferred methodology, because it forces the practitioner to think hard about the use case and the data required before going "in the weeds" of the dataset. That said, it's not uncommon to be handed a dataset and be asked to build something cool!

8.1.1 A first glance at the dataset

Our dataset consists of written movie reviews from the Internet Movie Database, IMDb (www.imdb.com). The training data consists of 50,000 reviews, selected so that each movie has no more than 30 reviews in the dataset. For each review, the outcome variable is encoded as a binary feature, with the value 1 if the manual IMDb rating for that review is greater than 6, and the value 0 if the rating is less than 5. No reviews in the intermediate ratings of 5–6 are included in the dataset.

The challenge with this dataset is to devise an ML system to learn the patterns and structure of language that constitute positive reviews versus those that constitute negative reviews. Critically, you'll train your model to learn only from the text of the reviews and not from other contextual data such as the movie actors, director, genre, or year of release. Presumably, that data would help the accuracy of your model predictions, but it isn't available in this dataset.

In addition to a training dataset, a separate testing dataset of 25,000 reviews of movies that don't appear in the training dataset is provided. In principle, this set of data could be used to validate the performance of your model and to estimate how well the model will perform when deployed to a real-world production setting. But Kaggle doesn't supply the labels for the testing set. Therefore, you'll construct your own testing set by splitting Kaggle's training set into 70% training and 30% testing.

Note the importance of ensuring that no movies in the training set appear in the testing set.[1] If, for instance, reviews from the same movies were included in both the training and testing sets, then your model could learn which movie titles were good and bad, instead of focusing on the language constituting positivity and negativity. But in production you'll be applying this ML model to new movies, with titles you've never seen. This leakage of movies from the training to the testing set could lead you to believe that your model is better than it is when predicting the sentiment of reviews of new movies. For this reason, we recommend that holdout testing sets always be constructed with temporal cutoffs, so that the testing set consists of instances that are newer than the training instances.

8.1.2 Inspecting the dataset

The individual reviews in this dataset vary in length, from a single sentence up to several pages of text. Because the reviews are pulled from dozens of film critics, the vocabulary can vary dramatically from review to review. The key is to build a machine-learning model that can detect and exploit the differences between the positive and negative reviews so that it can accurately predict the sentiment of new reviews.

The first step of the ML process is to look at the data to see what's there and to begin thinking about the other steps of the ML process, such as model type and featurization. To start the data review process, take a look at the 10 shortest reviews in figure 8.1. Look at the first row (`id = 10962_3`). This particular review demonstrates how nuanced this problem can be: although the review clearly states that the "movie is terrible," it also says that there are "good effects." Despite the use of the word *good*, any person would clearly agree that this is a negative movie review. The challenge now is to teach the ML model that even if positive words such as *good* are used, the use of the phrase "movie is terrible" trumps all!

Similarly, these 10 sample reviews include several examples of negative statements. Phrases such as "never get tired" and "no wasted moments" clearly indicate positive

[1] In our training set, we don't have an indicator of which movie each review describes. Therefore, we make the assumption that the training set is provided presorted by date, and we divide the set so that multiple reviews of the same movie fall together in the training or testing set.

id	sentiment	review
10962_3	0	This movie is terrible but it has some good effects.
2331_1	0	I wouldn't rent this one even on dollar rental night.
12077_1	0	Ming The Merciless does a little Bardwork and a movie most foul!
266_3	0	You'd better choose Paul Verhoeven's even if you have watched it.
4518_9	1	Adrian Pasdar is excellent is this film. He makes a fascinating woman.
874_1	0	Long, boring, blasphemous. Never have I been so glad to see ending credits roll.
3247_10	1	I don't know why I like this movie so well, but I never get tired of watching it.
7243_2	0	no comment - stupid movie, acting average or worse... screenplay - no sense at all... SKIP IT!
5327_1	0	A rating of \1\" does not begin to express how dull, depressing and relentlessly bad this movie is."
2469_10	1	This is the definitive movie version of Hamlet. Branagh cuts nothing, but there are no wasted moments.

Figure 8.1 Ten example reviews in the training set, chosen from the shortest reviews. For each review, you're provided only an ID, the binary sentiment, and the text of the review.

qualities of movies, even if the component words are all negative in nature. This demonstrates that to do well in predicting sentiment, you must combine information across multiple (neighboring) words.

Looking through a few of the other (longer) reviews, it's apparent that these reviews typically consist of verbose, descriptive, flowery language. The language is often sarcastic, ironic, and witty. This makes it a great dataset to demonstrate the power of ML to learn nuanced patterns from real data and to make accurate predictions under uncertainty.

8.1.3 So what's the use case?

Often practitioners of (non-real-world) machine learning dive into a problem without thinking hard about the practical use of their ML model. This is a mistake, because the choice of use case can help determine how you structure the problem and solution, including the following:

- How to encode the target variable (for example, binary versus multiclass versus real value)
- Which evaluation criterion to optimize
- What kinds of learning algorithms to consider
- Which data inputs you should and should not use

So before you get started with ML modeling, you first need to determine what real-world use case you want to solve with this dataset.

For each of three possible use cases, you'll consider the following:

- Why would the use case be valuable?
- What kind of training data would you need?
- What would an appropriate ML modeling strategy be?

- What evaluation metric should you use for your predictions?
- Is the data you have sufficient to solve this use case?

Based on the answers to those questions, you'll choose a single use case, which you'll spend the remainder of the chapter solving.

USE CASE 1: RANKING NEW MOVIES

The first and most obvious use case for a movie review dataset is to automatically rank all new movies based on the text of all their reviews:

- *Why would the use case be valuable?*

  This could be a powerful way to decide which movie to watch this weekend. Scoring individual reviews is one thing, but obviously the more valuable use case is to score each movie on the overall positivity of its reviews. Sites such as Rotten Tomatoes get heavy traffic because of their ability to reliably rate each movie.
- *What kind of training data would you need?*

  The basic necessities would be the review text, an indication of the sentiment of each review, and knowledge about which movie each review refers to. With these three components, building a movie-ranking system would be feasible.
- *What would an appropriate ML modeling strategy be?*

  There are a couple of options: (a) You could treat each movie as an ML instance, aggregate the individual reviews for each movie, and roll up the review sentiment into either an average score or a multiclass model. (b) You could continue to treat each review as an ML instance, score every new review on its positivity, and then assign each new movie its average positivity score. We prefer option (b), because aggregating all reviews for a single movie together could result in some confusing patterns for ML—particularly if the individual reviews are highly polarized! Scoring the individual results and then averaging them into a "metascore" is a more straightforward approach.
- *What evaluation metric should you use for your predictions?*

  Assume here that you have a binary outcome variable for each review and that your ML algorithm assigns a score to each review on its likelihood of being a positive review, which you aggregate into a single score per movie. What you care about here is how closely your score matches the true average rating for that movie (for example, percentage of positive reviews), which could lead you to use a metric such as R^2.

  But you could imagine using a different evaluation metric that focuses more weight at the top of the ranking list. In reality, you're probably interested in a movie ranking in order to pick a flick from the top of the list to see this Saturday. Therefore, you'd instead select a metric that focuses on your ability to get the top of the ranking list right. In this case, you'd select a metric such as the true-positive rate at a small false-positive rate (for example, 5% or 10%).

- *Is the data you have sufficient to solve this use case?*

  Unfortunately, no. You have everything you need except knowledge of which movie each review is describing!

USE CASE 2: RATING EACH REVIEW FROM 1 TO 10

A second possible use case is to auto-rate each review on a scale of 1 to 10 (the IMDb scale) based on the set of user reviews about each movie:

- *Why would the use case be valuable?*

  Any new review could be automatically assigned a rating without any manual reading or scoring. This would cut down on a lot of manual labor that's required to curate the IMDb website and movie ratings; or, if users are providing a score along with their rating, it could provide a more objective score based on the text of the user's review.
- *What kind of training data would you need?*

  Just the text of each review and a score, from 1 to 10, for each review.
- *What would an appropriate ML modeling strategy be?*

  Again, there are two options: (a) Treat the outcome variable as a real-valued number and fit a regression model. (b) Treat the outcome variable as categorical and fit a multiclass classification model. In this case, we much prefer option (a) because, unlike classification, it considers the scores on a numerical scale.
- *What evaluation metric should you use for your predictions?*

  If you choose to run a regression model, the typical regression evaluation metrics such as R^2 or mean squared error are natural choices.
- *Is the data you have sufficient to solve this use case?*

  Again, it's not. You have only a Boolean version of each review (positive versus negative) and not the finely grained numerical score.

USE CASE 3: SEPARATING THE POSITIVE FROM THE NEGATIVE REVIEWS

The final use case to consider is separating all the positive reviews from the rest:

- *Why would the use case be valuable?*

  This use case would represent a less granular version of use case 2, whereby each new review could be automatically classified as positive or negative (instead of scored from 1 to 10). This classification could be useful for IMDb to detect the positive reviews, which it could then promote to its front page or (better yet) sell to movie producers to use as quotes on their movie posters.
- *What kind of training data would you need?*

  Only the review text and the binary positive versus negative indicator.
- *What would an appropriate ML modeling strategy be?*

  You'd fit a binary classification model. From there, you could assign a prediction score for each new review on the likelihood that it's a positive review.

- *What evaluation metric should you use for your predictions?*

  It depends on how you want to use your predictions. If the use case is to automatically pull out the 10 most positive reviews of the week (for example, to use on the IMDb front page), then a good evaluation metric would be the true-positive rate at a very small false-positive rate (for example, 1%). But if the goal is to try to find *all* positive reviews while ignoring the negative reviews (for example, for complete automated sentiment tagging of every review), then a metric such as accuracy or area under the curve (AUC) would be appropriate.
- *Is the data you have sufficient to solve this use case?*

  Finally, yes! You have a training set of the movie review text and the binary sentiment variable. In the remainder of the chapter, you'll build out a machine-learning solution for this use case.

To recap, you first learned the basic details about the dataset: hand-written movie ratings from IMDb. Then, you dove a little deeper to explore some of the patterns and trends in the data. Finally, you considered possible ML use cases. For each use case, you explored the value of a machine-learning solution to the problem, the basic data requirements to build out an ML solution, and how to go about putting together a solution.

Next, you'll build out an ML solution to separate positive from negative movie reviews.

8.2 Extracting basic NLP features and building the initial model

Because the movie review dataset consists of only the review text, you need to use text and natural-language features to build a meaningful dataset for your sentiment model. In the previous chapter, we introduced various methods for extracting features from text, and we use this chapter to discuss various practical aspects of working with ML and free-form text. The steps you'll go through in this section are as follows:

1. Extracting features from movie reviews with the bag-of-words method
2. Building an initial model using the naïve Bayes ML algorithm
3. Improving your bag-of-words features with the tf-idf algorithm
4. Optimizing model parameters

8.2.1 Bag-of-words features

As you may recall from our discussion of NLP features in the previous chapter, we started out with a simple technique to featurize natural-language data: bag of words. This method analyzes the entire corpus of text, builds a dictionary of all words, and translates every instance in the dataset into a list of numbers, counting how many times each word appears in the document. To refresh your memory, let's revisit bag of words in figure 8.2.

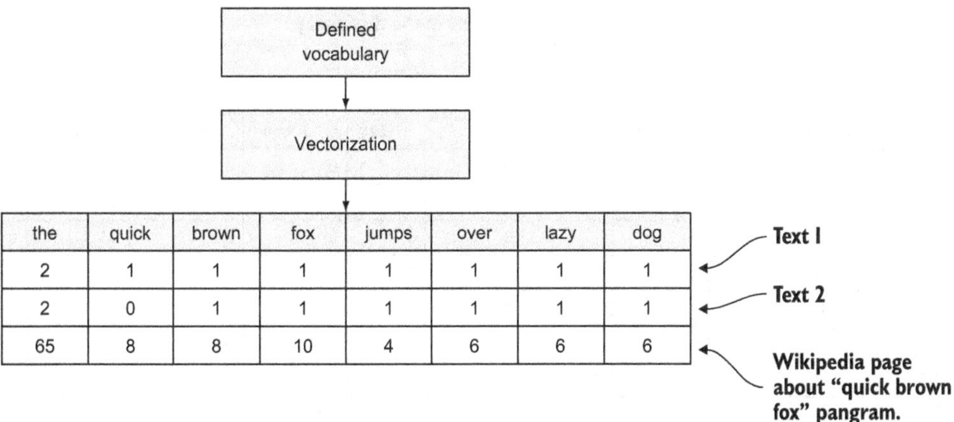

Figure 8.2 The bag-of-words vectorization algorithm. From a dictionary of words, you can transform any new document (for example, Text 1, Text 2 in the figure) into a list of numbers that counts how many times each word appears in the document.

In listing 8.1, you load the dataset, create a 70%–30% train-test split, and use a simple word-count method for extracting features. An important point to realize in this process is that you can't contaminate the bag-of-words dictionary with words from the test set. This is why you split the dataset into training and testing subsets *before* you build the vectorizer dictionary—to get a realistic estimate of the accuracy of the model on previously *unseen* data.

Listing 8.1 Building word-count features from the movie review dataset

```
import pandas
d = pandas.read_csv("movie_reviews/labeledTrainData.tsv", delimiter="\t")

split = 0.7
d_train = d[:int(split*len(d))]
d_test = d[int((1-split)*len(d)):]

from sklearn.feature_extraction.text import CountVectorizer
vectorizer = CountVectorizer()

features = vectorizer.fit_transform(d_train.review)
test_features = vectorizer.transform(d_test.review)
i = 45000
j = 10
words = vectorizer.get_feature_names()[i:i+10]
pandas.DataFrame(features[j:j+7,i:i+10].todense(), columns=words)
```

Loads the data

Splits the data into training and testing subsets

Initializes the word-count vectorizer

Fits the dictionary and generates training set features

enerates features for the sting set

Take a look at a subset of the features generated in figure 8.3.

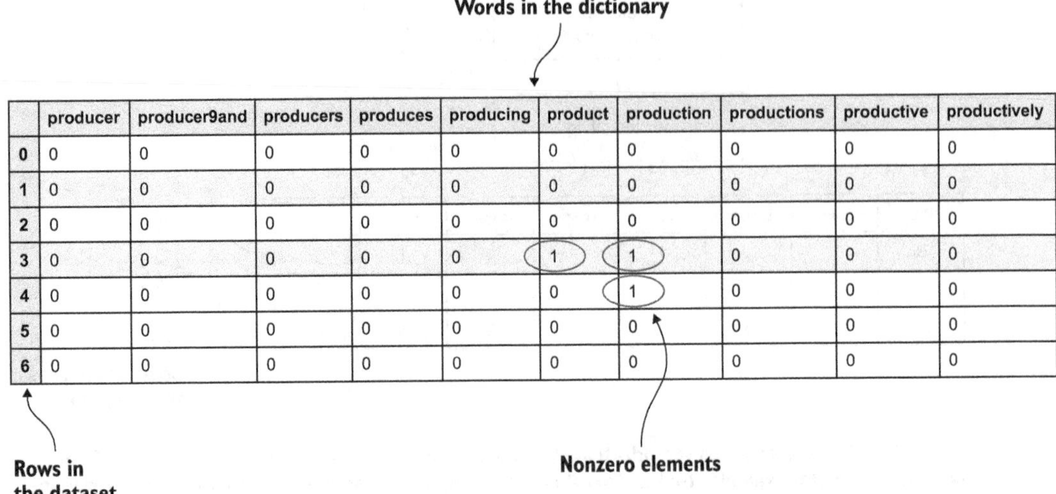

	producer	producer9and	producers	produces	producing	product	production	productions	productive	productively
0	0	0	0	0	0	0	0	0	0	0
1	0	0	0	0	0	0	0	0	0	0
2	0	0	0	0	0	0	0	0	0	0
3	0	0	0	0	0	1	1	0	0	0
4	0	0	0	0	0	0	1	0	0	0
5	0	0	0	0	0	0	0	0	0	0
6	0	0	0	0	0	0	0	0	0	0

Figure 8.3 A small 7 × 10 subset view of the word-count features that you'll use for building the model. The full dataset is a sparse matrix of size 17,500 × 65,005 (17,500 documents in the training set by 65,005 unique words in the training set). A sparse matrix is useful when most of the values are 0, which is the case in most bag-of-words–based features; in the full dictionary of words, individual words are unlikely to appear in a particular document.

From figure 8.3, it's clear that the dataset consists of mostly zeros with only a few exceptions. We call such a dataset *sparse*, a common attribute of NLP datasets. This has consequences when you want to use the dataset for features in an ML model, something we discuss in the next section before building an actual model to predict the sentiment of reviews.

8.2.2 Building the model with the naïve Bayes algorithm

Now that you have a proper featurized dataset, you can use the features to build the model as usual. For highly sparse datasets like this, some ML algorithms work much better than others. Specifically, some algorithms have built-in support for sparse data, and those algorithms are generally much more efficient, at least in memory usage but often also in CPU usage and time to build. If you inspect the generated feature set from listing 8.1, you'll find that only 0.2% of the cells in the dataset have nonzero elements. Using the dense representation of the dataset would significantly increase the size of the data in memory.

> **The basics of the naïve Bayes classifier**
>
> The naïve Bayes (NB) classifier algorithm is a simple ML algorithm that was created for use in text classification, an area of ML where it can still be competitive with more-advanced general-purpose algorithms. The name stems from the fact that the Bayes formula is applied to the data with very "naïve" assumptions about independence.

This assumption is what usually makes the algorithm less useful for general (dense) problems, because the features are rarely anywhere near independent. For sparse-text features, this assumption still isn't true, but it's true enough for the algorithm to work surprisingly well in practice. The NB classifier is one of the few ML algorithms that's simple enough to derive in a few lines, and we explain some of the highlights in this sidebar.

In this chapter, our goal is to classify a review by finding the probability $p(C_k|x)$ of the review sentiment being "bad" (k = 0) or "good" (k = 1) based on the features x of the instance. In probability theory using the Bayes formula, this can be written like so:

$$p(C_k|x) \sim p(C_k)p(x|C_k)$$

$p(x|C_k)$ is known as the joint probability of the features x if the instance was of class C_k. Because of the independence assumption (the *naïve* part), there's no cross-feature probability, and this becomes simply the product of the probability of each of the features given the class:

$$p(C_k|x) \sim p(C_k)p(x_1|C_k)p(x_2|C_k)p(x_3|C_k)p(x_4|C_k)...$$

$$= p(C_k)\prod_i^N p(x_i|C_k)$$

Because $p(C_k)$ is the marginal class distribution—the overall breakdown of good and bad sentiment reviews—which you can easily find from the data, you only need to figure out what $p(x_i|C_k)$ is. You can read this expression as "the probability of a specific feature for a specific class." For example, you'd expect the probability of having the word *great* in a good-sentiment review being higher than in a bad-sentiment review.

You can imagine learning this from the data by counting the feature (word) presence across all documents in each class. The probability distribution that generates such counts is called the *multinomial* distribution, and $p(x_i|C_k)$ becomes

$$p(x_i|C_k) \sim \prod_i p_{k_i}^{x_i}$$

You use this in the previous equation and move to log space for convenience:

$$\log[p(C_k|x_i)] \sim \log\left[p(C_k)\prod_i p_{k_i}^{x_i}\right]$$

$$= \log[p(C_k)] + \sum_i^n x_i \log(p_{k_i})$$

$$= b + w_k x$$

Here b is $\log[p(C_k)]$ (known from the data), x represents the features of the instance you want to predict, and w_k is $\log(p_{k_i})$—the fraction of times a word appears in a good or bad document, which you'll learn at model build time. Please note that we've left out various constants throughout this calculation, and there are multiple implementation details to consider when coding this algorithm from scratch, but the basics outlined here remain true.

One of the algorithms that works well for classification with sparse natural language processing (NLP) features is the naïve Bayes algorithm, specifically the multinomial (see the sidebar). In the following listing, you build the model on the features from listing 8.1.

Listing 8.2 Building the first review sentiment model using multinomial naïve Bayes

```
from sklearn.naive_bayes import MultinomialNB

model1 = MultinomialNB()
model1.fit(features, d_train.sentiment)
pred1 = model1.predict_proba(test_features)
```

To evaluate the performance of the model, you define a function in listing 8.3 and call it on the initial model predictions. The accuracy metrics that you'll report in this chapter are the general classification accuracy (fraction of correctly classified documents), the receiver operating characteristic (ROC) curve, and the corresponding area under the curve (AUC) number. These were all introduced in chapter 4 and used in many of our examples.

Listing 8.3 Evaluating the initial model

```
from sklearn.metrics import accuracy_score, roc_auc_score, roc_curve

def performance(y_true, pred, color="g", ann=True):
  acc = accuracy_score(y_true, pred[:,1] > 0.5)
  auc = roc_auc_score(y_true, pred[:,1])
  fpr, tpr, thr = roc_curve(y_true, pred[:,1])
  plot(fpr, tpr, color, linewidth="3")
  xlabel("False positive rate")
  ylabel("True positive rate")
  if ann:
    annotate("Acc: %0.2f" % acc, (0.2,0.7), size=14)
    annotate("AUC: %0.2f" % auc, (0.2,0.6), size=14)

performance(d_test.sentiment, pred1)
```

The result of running this code is shown in figure 8.4.

Looking at figure 8.4, you can see that the performance of your bare-bones model isn't bad at all. You classify 88% of the reviews correctly, but you can dial the number of false positives versus true positives up or down, depending on your preference for more noise or better detection rate.

Let's try this with a few new example reviews by passing some text through the vectorizer and model for sentiment predictions:

```
>>> review = "I love this movie"
>>> print model1.predict(vectorizer.transform([review]))[0]
1
```

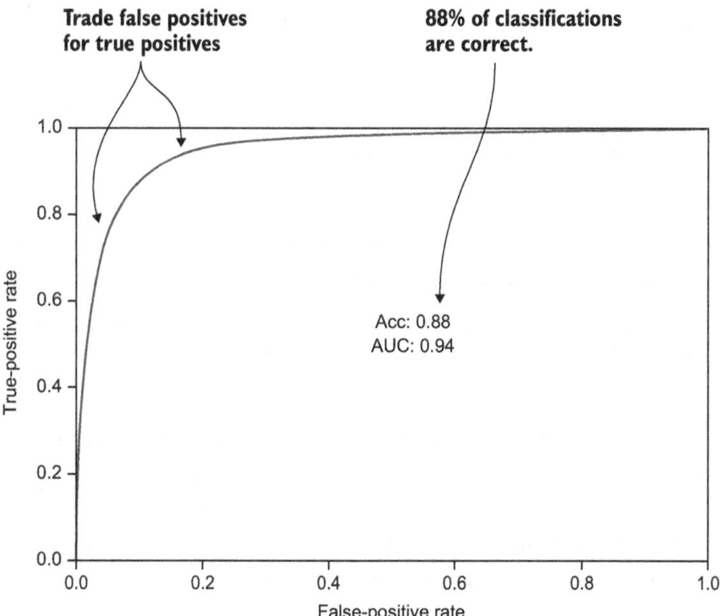

Figure 8.4 ROC curve of the classification performance of the simple bag-of-words model. The classification accuracy—the fraction of correctly classified reviews—as well as the AUC (area under the ROC curve) metrics are printed in the figure. The accuracy shows that you'd expect to correctly classify 88% of the reviews with this model, but by using the ROC curve, you can trade false-positive rate (FPR) for true-positive rate (TPR), and vice versa. If there were many reviews that humans needed to look through based on this classification, you might want to fix the FPR at a low value, which would in turn lower the true-positive detection rate.

A positive sentiment is indicated by 1, so this sounds about right. Let's try another one:

```
>>> review = "This movie is bad"
>>> print model1.predict(vectorizer.transform([review]))[0]
0
```

A negative sentiment is indicated by 0, so again this is indeed correct. Okay, let's try to trick the model:

```
>>> review = "I was going to say something awesome, but I simply can't
    because the movie is so bad."
>>> print model1.predict(vectorizer.transform([review]))[0]
0
```

No luck, the prediction is still correct. Maybe if you introduce more positive words into the negative review?

```
>>> review = "I was going to say something awesome or great or good, but I
    simply can't because the movie is so bad."
>>> print model1.predict(vectorizer.transform([review]))[0]
0
```

Nope, this is one clever model. The word *bad* must have a strong influence on the classification, so perhaps you can cheat the model by using that in a positive review:

```
>>> review = "It might have bad actors, but everything else is good."
>>> print model1.predict(vectorizer.transform([review]))[0]
0
```

Finally, you succeed in somewhat cheating the model. This little exercise is fun, but it also shows the power of the model in understanding arbitrary natural language in the movie review domain. In the next section, you'll try to improve the initial model by going a bit further than our simple word-count features and by finding better values for the parameters of the feature and modeling algorithms.

8.2.3 Normalizing bag-of-words features with the tf-idf algorithm

In the previous chapter, we introduced tf-idf as an upgrade to simple word-count features. In essence, tf-idf normalizes the word counts based on the frequency of how often each word appears across the documents. The main idea is that common words get smaller weighting factors, and relatively rare words get larger weighting factors, which enables you to dig deeper into the (often highly informative) words that appear less often in the dataset.

In this section, you'll use tf-idf for your features to see whether you can gain extra accuracy. The change is easy with scikit-learn, because you simply need to switch out your `CountVectorizer` for a `TfidfVectorizer`. The code is shown in the next listing.

Listing 8.4 Using tf-idf features in your model

```
from sklearn.feature_extraction.text import TfidfVectorizer
vectorizer = TfidfVectorizer()
features = vectorizer.fit_transform(d_train.review)

model2 = MultinomialNB()
model2.fit(features, d_train.sentiment)
pred2 = model2.predict_proba(vectorizer.transform(d_test.review))

performance(d_test.sentiment, pred2)
```

Uses the Tfidf vectorizer to build features

Trains a new naïve Bayes model on the features and makes predictions

Plots the results

The performance of the tf-idf model is shown in figure 8.5. You can see how the tf-idf features improved the model accuracy slightly. Specifically, the ROC curve shows that it should be better at avoiding false positives. Imagine that you had numerous reviews

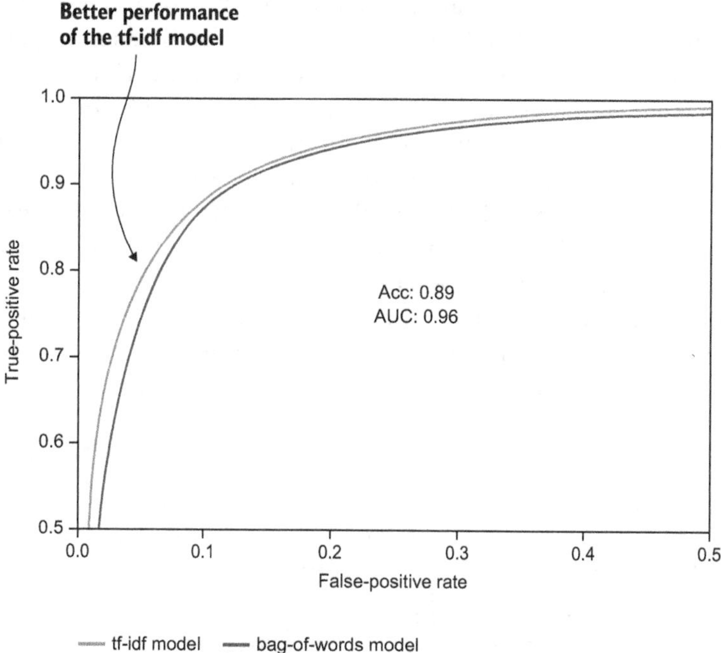

Figure 8.5 ROC curves for the tf-idf model on top of the previous bag-of-words model. You can see a slight improvement in both classification accuracy and AUC (area under the ROC curve). The tf-idf model curve specifically shows improvements in the low FPR range; the model would yield fewer false positives for the same number of correctly classified reviews. If humans were in the classification review loop, you'd have less noise to sift through.

coming in but wanted to flag bad reviews for human inspection. A lower false-positive rate would present fewer reviews to the reviewer that were actually positive, so they could work through the queue faster.

Both our tf-idf NLP feature-extraction algorithm and our naïve Bayes modeling algorithm have knobs that can be turned to tune the algorithm for specific details in the dataset. We call such knobs *hyperparameters*. This comes from the fact that the variables (features) of the model can be considered parameters as well, whereas these algorithm parameters work at a higher level. Before you accept your model performance, it's important that you try different values for these parameters, and this is the topic of the next section.

8.2.4 Optimizing model parameters

The simplest way to find the best parameters of a model is to try to build a bunch of models with different parameters and look at the performance metric of interest. The problem is that you can't assume that the parameters are independent of each other—varying one parameter may affect the optimal value of another. This can be solved in a brute-force way by building a model for any combination of parameters. But if there are many parameters, this quickly becomes intractable, especially if it takes a while to build the model just once. We discussed some solutions in chapter 4, but you'll probably be surprised by how often ML practitioners still rely on the brute-force way. You'll need to build up intuition about which parameters may be more independent of each other and which have the largest effect on which types of dataset. For this exercise, you have three parameters to optimize: two tf-idf parameters (`max_features`, `min_df`) and one naïve Bayes parameter (`nb_alpha`).

The first thing you need is a function that you can call repeatedly to build a model and return the parameters and the metric of interest (in this case, the AUC). The following listing defines this function.

Listing 8.5 Model building method useful for parameter optimization

```
def build_model(max_features=None, min_df=1, nb_alpha=1.0):
  vectorizer = TfidfVectorizer(max_features=max_features, min_df=min_df)
  features = vectorizer.fit_transform(d_train.review)
  model = MultinomialNB(alpha=nb_alpha)
  model.fit(features, d_train.sentiment)
  pred = model.predict_proba(vectorizer.transform(d_test.review))
  return {
    "max_features": max_features,
    "min_df": min_df,
    "nb_alpha": nb_alpha,
    "auc": roc_auc_score(d_test.sentiment, pred[:,1])
  }
```

With the repeatable model building function defined in listing 8.5, you can go ahead and run your optimization pipeline by defining the possible values of your parameters (chosen randomly or by intuition) and run the loop. This is done in the next listing.

Listing 8.6 Parameter optimization loop

```
from itertools import product

param_values = {
  "max_features": [10000, 30000, 50000, None],
  "min_df": [1,2,3],
  "nb_alpha": [0.01, 0.1, 1.0]
}

results = []
for p in product(*param_values.values()):
  res = build_model(**dict(zip(param_values.keys(), p)))
  results.append( res )
  print res
```

Defines parameter values to try to optimize (annotation on `param_values`)

For each parameter value combination (annotation on the `for` loop)

Builds the model and saves the result (annotation on `res = build_model(...)` and `results.append( res )`)

The parameters you optimize over are these:

- *max_features*—The maximum number of word columns for the tf-idf algorithm to create. From looking at the data, you know that all words amount to about 65,000 columns, so you try out a number of a similar size in a range. `None` specifies to use all words.
- *min_df*—The minimum number of times a word must appear in the dataset to be included in the features. This is an example of potential parameter dependency, because the number of words in the dictionary (and hence `max_features`) could be changed by changing `min_df`.
- *nb_alpha*—The alpha (smoothing) parameter of the naïve Bayes classifier. This is the only parameter that you can tune on this specific ML algorithm. The values to choose here require a bit more research into what the parameter means and how others have been using it in other circumstances.

The last thing to mention about the code in listing 8.6 is the use of the `product` function from the `itertools` module—a collection of Python functions that makes it easier to work with data. This function is a clever way to generate all combinations of a set of lists (Cartesian product). The results from running the code in listing 8.6 are shown in figure 8.6.

Figure 8.6 shows the output of some of the optimization runs. You had only three parameters with 36 possible value combinations, so this didn't take more than 10 minutes because the naïve Bayes training time is relatively low, but you could easily imagine wanting to try many more values of many more parameters, and the optimization

	AUC	max_features	min_df	nb_alpha
17	0.955985	30000	3	1.00
18	0.970304	50000	1	0.01
19	0.967335	50000	2	0.01
20	0.963369	50000	3	0.01
21	0.968388	50000	1	0.10
22	0.965854	50000	2	0.10
23	0.962516	50000	3	0.10
24	0.958776	50000	1	1.00
25	0.957700	50000	2	1.00
26	0.956112	50000	3	1.00
27	0.973386	NaN	1	0.01
28	0.967335	NaN	2	0.01

The highest AUC score is for iteration 27.

Figure 8.6 A subset of results from the parameter optimization loop. The parameter combination in iteration 27 produces the best model overall.

would take a long time. Another trick for finding the optimal parameters is to start with a broad range of values and then dive more deeply into the optimal value range with subsequent optimization runs over different parameter values. It's clear from the table how different parameters seem to improve the AUC of the model. Iteration 27 had the best results with these values:

- *max_features*—None (all words, default)
- *min_df*—1 (default)
- *nb_alpha*—0.01

So, interestingly, you managed to improve on the model performance quite a bit by finding a better value for the alpha parameter of the naïve Bayes algorithm. Let's look at the evolution of the AUC when varying each parameter (fixing the others at their optimal values) in figure 8.7.

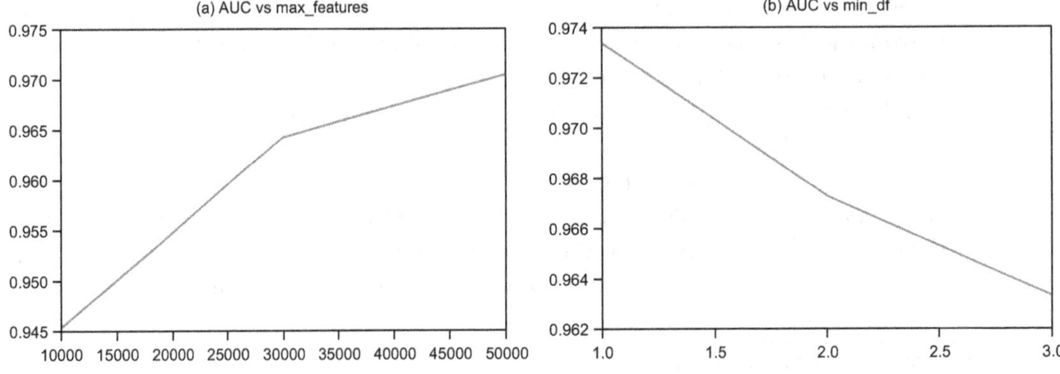

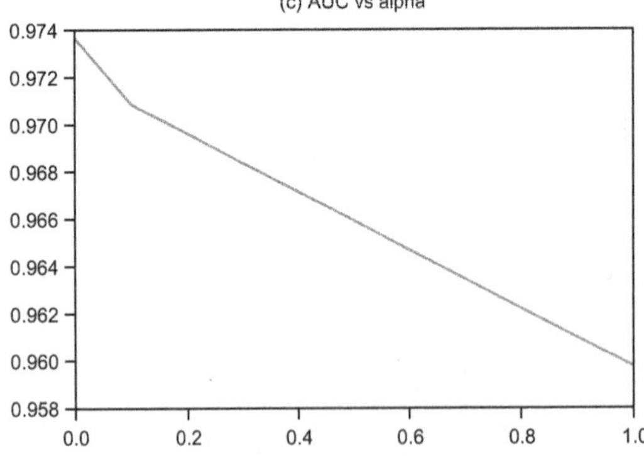

Figure 8.7 The AUC improvements from varying three parameters of the feature and ML algorithms. You can see that (a) a higher `max_features` gives a better AUC, (b) a lower `min_df` gives a better AUC, and (c) a lower alpha gives a better AUC. This doesn't mean that the best values for each of them individually necessarily yields the best combined. The best combined parameters from our optimization run are `max_features=None` (all words, default), `min_df=1` (minimum, default), `alpha=0.01` (main reason for improvement). The best AUC is 0.974. All graphs shown can be reproduced using the code in the accompanying Python notebook.

Each of these plots is only one perspective on the AUC evolution, because you'd need a four-dimensional plot to plot the AUC as a function of all the parameters. But it's still interesting to see how the model responds to varying each value. For instance, the higher the number of features, the better (the largest possible value won). The smaller the number of `min_df`, the better (the smallest possible value won). And then, the smaller the `nb_alpha`, the better. Because this has no theoretical lower limit, this should prompt you to try even lower values in another run. We leave this as an exercise for you (but, anecdotally, we weren't able to find a much better value).

The ROC curve of the optimized model is plotted with the previous models in figure 8.8. You can see a substantial improvement in model performance for both metrics and all points on the ROC curve. This is a great example of how it can pay off to tune your model hyperparameters to gain extra prediction power. One last thing to note here: you could, of course, imagine that new choices of model parameters could, in turn, affect which feature and modeling algorithms (for example, word count versus tf-idf) would perform best, and each algorithm would potentially have a new set of parameters to optimize. To be fully rigorous, you'd need to optimize across all choices of algorithms and their parameters, but this is infeasible for most real-world problems, and the trade-off here is to go through your optimization in milestones. For example, first you fix the NLP algorithm to use and then the ML model, and then you optimize those parameters. Your project could require a different set of milestones—again, you'll develop intuition about these things as you build successive ML models.

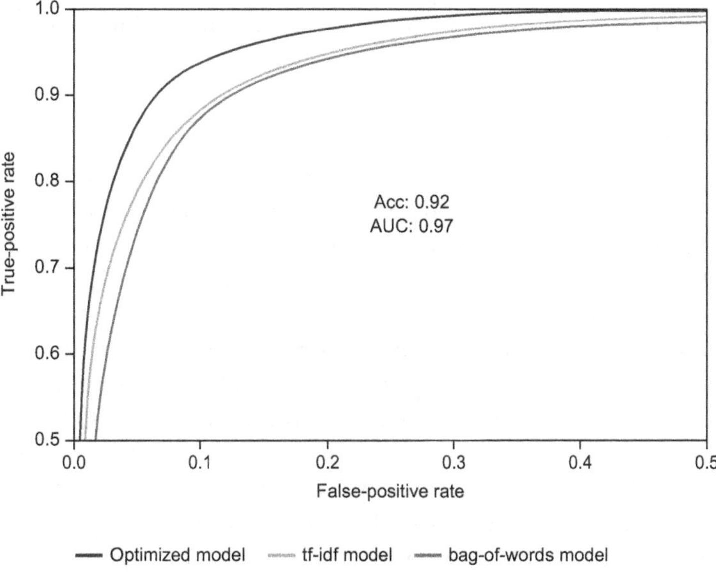

Figure 8.8 The ROC curve of the optimized model versus the previous models. In our test set evaluation, this model seems to be universally better (at every point on the curve), and the expected accuracy increased considerably.

The ROC curves in figure 8.8 conclude our initial modeling experiments. From basic algorithms and very little code, you've managed to build a model with pretty good accuracy on natural-language data alone. In the next section, you'll go a step further in your feature-engineering and modeling efforts and see various aspects of deploying such a model into a real-world production-ready system.

8.3 Advanced algorithms and model deployment considerations

In the previous section, we were concerned with building a model using relatively simple features and ML algorithms. The accuracy of any of the models in that section may have been good enough for our needs. You can try the next idea for optimizing the model, but there's always a trade-off between the time you spend and the potential value brought by incremental improvements in model accuracy. We encourage you to get a handle on the value of each percentage improvement, for example, in the form of saved human-reviewer time, and how much you can afford to spend up front. As you saw, our very first model was certainly capable of understanding review sentiment in many cases and may well have been a good enough model to begin with. Often it's more valuable to put a slightly lower-accuracy model into production and get live feedback from the system if possible.

With that advice out of the way, let's go against it and try to optimize this model a bit further. Next, you'll look into generating features from a new natural-language modeling technique, originally developed by Google: *word2vec*. After you've extracted the word2vec features, you'll switch to the random forest algorithm to better support the new features.

8.3.1 Word2vec features

A relatively new approach to natural language processing has been introduced by Google in the form of the word2vec project. A word2vec model is itself an ML model that's built using deep neural networks, a branch of ML that has recently been producing state-of-the-art results, especially on human-related domains such as natural language, speech, and images.

To build a word2vec model on your training set, you'll use the Gensim NLP library for Python, which has a nice word2vec implementation built in. You previously used Gensim in chapter 7 to work with LDA, another topic model similar to word2vec.

In Gensim, you need to do a bit of extra work to prepare your documents for modeling, because the Gensim algorithms work on sentences (lists of words already split up) instead of arbitrary documents. This can be more work up front, but it also gives you a better understanding of what goes into your model. In listing 8.7, you'll build a simple tokenization function that removes stop words and punctuation characters, and converts all words to lowercase. Note that this was all done automatically in the scikit-learn word vectorizers; we could have used the same functionality or similar functions from the NLTK Python NLP toolkit, but we chose to write it out ourselves here for educational purposes.

Listing 8.7 Document tokenization

```
import re, string

stop_words = set(['all', "she'll", "don't", 'being', 'over', 'through',
'yourselves', 'its', 'before', "he's", "when's", "we've", 'had', 'should',
"he'd", 'to', 'only', "there's", 'those', 'under', 'ours', 'has',
"haven't", 'do', 'them', 'his', "they'll", 'very', "who's", "they'd",
'cannot', "you've", 'they', 'not', 'during', 'yourself', 'him', 'nor',
"we'll", 'did', "they've", 'this', 'she', 'each', "won't", 'where',
"mustn't", "isn't", "i'll", "why's", 'because', "you'd", 'doing', 'some',
'up', 'are', 'further', 'ourselves', 'out', 'what', 'for', 'while',
"wasn't", 'does', "shouldn't", 'above', 'between', 'be', 'we', 'who',
"you're", 'were', 'here', 'hers', "aren't", 'by', 'both', 'about', 'would',
'of', 'could', 'against', "i'd", "weren't", "i'm", 'or', "can't", 'own',
'into', 'whom', 'down', "hadn't", "couldn't", 'your', "doesn't", 'from',
"how's", 'her', 'their', "it's", 'there', 'been', 'why', 'few', 'too',
'themselves', 'was', 'until', 'more', 'himself', "where's", "i've", 'with',
"didn't", "what's", 'but', 'herself', 'than', "here's", 'he', 'me',
"they're", 'myself', 'these', "hasn't", 'below', 'ought', 'theirs', 'my',
"wouldn't", "we'd", 'and', 'then', 'is', 'am', 'it', 'an', 'as', 'itself',
'at', 'have', 'in', 'any', 'if', 'again', 'no', 'that', 'when', 'same',
'how', 'other', 'which', 'you', "shan't", 'our', 'after', "let's", 'most',
'such', 'on', "he'll", 'a', 'off', 'i', "she'd", 'yours', "you'll", 'so',
"we're", "she's", 'the', "that's", 'having', 'once'])

def tokenize(docs):
  pattern = re.compile('[\W_]+', re.UNICODE)
  sentences = []
  for d in docs:
    sentence = d.lower().split(" ")
    sentence = [pattern.sub('', w) for w in sentence]
    sentences.append( [w for w in sentence if w not in stop_words] )
  return sentences
```

Splits the document into words after converting all characters to lowercase

Removes every nonword character, such as punctuation

Removes English stop words

From this function, you can tokenize any list of documents, and you can now proceed to build your first word2vec model. For more information on the parameters of the algorithm, please see the Gensim documentation.[2]

[2] https://radimrehurek.com/gensim/models/word2vec.html

Listing 8.8 Word2vec model

```
from gensim.models.word2vec import Word2Vec

sentences = tokenize(d_train.review)
model = Word2Vec(sentences, size=300, window=10, min_count=1,
   sample=1e-3, workers=2)
model.init_sims(replace=True)
print model['movie']
#> array([ 0.00794919, 0.01277687, -0.04736909, -0.02222243, …])
```

Generates sentences from tokenize function

Builds and normalizes word2vec model

Prints the vector from word2vec model for the word movie

You can see how a single word is represented as a vector (of 300 numbers, in this case). In order to use the word2vec model to generate features for your ML algorithm, you need to convert your reviews into feature vectors. You know how to represent single words as vectors, so a simple idea is to represent a review document (list of words) as the average vector of all the words in the document. In the next listing, you'll build a function to do exactly this.

Listing 8.9 Word2vec featurization

```
def featurize_w2v(model, sentences):
  f = zeros((len(sentences), model.vector_size))
  for i,s in enumerate(sentences):
    for w in s:
      try:
        vec = model[w]
      except KeyError:
        continue
      f[i,:] = f[i,:] + vec
    f[i,:] = f[i,:] / len(s)
  return f
```

Initializes a NumPy array for the feature vectors

Loops over each sentence, add the vectors for each word, and takes the mean

You're now ready to build a model on your newly generated word2vec features. As you may recall from our ML algorithm discussions in section 8.2.2, the naïve Bayes classifier works well with sparse data but not so well with dense data. The word2vec features have indeed converted your documents from the ~65,000 sparse word-count features into only hundreds of dense features. The deep-learning model has learned higher-level topics of the model (listing 8.8), and each document can be represented as a combination of topics (listing 8.9).

8.3.2 Random forest model

The multinomial naïve Bayes algorithm introduced in the previous section is incompatible with the new word2vec features, because they can't be considered generated by a multinomial distribution. You could use other distributions to continue to work with the naïve Bayes algorithm, but you'll instead rely on an old friend of ours: the random forest algorithm. In the following listing, you'll build a 100-tree random forest model on the word2vec features and analyze the performance as usual on the test set.

Listing 8.10 Building a random forest model on the word2vec features

```
features_w2v = featurize_w2v(model, sentences)

model4 = RandomForestClassifier(n_estimators=100, n_jobs=-1)
model4.fit(features_w2v, d_train.sentiment)

test_sentences = tokenize(d_test.review)
test_features_w2v = featurize_w2v(model, test_sentences)
pred4 = model4.predict_proba(test_features_w2v)
performance(d_test.sentiment, pred4, color="c")
```

The performance of the word2vec random forest model is compared to your previous models in figure 8.9. You can see how your new model indeed improves the model accuracy in your chosen evaluation metric and across all points on the ROC curve.

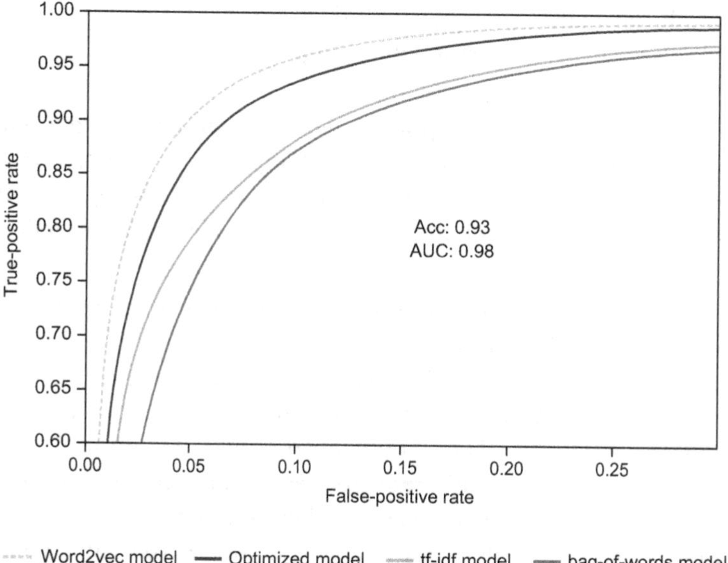

Figure 8.9 The ROC curve of the word2vec model along with previous models. You can see an improvement for all values of the ROC curve, also reflected in the increased accuracy and AUC numbers.

With your final model illustrated in figure 8.9, you're satisfied with the performance and will stop optimization work for now. You could try many more things to improve the accuracy even further. Most likely, not even humans would be capable of correctly classifying the sentiment of all the reviews; there may be some incorrect labels or some reviews for which the sentiment isn't easily understandable.

But the model can likely get much better than what you've achieved so far. We'll leave you, dear reader, with an initial list of things that we would try out, in rough order of priority:

- *Use unlabeled data to build a better topic model.*
  The data section of the Kaggle competition website contains an unlabeled set of reviews that you can use for training. Because you're building a supervised model, they don't seem useful at first. But because you're building a word2vec model that needs to learn the nuances of the world of IMDb movie reviews—and especially the connections between different words and concepts—it would be beneficial to use this data in order to improve your word2vec model that goes into the features of your training set (the one that has labels) before you build the model.
- *Optimize parameters.*
  You saw great improvement in model performance in the initial models of this chapter after finding better values for the hyperparameters of the model. We since introduced a new NLP model (word2vec) and ML algorithm (random forest), so there are many new parameters to optimize.
- *Detect phrases.*
  The Gensim library includes support for detecting phrases in text, such as "New York City," which would be missed in our "dump" word-only tokenization function. The English language tends to include multiword concepts, so this could be an interesting thing to include in your sentence-generation function.
- *Handle multiple languages.*
  If you were uncertain about all the reviews being in a single language (in this case, English), you'd have to deal with multiple languages in various places of the modeling pipeline. First, you'd need to know which language the review was in, or you'd need to detect the language (for which there are several libraries of varying quality available). Then you'd need to use this information in your tokenization process to use different stop words and, potentially, punctuation characters. If you were really unlucky, you'd even have to deal with totally different sentence structures, such as Chinese text, where you can't just split the words when there's a whitespace.

Now, imagine you're satisfied with the model at hand. If this were a real-world use case, you'd want to put the model into production. You should then consider some of the following aspects, depending on the exact use case:

- *How much training data do you have, and does the model get better with more training data?*
  This can affect the choice of ML algorithm because you need to pick a model that scales well with more training data. For example, the naïve Bayes classifier supports partial training, also known as online learning, whereas the random forest algorithm can be difficult to scale to larger datasets.

- *What is the volume of predictions, and do they need to be delivered in real time?*

  We'll talk a great deal more about scaling up predictions with volume and speed in the next chapter, but the takeaway is that this can have consequences for the choice of algorithm and the infrastructure in which it's deployed.

8.4 Summary

In this chapter, you learned how to go end to end on a real machine-learning use case, along with the basics of natural language processing and optimizing model parameters. Key takeaways for this chapter included the following:

- It's essential to focus on the right problem. You should always start by asking, for each possible use case, "What's the value of solving this problem?"
- For each use case, you need to inspect the data and systematically determine whether the data is sufficient to solve the problem at hand.
- Start with simple off-the-shelf algorithms to build an initial model whenever possible. In our example, we predicted review sentiment with almost 90% accuracy.
- Accuracy can be improved by testing and evaluating alternative models and combinations of model parameters.
- There are often trade-offs between different model parameters and evaluation criteria. We looked at how the trade-off between false positive and false negative rates for movie reviews is represented by the model's ROC curve.
- State-of-the-art natural-language and ML modeling techniques like word2vec are examples of how advanced feature engineering may enable you to improve your models.
- Your choice of algorithms may depend on factors other than model accuracy, such as training time and the need to incorporate new data or perform predictions in near-real time.
- In the real world, models can always be improved.

8.5 Terms from this chapter

Word	Definition
word2vec	An NLP modeling framework, initially released by Google and used in many state-of-the-art machine-learning systems involving natural language
hyperparameter optimization	Various techniques for choosing parameters that control ML algorithms' execution to maximize their performance

9 Scaling machine-learning workflows

This chapter covers

- Determining when to scale up workflows for model accuracy and prediction throughput
- Avoiding unnecessary investments in complex scaling strategies and heavy infrastructure
- Ways to scale linear ML algorithms to large amounts of training data
- Approaches to scaling nonlinear ML algorithms—usually a much greater challenge
- Decreasing latency and increasing throughput of predictions

In real-world machine-learning applications, scalability is often a primary concern. Many ML-based systems are required to quickly crunch new data and produce predictions, because the predictions become useless after a few milliseconds (for instance, think of real-time applications such as the stock market or clickstream data). On the other hand, other machine-learning applications need to be able to scale during model training, to learn on gigabytes or terabytes of data (think about learning a model from an internet-scale image corpus).

In previous chapters, you worked mostly with data that's small enough to fit, process, and model on a single machine. For many real-world problems, this may be sufficient to solve the problem at hand, but plenty of applications require scaling to multiple machines and sometimes hundreds of machines in the cloud. This chapter is about deciding on a scaling strategy and learning about the technologies involved.

In the first part of this chapter, we introduce the various dimensions to consider when facing a large dataset or a requirement for high-volume predictions. We present ways that you can avoid investing a lot of time and resources in a fully scalable approach, and some technologies to consider if there's no way around it. The following section goes more deeply into the process of scaling up the ML workflow for training models on large datasets. Finally, we focus on scaling the prediction workflow to large volumes or decreased latency.

In the next chapter, you'll get to use everything you've learned in order to solve a real-world big-data example, so hang on as you get through the basics in this chapter.

9.1 Before scaling up

The type of scalability required for any given problem ultimately depends on the use case and the computational constraints that exist. This section starts by describing the kinds of scalability that are commonly required in modern machine-learning applications. You'll step through the various dimensions to consider and identify which could be bottlenecks in your ML code. Later, after you've identified the types of scalability required, you'll learn about standard techniques to ensure that your ML applications can handle real-world data rates and volumes.

Instead of diving right into specific methods to scale ML applications, we start with a high-level overview. Using our ML workflow as a guide, let's begin with a systems view of ML scalability.

9.1.1 Identifying important dimensions

Let's first deconstruct our machine-learning workflow into the two primary routines: model training and model prediction. For these two systems, how could resource constraints affect the workflow, and how could these inhibit or break the system? Consider table 9.1.

Table 9.1 Problems in model building that can occur due to lack of scalability, plus their ultimate consequences

Scalability problem	Consequence
Training dataset is too large to fit a model.	No model is fitted, so no predictions can be made.
Training dataset is so large that model fitting is slow.	Model optimization is infeasible (or impractical), so a suboptimal model is used, sacrificing accuracy.

During model building, the scalability issues that you'll face stem from large training sets. At one extreme, if your training dataset is so large that you can't even fit a model (for example, the data doesn't fit in memory), then this is a problem that you *must* find a way around. You can choose from three approaches: (1) find a smaller subset of the data that you can learn on, (2) use a machine with more RAM, or (3) use a more memory-efficient learning algorithm.

In a bit, we describe a few quick ways to reduce your dataset size without significantly impacting model quality. We follow this up with a discussion of how to scale compute cycles to fit your problem via scalable data systems. Later in the chapter, we introduce scalable learning algorithms, which can allow you to scale ML to your data without relying on shortcuts or extra hardware.

For slightly smaller datasets, it may be possible to fit only relatively simple models (such as linear/logistic regression) in lieu of more-sophisticated ones (such as boosting), because of the extra computational complexity and memory footprint of the latter. In this case, you may be sacrificing accuracy by not fitting more-sophisticated learning algorithms, but at least you're able to fit a model. In this case, the same options presented previously are viable approaches to try.

In a related scenario, the massive size of your training dataset could cause model fitting, and in turn model optimization, to be slow. Like the previous scenario, this can cause you to use a less accurate model, because you're forced to employ a coarse tuning-parameter-optimization strategy or to forego tuning altogether. But unlike the preceding situation, this predicament can be solved by spinning up more nodes (horizontal scaling) and fitting models (with different tuning parameter choices) on the different machines. We touch more on horizontal scaling in section 9.1.3.

In the prediction workflow, the scalability issues you face stem from data that comes in very fast, prediction or feature-engineering processes that are CPU-intensive, or prediction data batches that are very large. Consider table 9.2.

Table 9.2 Problems in ML prediction that can occur due to lack of scalability, plus their ultimate consequences

Scalability problem	Consequence
Data rates (streaming) are too fast for the ML system to keep up.	The backlog of data to predict on grows and grows until ultimately breaking.
Feature-engineering code and/or prediction processes are too slow to generate timely predictions.	The potential value of the predictions is lost, particularly in real-time use cases.
Data sizes (batch) are too large to process with the model.	The prediction system breaks, and no predictions are made.

Luckily, all three of these challenges can be resolved with the same strategy: spinning up more machines. The advantage of prediction, as opposed to model training, is that in the vast majority of use cases, predictions can be made independently for each data instance.[1] To generate predictions, at any one time you need to hold in memory only the features for a single instance (and the ML model that you've built). Contrast that scenario to model training: typically, the entire training set needs to be loaded into memory. Thus, unlike the scalability problems during model training, prediction scalability issues don't require larger machines; they just require more of them—and, of course, an efficient data management system to control them (more on this later).

Whether you need to generate predictions more quickly, handle a higher volume of instances, or deal with slow feature-engineering or prediction processes, the solution is to spin up more machines and send out different subsets of instances on each node for processing. Then, assuming that the fitted model is distributed on all the nodes, you can generate predictions in parallel across all machines and return them to a central database.

In section 9.3, you'll dive deeply into prediction systems. There, you'll explore a few approaches to building computational systems for fast and scalable ML prediction.

9.1.2 Subsampling training data in lieu of scaling?

In some cases, model training may be infeasible with the entire training set and the available CPU resources. If you're up against this challenge and no other option is viable, then *as a method of last resort*, you may consider subsampling the training data before model building.

Although in general we discourage subsampling data (you might lose important signals), some ways of discarding data are better than others. Some might even improve your model, depending on the ML algorithm at hand. You can throw away data in two ways: discard features or discard instances. For each option, we'll describe a statistically rigorous method to reduce the size of your training data.

Feature selection

Often, the broadness of a dataset creates the computational bottleneck. For example, in genome data, a training set may contain data for millions of genes (features) but for only hundreds of patients (instances). Likewise, for text analysis, the featurization of data into n-grams can result in training sets containing upward of millions of features. In these cases, you can make your model training scale by first eliminating unimportant features in a process called *feature selection*. Figure 9.1 shows a schematic of how feature selection works.

As we discussed in chapters 4 and 5, feature selection can lead to better models in some cases. By intelligently removing features, you can make the learning algorithms hone in on the important signals without becoming distracted by the features that don't matter. The actual loss or gain of feature selection depends on the choice of ML model and on how much information is unknowingly lost because you're throwing

[1] Note that in a handful of ML use cases, predictions can't be made on separate instances independently. For example, a time-series forecasting model, such as a financial or climate model, may rely on the predictions from multiple timestamps in generating a single forecast.

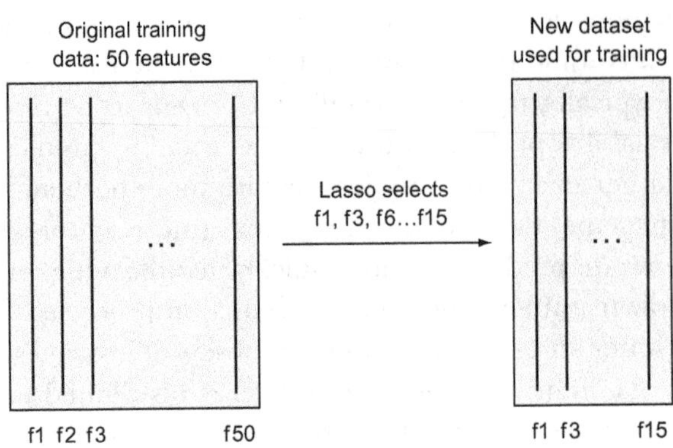

Figure 9.1 Feature selection using Lasso to reduce the dimensionality of a large dataset to train a machine-learning model

away data, so you should always test your changes by validating your model appropriately. In this section, we talk about feature selection primarily as a way of working with large datasets.

For massive training sets, our recommended method of feature selection is *Lasso.* Lasso is an efficient linear learning algorithm that automatically searches for the most predictive subset of features. Computing the entire trace of the algorithm is efficient, allowing the user insight into the entire ordering of all the features in terms of their predictive power in the linear model. Moreover, the best subset of features, in terms of the linear model predictions, is provided.

If you're (un)lucky enough to have such a large dataset that you can't even fit a Lasso model, you may consider fitting the Lasso to subsets of the instances in your training set (and potentially averaging across runs of the algorithm). This can give you a good sense of which features can be removed from the model without degrading the statistical performance of your ML algorithm.

The obvious downside to Lasso feature selection is that it uses a linear model to gauge the importance of each feature. A feature that's selected out via Lasso could indeed have a nonlinear relationship with the target variable that may not be appropriately captured by Lasso. As an alternative, nonparametric approaches to feature selection exist, such as random forest feature importance, but those methods typically don't scale to large datasets.

INSTANCE CLUSTERING

If after feature selection your training data is *still* too large to fit a model on, you may consider subselecting instances. As an absolute method of last resort, you can use statistical clustering algorithms to identify and remove redundancies in your training instances.

For this type of data reduction, we recommend using an agglomerative hierarchical clustering algorithm. This approach will initialize with each training set instance as the sole member of its own cluster. Then, the two closest clusters are subsequently joined (using a predefined distance measure to determine "closeness"). This joining of nearby clusters continues until a stopping criterion (for example, number of clusters) is reached. We recommend stopping this process as early as possible so you don't reduce too dramatically the information content of your data. The final reduced training set consists of a single instance for each of the resulting clusters.

9.1.3 Scalable data management systems

Independent of the strategy you want to take for scaling up your ML workflow, you need to be able to handle the data first. In the past decade, we've seen tremendous focus on so-called *big-data* technologies. In this book, we use the term *big data* to mean any data that's too large to be processed by a single machine in a reasonable amount of time. Here, we introduce some of the most successful big-data projects and how they can be used in an ML framework.

The basic principle in modern big-data systems is that you need to be able to handle more data by adding more machines. This is known as *horizontal* scalability. In contrast, the alternative way of handling larger resource requirements is *vertical* scaling, whereby you upgrade the small number of machines you have with more disk, memory, or CPU cores. Figure 9.2 compares horizontal and vertical scalability.

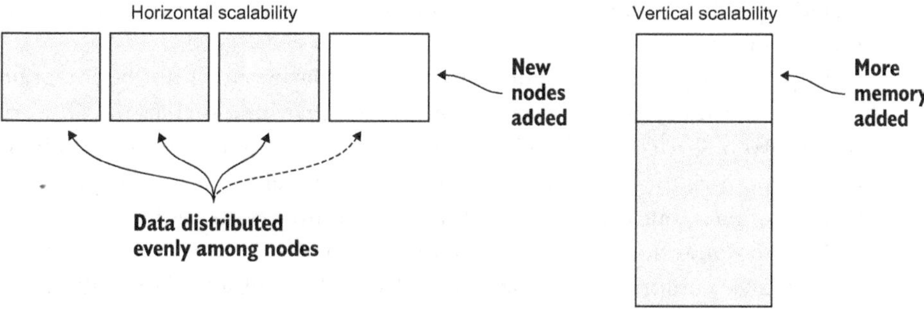

Figure 9.2 Horizontal vs. vertical scalability for big-data systems. In horizontal systems, you add new nodes (machines) to your infrastructure to handle more data or computation, as the load is distributed relatively evenly among nodes. An example of such a system is Apache Hadoop. In vertically scaling systems, you add more resources to your existing machines in order to handle higher loads. This approach is usually more efficient initially, but there's a limit to the amount of resources you can add. Examples of databases that work well with this approach are SQL servers such as PostgreSQL.

Sometimes, and perhaps more often than you might think, upgrading your machines will be enough to scale up your machine-learning workflow. As stated in the previous sections, after the raw data has been processed and readied for your classification or regression problem, the data may not be big enough to warrant the complexity of a true big-data system. But in some cases, when dealing with data from popular websites, mobile apps, games, or a large number of physical sensors, it's necessary to use a horizontally scalable system. From now on, this is what we'll assume.

Horizontally scalable big-data systems have two main layers: storage and computation. In the *storage layer*, data is stored and passed on to the *computational layer*, where data is processed. One of the most popular big-data software projects is Apache Hadoop, which is still widely used in science and industry and is based on ideas from a previously unseen level of scalability obtained at Google and other web-scale companies in the early 2000s.

The storage layer in Hadoop is called the *Hadoop Distributed File System* (HDFS). Datasets are partitioned and distributed over multiple machines so they can be processed in parallel. Also, each partition is replicated so data is unlikely to be lost in the event of hardware or software failures.

The computing layer of Hadoop uses a simple algorithm called *MapReduce* to distribute computation among the nodes in the cluster. In the MapReduce framework, the map step distributes data from HDFS onto workers that transform the data in some way, usually keeping the number of data rows the same. This is similar to our feature-engineering processes in earlier chapters, where you add new columns to each row of input data. In the reduce step, the mapped data is filtered and aggregated into its final form. Many data-processing algorithms can be transformed into MapReduce jobs. When algorithms are transformed to this framework, systems such as Hadoop will take care of the distribution of work among any number of machines in your cluster.

In principle, the storage and computational layers need not be integrated. Many organizations use a storage system from a cloud provider, such as the S3 service in the Amazon Web Services (AWS) cloud infrastructure, coupled with the Hadoop MapReduce framework for computation. This has the benefit that AWS manages your large volumes of data, but you lose one of the main points of the tight integration between HDFS and MapReduce: *data locality*. With data locality, your system becomes more efficient because computational tasks are performed on subsets of the data close to where that data is stored.

The Hadoop community has developed a machine-learning library called *Mahout* that implements a range of popular ML algorithms that work with HDFS and MapReduce in the Hadoop framework. If your data is in Hadoop, Mahout may be worth looking into for your machine-learning needs. Mahout is moving away from the simplistic MapReduce framework into more-advanced distributed computing approaches based on Apache Spark. *Apache Spark*, a more recent and widely popular framework based on the ideas of Hadoop, strives to achieve better performance by working on data in memory. Spark has its own library of machine-learning algorithms in the *MLlib* library included with the framework. Figure 9.3 shows a simple diagram of the Apache Spark ecosystem.

Scalable ML algorithms are often linear for natural reasons. Both Mahout and MLlib include mostly linear ML algorithms or approximations to nonlinear algorithms. In the next section, you'll look at how to approach scaling with both types of algorithms.

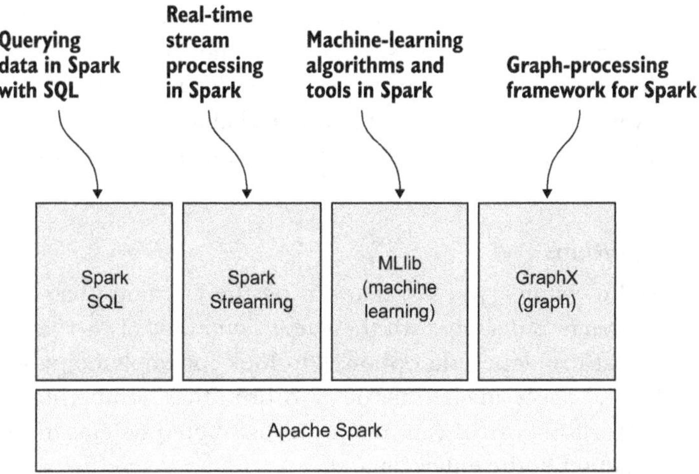

Figure 9.3 The Apache Spark ecosystem based on the Spark core for distributed computation. Spark SQL allows you to work with tables using Python pandas or R data frames. Spark Streaming allows you to process data in real time as it arrives, in contrast to the batch-processing nature of Hadoop and classic Spark. MLlib is the machine-learning library that includes a range of ML algorithms optimized for the Spark engine, and GraphX is a library allowing efficient computation on large graphs such as the social graph of a social network.

9.2 Scaling ML modeling pipelines

In the first section of this chapter, you looked at things that are good to know before you take the plunge and invest in scaling up your workflow to handle larger datasets. In this section, we assume that you've made the decision to scale out your ML workflow and chosen a big-data processing system to use. Figure 9.4 updates our familiar ML workflow diagram to the world of big data.

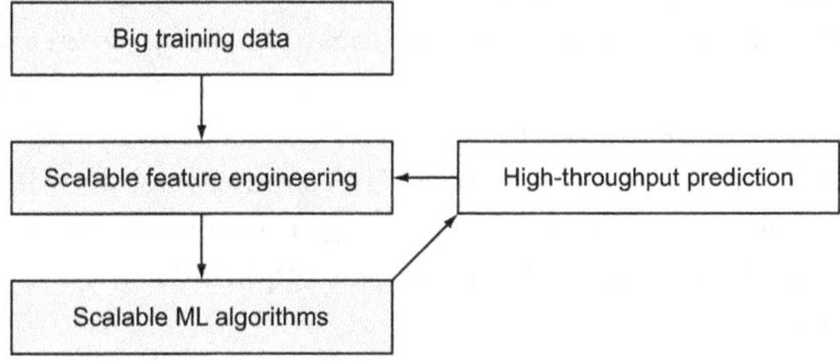

Figure 9.4 The modeling part of our familiar ML workflow diagram with scalable components

In section 9.1.3, we introduced a few big-data-capable systems that can be used to manage and process data of almost any size. Because they work on an instance-by-instance basis, the feature-engineering processes that we've talked about in the book so far can be done with simple map calls that are available in any of those systems. Next, you'll look at how some popular linear and nonlinear ML algorithms scale in the face of big data.

9.2.1 Scaling learning algorithms

In the beginning of the chapter, you saw that during the learning phase, the fundamental scalability challenge is dealing with the size, in memory, of very large training sets. To circumvent that problem, one option is to look for implementations of ML algorithms that either (a) use a smaller memory footprint than competing implementations of the same algorithm, or (b) can train over distributed systems in which each node requires only a subset of the entire dataset.

Out in the wild, countless implementations of the most common ML learning algorithms exist. From scikit-learn to mlpack, these implementations are continually stretching the frontiers of memory efficiency (and thus increasing the dataset size that can be trained on a single computer with a fixed amount of RAM). Yet, data volumes are still outpacing the gains in ML software and computer hardware. For some training sets, the only option is horizontally scalable machine learning.

The most commonly used distributed learning algorithm is linear (and logistic) regression. The *Vowpal Wabbit* (VW) library popularized this approach, and has been a mainstay for scalable linear learning across multiple machines. The basic way that distributed linear regression works is to first send subsets of the training data (subset by dataset rows) to the various machines in the cluster. Then, in an iterative manner, each machine performs an optimization problem on the subset of data on hand, sending back the result of the optimization to the central node. There, that information is combined to come up with the best overall solution. After a small number of iterations of this procedure, the final model is guaranteed to be close to the overall optimal model (if a single model were fit to all the data at once). Hence, linear models can be fit in a distributed way to terabytes or more of data!

As we've discussed numerous times in this book, linear algorithms aren't necessarily adequate for modeling the nuances of data for accuracy predictions. In these cases, it can be helpful to turn to nonlinear models. Nonlinear models usually require more computational resources, and horizontal scalability isn't always possible with nonlinear models. This can be understood loosely by thinking of nonlinear models as also considering complex interactions between features, thus requiring a larger portion of the dataset at any given node.

In many cases, it's more feasible to upgrade your hardware or find more-efficient algorithms or more-efficient implementations of the algorithms you've chosen. But in other situations, scaling a nonlinear model is needed, and in this section we discuss a few ways to approach this.

POLYNOMIAL FEATURES

One of the most widely used tricks to model nonlinear feature interactions is to create new features that are combinations of the existing features and then train a linear model including the nonlinear features. A common way to combine features is to multiply features in various combinations, such as *feature 1 times feature 2, feature 2 squared,* or *feature 1 times feature 2 times feature 5.* Say a dataset consists of two features, f1 = 4 and f2 = 15. In addition to using f1 and f2 in your model, you can generate new features f1 × f2 = 60, f1 ^ ² = 16 and f2 ^ ² = 225. Datasets usually contain a lot more than two features, so this technique can generate a huge number of new features. These features are nonlinear combinations of existing features. We call them *polynomial features.* The following listing shows how this can be achieved with the scikit-learn Python library. The results of running the code in this listing show the accuracy gained when adding polynomial features to a standard Iris flower classification model:

```
Accuracy (linear):      0.95 (+/- 0.12)
Accuracy (nonlinear):   0.98 (+/- 0.09)
```

Listing 9.1 Making a linear model nonlinear by using polynomial features

```
from sklearn import datasets
from sklearn.linear_model import LogisticRegression
from sklearn.preprocessing import PolynomialFeatures
from sklearn.cross_validation import cross_val_score

iris = datasets.load_iris()

linear_classifier = LogisticRegression()
linear_scores = cross_val_score(linear_classifier, \
    iris.data, iris.target, cv=10)
print "Accuracy (linear):\t%0.2f (+/- %0.2f)" % \
    (linear_scores.mean(), linear_scores.std() * 2)

pol = PolynomialFeatures(degree=2)
nonlinear_data = pol.fit_transform(iris.data)

nonlinear_classifier = LogisticRegression()
nonlinear_scores = cross_val_score(nonlinear_classifier, \
    nonlinear_data, iris.target, cv=10)
print "Accuracy (nonlinear):\t%0.2f (+/- %0.2f)" % \
    (nonlinear_scores.mean(), nonlinear_scores.std() * 2)
```

Loads the sample data. Each instance describes pictures of Iris flowers that the model will learn to tell apart.

Builds and prints cross-validated results of linear model

Adds degree-2 polynomial interaction features to the dataset

Builds and prints cross-validated results of linear model on nonlinear data

An example of another machine-learning toolkit that has polynomial feature extraction integrated is the Vowpal Wabbit library. VW can be used to build models on large datasets on single machines because all computation is done iteratively and *out of core,* meaning that only the data used in the particular iteration needs to be kept in memory. VW uses stochastic gradient descent and feature hashing to deal with unstructured and sparse data in a scalable fashion. VW can generate nonlinear models by supplying the `-q` and `-cubic` flags to generate quadratic or cubic features, corresponding to polynomial features where all pairs or all triplets of features have been multiplied together.

DATA AND ALGORITHM APPROXIMATIONS

As you saw in the preceding section, the polynomial feature approach has the ability to increase the accuracy of the model significantly, but also increases the number of features polynomially. That might not be feasible for a large number of input features, so here you'll look at a few nonlinear algorithms that have well-known approximations useful for scalable implementations. Other algorithms may have their own approximations for scalability, so we encourage you to investigate your favorite algorithm further.

A widely used nonlinear learning algorithm is random forest, which you've already read about in previous chapters. The random forest model consists of numerous decision trees, and on first sight it may look trivial to scale random forest to many machines by building only a subset of the trees on each node. Be aware that if the data subsamples available at each node aren't sufficiently similar, the accuracy of the model can suffer. But building more trees or splitting the data more intelligently could mitigate the loss in accuracy.

Another approximation that can be used to scale random forests and other algorithms is a *histogram approximation*: each column in the dataset is replaced with the histogram of that column, which usually decreases the number of values in the column significantly. If the number of bins in the histogram is too small, a lot of nuance may be lost and model performance suffers.

Another algorithm that has natural approximations is k-nearest neighbors; special approximate tree structures can be used to increase the scalability of the model. Support vector machines have seen multiple approximation methods to make the nonlinear versions more scalable, including Budgeted Stochastic Gradient Descent (BSGD) and Adaptive Multi-hyperplane Machines (AMM).

DEEP NEURAL NETS

A recent revolution in neural network research has spawned a new field of deep learning that produces highly nonlinear models and has proven to be scalable to very large datasets. In the early days of machine learning, neural networks (NNs) were researched heavily and applied widely in science and industry. Later, with the advent of algorithms that were easier to reason about mathematically, NNs were used less frequently. Recently, NNs again started producing state-of-the-art results on large and diverse datasets after going through a few important evolutionary steps and entering the realm of deep learning.

Deep learning refers to a family of algorithms that extends the traditional neural network. Commonly, these models include many hidden layers in the neural network or many single-layer networks combined. Figure 9.5 illustrates an example neural network.

One of the disadvantages of deep neural nets are that even on GPU hardware, the computational resources needed to build and optimize models can take a long time. In practice, you may be able to get just as good performance with other algorithms, such as random forests, using far less time and resources. This depends on the dataset

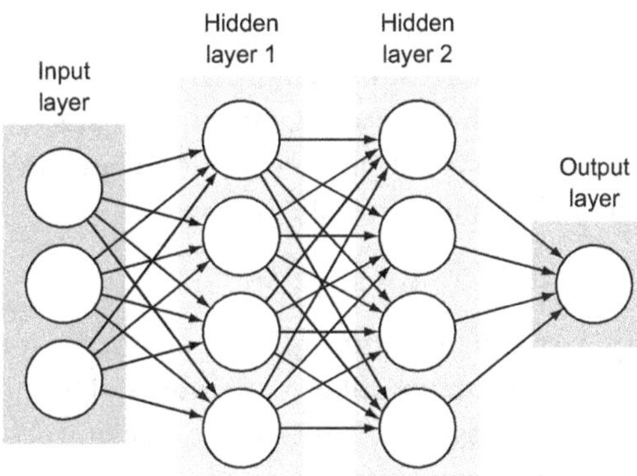

Figure 9.5 A neural network of two hidden layers. Loosely modeled on the human brain, the neurons (circles in each layer) are connected with weights that are learned during model training. The output variables can be predicted by running the input variables through the weighted connections. In deep learning, this classical neural network concept is expanded to include more hidden layers of various shapes and various degrees of connectivity between layers.

and problem at hand, as always. Another disadvantage is that it can be difficult to understand what's going on under the hood of these neural net models. Some refer to them as *black-box models*, because you have to trust the results of your statistical analysis of the models without doing any introspection of their internals. This again depends on the use case. If you're working with images, for example, the neurons can take on intuitive representations of various visual patterns that lead to specific predictions.

Many deep-learning methods have shown to scale to large datasets, sometimes by using modern graphic cards (GPUs) for performing certain computations. For a deep-learning library in Python that supports GPUs, take a look at *Theano* (http://deeplearning.net/software/theano/) or *Keras* (http://keras.io/), which is based on Theano).

9.3 Scaling predictions

Scaling ML isn't only about scaling to larger datasets. Imagine you're building an email service, and you suddenly have millions of users. You built a nice spam-detection model, and it even scales to large datasets, but now you need to make hundreds of millions of predictions per day. That's more than 10 thousand per second! Figure 9.6 illustrates this common pattern. In this section, we discuss ways to scale the volume of predictions and scale the velocity when predictions need to be used in real time.

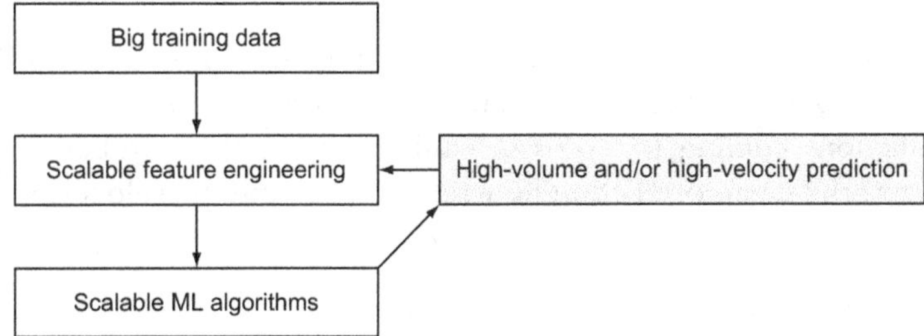

Figure 9.6 Scaling the prediction part of the ML workflow to high volumes or high-velocity predictions

First, you'll look at infrastructure architectures for scaling with the volume of predictions so you can handle the large user base of your email client, for example. Next, you'll look at how to scale the velocity of predictions and guarantee an answer within a given timeframe. This is important when your ML models are used in the real-time feedback loop of, for example, humans on web or mobile devices.

9.3.1 Scaling prediction volume

In order to handle many predictions, you can use patterns known from computational architecture for scaling workers to support any number of requests. The traditional approach is to have a queue of prediction jobs from which a number of worker nodes pull predictions, load the model (if needed), make the prediction, and push back the results in whatever way makes sense for the application. Figure 9.7 shows how this architecture might look for scaling predictions by volume.

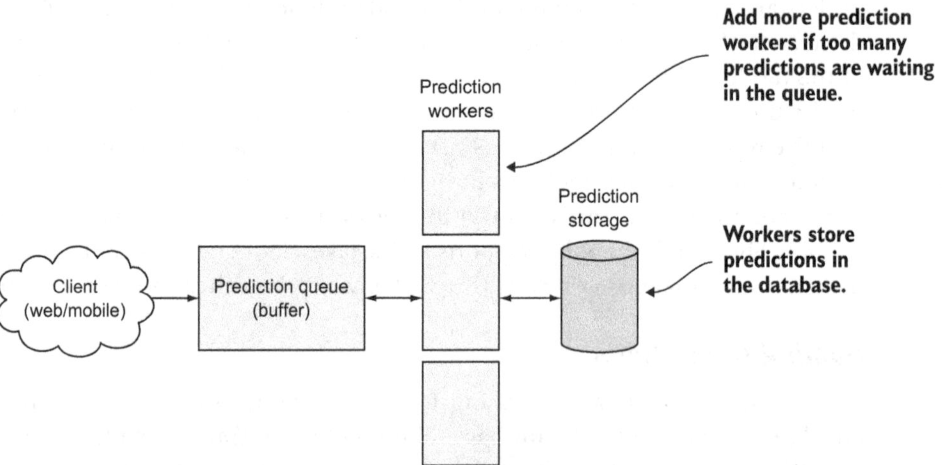

Figure 9.7 A possible infrastructure for a scalable prediction service. Prediction requests are sent from the consumer to a queue, which delegates the job to a prediction worker. The worker stores the prediction in a database and delivers it back to the client when done. If the queue is clogging up when more predictions are streaming in than the workers can handle, more workers can be spun up.

This approach requires that the model can be loaded on all worker nodes, of course, and that there are enough workers (or an autoscaling solution in place) to handle the number of predictions coming in. You can easily calculate the number of workers needed if you know the mean prediction time for a worker and the velocity of requests coming in:

```
n_workers = request_velocity * prediction_time
```

For example, if you have 10 prediction requests coming in per second, and your workers take 2 seconds to finish, you need at least 20 workers to keep up. The optimal autoscaling solution here is to be able to spawn new workers from the number of requests waiting in the queue over a certain period of time.

9.3.2 Scaling prediction velocity

In some cases, you need your predictions to be returned within a certain time after the request was made by a client. Prediction velocity can be important, for example, when predictions are made in response to a user action. Users expect feedback in real time, and waiting even a few seconds can be detrimental to the user experience. Imagine a Google search that takes 20 seconds—likely, you'd be long gone. Or, if you're making predictions about financial transactions, mere milliseconds could mean making or losing a lot of money.

Various approaches are available to make your predictions faster, such as upgrading your hardware or using more-efficient algorithms or implementations of an algorithm. You can also optimize the network and make sure that the client is as physically close to your servers as possible. In addition, you shouldn't call any other service that may introduce additional latency, such as recording the predictions to a database, or waiting for the data to be written to disk and replicated across a cluster. In the following example, we'll assume that you've already considered these points. Now you'll take a look at two architectures for serving real-time predictions.

The first architecture for fast predictions is similar to the architecture introduced in the preceding scale-by-volume section, but requires more workers. The basic idea is that each prediction request is sent to multiple workers at once, and the first prediction that finishes is sent back to the customer. Figure 9.8 shows an example of this architecture.

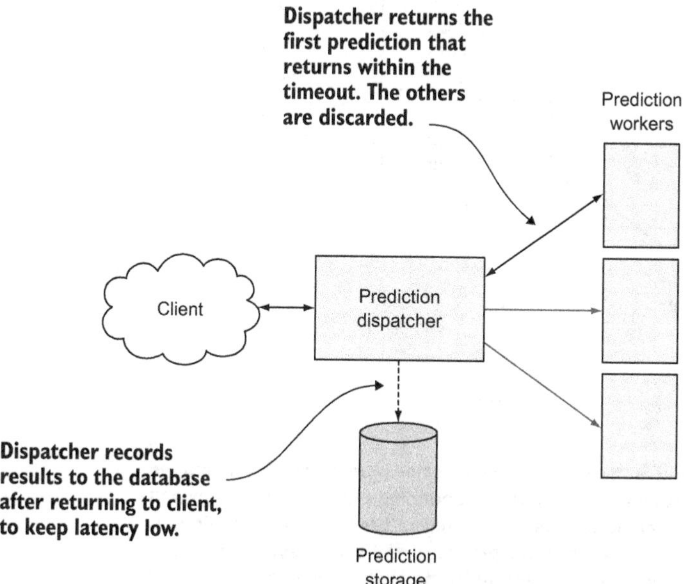
Dispatcher returns the first prediction that returns within the timeout. The others are discarded.
Prediction workers
Client
Prediction dispatcher
Dispatcher records results to the database after returning to client, to keep latency low.
Prediction storage

Figure 9.8 A possible architecture for a prediction pipeline with low-latency requirements. A prediction dispatcher sends the prediction job to multiple workers, hoping that at least one will return predictions in time. It will return the first one that comes back to the client, and afterward record it in a log or database for later inspection and analytics (in the background, possibly while already working on the next prediction).

Another approach to real-time predictions is to make predictions in parts so the computation can be distributed among multiple machines. Ensemble methods comprise a class of algorithms that lend themselves well to this approach. We'll again use random forests as an example here.

Random forest models consist of an ensemble of decision trees. The algorithm makes a prediction from each tree and (in the case of classification) counts the votes from each tree into the final probability. For example, if there are 10 trees and 6 of them vote yes for a particular prediction instance, the forest returns 6/10, or 60%, as the answer. Usually, the larger the total number of trees queried, the more accurate and confident the results. This can be used in a real-time prediction system to trade accuracy for speed. If each prediction node is responsible for a tree or list of trees from the forest, you ask each for a prediction. Whenever a node finishes predicting on its own trees, the result is returned to a collector service that collects results from all nodes and makes the final prediction. The collector can observe a time limit and at any time return the prediction in its current state, if necessary. For example, if only 20 of 1,000 trees have returned anything, the user gets an answer, but it's not as accurate as it could have been had all 1,000 trees had time to return an answer.

Figure 9.9 shows a diagram of this architecture in action.

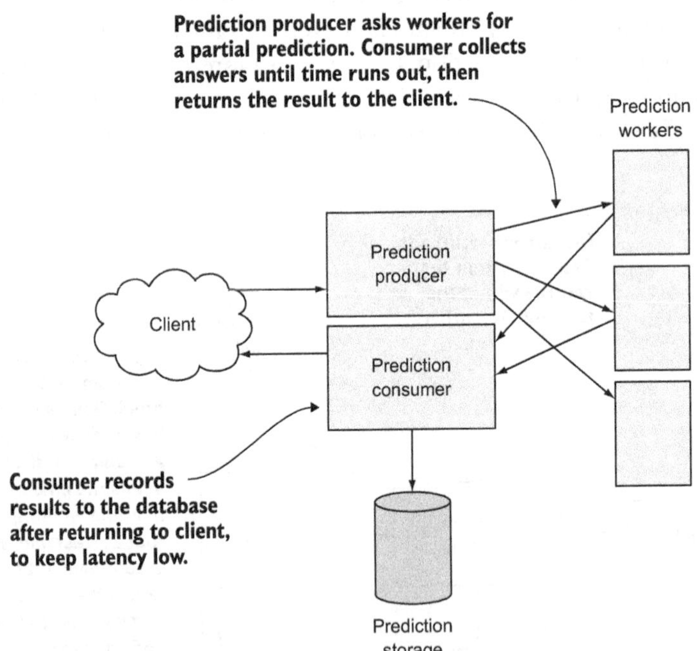

Figure 9.9 Suggested architecture for a prediction pipeline that's guaranteed to return within a certain time, potentially sacrificing prediction accuracy and confidence if some of the partial predictions haven't returned yet. Prediction requests are shipped to workers by the producer, while a consumer service collects partial predictions ready to return to the client if time is up.

A few systems are showing promise in supporting these scalable, real-time systems. One is part of the previously mentioned Apache Spark ecosystem: Spark Streaming. With Spark Streaming, you get a set of tools and libraries that makes it easier to build real-time, stream-oriented data-processing pipelines. Don't forget that any prediction made usually has to go through the same feature-engineering processes that the training data went through at model-building time.

Other projects include Apache Storm, Apache Kafka, AWS Kinesis, and Turi. Each project has pros and cons for particular use cases, so we encourage you to investigate the appropriate tool for your needs.

9.4 Summary

In this chapter, you've investigated various ways to scale machine-learning systems to large datasets by transforming the data or building a horizontally scalable multimachine infrastructure. The main takeaways from the chapter are as follows:

- Scaling up your machine-learning system is sometimes necessary. These are some common reasons:
  - The training data doesn't fit on a single machine.
  - The time to train a model is too long.
  - The volume of data coming in is too high.
  - The latency requirements for predictions are low.
- Sometimes you can avoid spending time and resources on a scalable infrastructure by doing the following:
  - Choosing a different ML algorithm that's fast or lean enough to work on a single machine without sacrificing accuracy
  - Subsampling the data
  - Scaling up vertically (upgrading the machine)
  - Sacrificing accuracy or easing other constraints if it's still cheaper than scaling up
- If it's not possible to avoid scaling up in a horizontal fashion, widely used systems are available for setting up a scalable data-management and processing infrastructure:
  - The Hadoop ecosystem with the Mahout machine-learning framework
  - The Spark ecosystem with the MLlib machine-learning library
  - The Turi (formerly GraphLab) framework
  - Streaming technologies such as Spark Streaming, Apache Storm, Apache Kafka, and AWS Kinesis
- When scaling up a model-building pipeline, consider the following:
  - Choosing a scalable algorithm such as logistic regression or linear SVMs
  - Scaling up other (for example, nonlinear) algorithms by making data and algorithm approximations
  - Building a scalable version of your favorite algorithm using a distributed computing infrastructure

- Predictions can be scaled in both volume and velocity. Useful approaches include the following:
  - Building your infrastructure so that it allows you to scale up the number of workers with the prediction volume
  - Sending the same prediction to multiple workers and returning the first one in order to optimize prediction velocity
  - Choosing an algorithm that allows you to parallelize predictions across multiple machines

9.5 Terms from this chapter

Word	Definition
big data	A broad term usually used to denote data management and processing problems that can't fit on single machines.
horizontal/vertical scaling	Scaling out horizontally means adding more machines to handle more data. Scaling up vertically means upgrading the hardware of your machines.
Hadoop, HDFS, MapReduce, Mahout	The Hadoop ecosystem is widely used in science and industry for handling and processing large amounts of data. HDFS and MapReduce are the distributed storage and parallel processing systems respectively, and Mahout is the machine-learning component of the Hadoop ecosystem.
Apache Spark, MLlib	Apache Spark is a newer project that tries to keep data in memory to make it much more efficient than the disk-based Hadoop. MLlib is the machine-learning library that comes with Spark.
data locality	Doing computation on the data where it resides. Data transfer can often be the bottleneck in big-data projects, so avoiding transferring data can result in a big gain in resource requirements.
polynomial features	A trick to extend linear models to include nonlinear polynomial feature interaction terms without losing the scalability of linear learning algorithms.
Vowpal Wabbit	An ML tool for building models efficiently on large datasets without necessarily using a full big-data system such as Hadoop.
out-of-core	Computations are done out of core if you need to keep only the current iteration of data in memory.
histogram approximations	Approximations of the training data that convert all columns to histograms for the learning process.
feature selection	Process of reducing the size of training data by selecting and retaining the best (most predictive) subset of features.
Lasso	Linear algorithm that selects the most predictive subset of features. Very useful for feature selection.

Word	Definition
deep neural nets	An evolution of neural nets that scales to larger datasets and achieves state-of-the-art accuracy. Requires more knowledge and computational resources in practice than other algorithms, depending on the dataset and problem at hand.
prediction volume/velocity	Scaling prediction volume means being able to handle a lot of data. Scaling velocity means being able to do it fast enough for a specific real-time use case.
accuracy vs. speed	For real-time predictions, you can sometimes trade accuracy of the prediction for the speed with which the prediction is made.
Spark Streaming, Apache Storm, Apache Kafka, AWS Kinesis	Upcoming technologies for building real-time streaming systems.

10 Example: digital display advertising

This chapter covers

- Visualizing and preparing a real-world dataset
- Building a predictive model of the probability that users will click a digital display advertisement
- Comparing the performance of several algorithms in both training and prediction phases
- Scaling by dimension reduction and parallel processing

Chapter 9 presented techniques that enable you to scale your machine-learning workflow. In this chapter, you'll apply those techniques to a large-scale real-world problem: optimizing an online advertising campaign. We begin with a short introduction to the complex world of online advertising, the data that drives it, and some of the ways it's used by advertisers to maximize *return on advertising spend* (ROAS). Then we show how to put some of the techniques in chapter 9 to use in this archetypal big-data application.

We employ several datasets in our example. Unfortunately, only a few large datasets of this type are available to the public. The primary dataset in our example isn't available for download, and even if it were, it would be too large for personal computing.

One dataset that can be downloaded and used for noncommercial purposes is from the Kaggle Display Advertising Challenge sponsored by Criteo, a company whose business is optimizing the performance of advertising campaigns. The Criteo dataset contains more than 45 million observations of 39 features, of which 13 are numerical and 26 categorical. Unfortunately, as is common for datasets used in data science competitions, the meaning of the features is obfuscated. The variable names are V1 through V40. V1 is the label, and V2 through V40 are features. In the real world, you'd have the benefit of knowing what each feature measures or represents. But as the competition proved, you can nonetheless explore their predictive value and create useful models.

The Criteo dataset is available at https://s3-eu-west-1.amazonaws.com/criteo-labs/dac.tar.gz.

10.1 Display advertising

> Half the money I spend on advertising is wasted; the trouble is, I don't know which half.
>
> —John Wannamaker

In the days of *Mad Men*, this was an inescapable truth. But with digital advertising comes the opportunity to discover what works and what doesn't via the data collected as users interact with online ads.

Online advertising is delivered through a myriad of media. *Display ads* appear within web pages rendered in browsers, usually on personal computers or laptops. Because the rules for identifying users and the handling of internet cookies are different on mobile browsers, mobile ad technology relies on a different set of techniques and generates quite different historical data. *Native ads,* embedded in games and mobile apps, and *pre-roll ads* that precede online video content, are based on distinct delivery technologies and require analyses tailored to their unique processes. Our examples are limited to *traditional* display advertising.

Much of the terminology of display advertising was inherited from the print advertising business. The websites on which ads can be purchased are known as *publications,* within which advertising space is characterized by size and format, or *ad unit,* and location within the site and page is referred to as *placement.* Each presentation of an ad is called an *impression.* Ads are sold in lots of 1,000 impressions, the price of which is known as CPM, (cost per thousand).

When a user browses to a web page—say, xyz.com—it appears that the publisher of xyz.com delivers the entire page. In reality, the page contains placeholders for advertisements that are filled in by various advertisers through a complex network of intermediaries. Each web server that delivers ads maintains logs that include information about each impression, including the publisher, the internet address of the user, and information contained in internet *cookies*, where information about previous deliveries from the advertiser's server may be stored. In the next section, you'll look at the sorts of data that's captured during a display ad campaign.

10.2 Digital advertising data

Web servers capture data for each user request, including the following:

- *Client address*—The IP address of the computer that made the request.
- *Request*—The URL and parameters (for example, http://www.abc.com?x=1234&y=abc01).
- *Status*—The response code issued by the server; usually 200, indicating successful response.
- *Referrer*—The web page from which the user linked to the current page.
- *User agent*—A text string that identifies the browser and operating system making the request.
- *Cookie*—A small file stored when a browser visits a website. When the site is visited again, the file is sent along with the request.

In addition, many modern advertisements are served in conjunction with measurement programs—small JavaScript programs that capture information such as the following:

- *Viewability*—Whether and for how long the advertisement was displayed.
- *User ID*—Browser cookies are used to leave behind unique identifiers so that users can be recognized when encountered again.
- *Viewable seconds*—Number of seconds advertisement was in view.

Figure 10.1 shows sample data from a campaign. Viewability data is extracted from a query string, and `user_id` is a randomly generated identifier that associates users with previous visits.

	timestamp	click	viewed	v_secs	user_id	operating_system	pub_domain
0	2015-09-28 09:01:35	False	False	0	9b644f47729749cc80ac9a67df399cb0	Windows	D10037853.com
1	2015-09-21 00:25:42	False	True	3	f5b295de8cf1448c8fde3b4cb1650873	Windows	D10031681.com
2	2015-09-08 00:08:49	False	False	0	06c757b7637647fb96b2d911303d5ed5	Windows	D10013014.com
3	2015-09-15 09:37:24	False	False	0	0dfabf89-5da8-459d-a4f7-3dfea37497f5	Windows	D10013014.com
4	2015-09-25 06:23:47	False	False	0	4171bedc8a99412a980c8521eee86c83	Windows	D10013014.com

Figure 10.1 Impression data. Domain names are randomly generated substitutes for the real names.

10.3 Feature engineering and modeling strategy

Click is our target variable. You want to predict the likelihood that impressions will result in clicks (sometimes called *click-throughs* or *click-thrus*). More specifically, given a specific user visiting a particular site, you'd like to know the probability that the user will click the advertisement. You have several choices in formulating the problem. You can try to predict the probability that a given user will click through, and you can try to predict the click-through rate (CTR) for each publisher that presents the ad.

As is often the case, precisely what you model and the precise values you endeavor to predict will ultimately be driven by asking these questions: *How will the prediction be used? In what manner will it be acted on?* In this case, our advertiser has the option of blacklisting certain publications, so the advertiser's primary concern is identifying the publications least likely to yield clicks. In recent years, *real-time bidding* technologies have been developed that enable advertisers to bid for individual impressions based on user and publication features provided by the bidding system, but our example advertiser hasn't adopted real-time bidding yet.

You might wonder at this point why the advertiser doesn't just look at some historical data for all the publications and blacklist those with low CTRs. The problem is that when the overall CTR for a campaign is in the neighborhood of 0.1%, the expected value of clicks for a publication with only a few impressions is zero. The absence of clicks doesn't indicate a low CTR. Further, when we aggregate the best-performing, low-volume publications, we often observe above-average CTR (so just blacklisting all the low-volume pubs isn't a good strategy). You're looking for a model that will enable you to predict publications' performance without the benefit of a great deal of performance history.

At first glance, you might imagine you don't have much to work with. You can count impressions, clicks, and views for users, publishers, and operating systems. Maybe time of day or day of the week has some effect. But on further reflection, you realize that the domains a user visits are features that describe the user, and the users who visit a domain are features of the domain. Suddenly, you have a wealth of data to work with and a real-world opportunity to experience *the curse of dimensionality*—a phrase used to describe the tribulations of working in *high-dimensional space.* As you explore the data, you'll see that a wealth of features can be, if not a curse, a mixed blessing.

You may recognize the logic you'll apply here as the basis of *recommenders*, the systems that suggest movies on Netflix, products on Amazon, and restaurants on Yelp. The idea of characterizing users as collections of items, and items as collections of users, is the basis of *collaborative filtering*, in which users are clustered based on common item preferences, and items are clustered based on the affinities of common users. Of course, the motivation for recommenders is to present users with items they're likely to purchase. The advertising problem is a variation; instead of many items, the same advertisement is presented in a wide variety of contexts: the publications. The driving principle is that the greatest likelihood of achieving user responses (clicks) will be on publications that are similar to those that have a history of achieving responses. And because similarity is based on common users, pubs chosen in this manner will attract people who are similar in their preferences to past responders.

10.4 Size and shape of the data

You'll start with a sample of 9 million observations, a small-enough sample to fit into memory so you can do some quick calculations of cardinality and distributions.

Listing 10.1 A first look at the data

```
%matplotlib inline
import pandas as pd
import seaborn as sns
import numpy as np
import matplotlib.pyplot as plt

df = pd.read_pickle('combined.pickle')        <-- Loads data from a compressed archive

nImps = len(df)
nPubs = len(df.pub_domain.unique())
nUsers = len(df.user_id.unique())

print('nImps={}\nnPubs={}\nnUsers={}'.format(nImps, nPubs, nUsers))

nImps=9098807       <-- Number of impressions
nPubs=41576         <-- Number of publisher domains
nUsers=3696476      <-- Number of distinct users

(nPubs * nUsers) / 1000000    <-- Size of the user/item matrix divided by 1 million for readability

153684    <-- 153.684 billion cells—a rather large matrix
```

Fortunately, most users never visit most of the domains, so the user/item matrix is sparsely populated, and you have tools at your disposal for dealing with large, sparse matrices. And nobody said that users and domains must be the rows and columns of a gigantic matrix, but it turns out that some valuable algorithms work exceptionally well when it's possible to operate on a user/item matrix in memory.

Oh, and one more thing: the 9 million observations referenced in listing 10.1 represent roughly 0.1% of the data. Ultimately, you need to process roughly 10 billion impressions, and that's just one week's worth of data. We loaded the data from 9 million impressions into about 53% of the memory on an Amazon Web Services (AWS) instance with 32 GB of RAM, so this will certainly get more interesting as you go.

Next, let's look at how the data is distributed over the categorical variables. In listing 10.1, we already started this process by computing the cardinality of `pub_domain` and `user_id`.

Listing 10.2 Distributions

```
import seaborn as sns        <-- Seaborn is a statistical visualization library.

nClicks = df.click.value_counts()[True]
print('nClicks={} ({}%)'
.format(nClicks, round(float(nClicks) * 100 / nImps, 2)))
```

```
nClicks=10845 (0.12%)

nViews = df.viewed.value_counts()[True]
print('nViews={} ({}%)'.format(nViews,
round(float(nViews) * 100 / nImps, 2)))

nViews=3649597 (40.11%)

df.groupby('pub_domain').size()          <-- Group by domain and look
                                             at number of impressions
                                             per domain
pub_domain
D10000000.com        321
D10000001.com        117
D10000002.com        124
D10000003.com         38
D10000004.com       8170
...

f = df.groupby('pub_domain').size()
f.describe()

count       41576.000000
mean          218.847580
std          6908.203538
min             1.000000
25%             2.000000
50%             5.000000
75%            19.000000
max       1060001.000000

sns.distplot(np.log10(f));
```

Figure 10.2 shows that many domains have a small number of impressions, and a few have large numbers of impressions. So that you can see the distribution graphically, we plotted the base 10 log rather than the raw frequencies (we use base 10 so you can think of the x-axis as 10^0, 10^1, 10^2...).

Perhaps most significantly, you can see that clicks are relatively rare, only 0.12%, or 0.0012. This is a respectable overall click-through rate. But for this example, you need large datasets in order to have enough target examples to build your model. This isn't

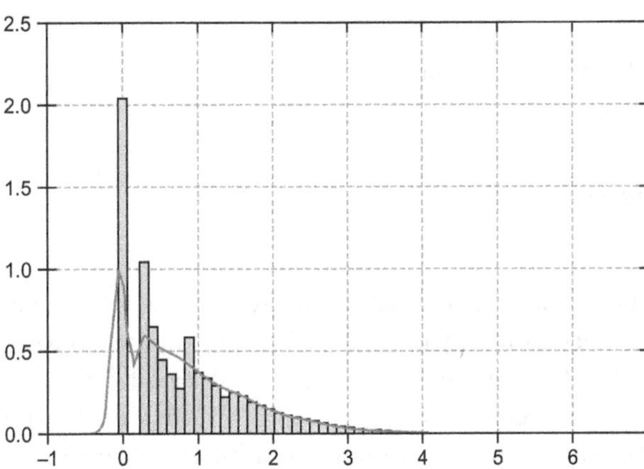

Figure 10.2 The histogram of impression data shows that the distribution of the number of impressions over publisher domains is heavily skewed.

unusual. We're often trying to predict relatively rare phenomena. The capacity to process huge datasets by using big-data technologies has made it possible to apply machine learning to many whole new classes of problems.

Similarly, impression frequency by `user_id` is highly skewed. An average user has 2.46 impressions, but the median is 1, so a few heavy hitters pull the mean higher.

10.5 Singular value decomposition

Chapters 3 and 7 mentioned principal component analysis, or PCA, an unsupervised ML technique often used to reduce dimensions and extract features. If you look at each user as a feature of the publications they've interacted with, you have approximately 3.6 million features per publication, 150 billion values for your exploratory sample of data. Obviously, you'd like to work with fewer features, and fortunately you can do so fairly easily.

As it turns out, PCA has several algorithms, one of which is *singular value decomposition*, or SVD. You can explain and interpret SVD mathematically in various ways, and mathematicians will recognize that our explanation here leaves out some of the beauty of the underlying linear algebra. Fortunately, like the latent semantic analysis covered in chapter 7, SVD has an excellent implementation in the scikit-learn Python library. But this time, let's do just a little bit of the matrix algebra. If you've done matrix multiplication, you know that dimensions are important. If $A_{[n \times p]}$ denotes an n-by-p matrix, you can multiple A by another matrix whose dimensions are p by q (for example, $B_{[p \times q]}$), and the result will have dimensions of n by q (say, $C_{[n \times q]}$). It turns out that any matrix can be factored into three components, called the left and right singular vectors and the singular values, respectively.

In this example, n is the number of users, each of which is represented by a row in matrix A, and p is the number of pubs, each of which is represented by a column:

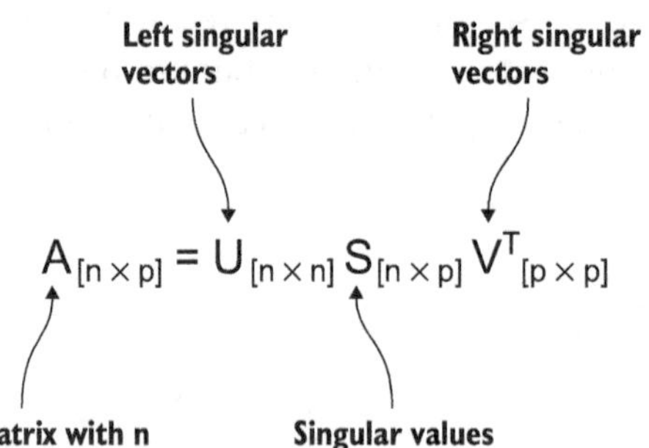

What makes this interesting is that the singular values tell you something about the importance of the features represented by the left and right singular vectors (the vectors are the rows of U and V^T). In particular, the singular values tell you the extent to which the corresponding feature vectors are independent. Consider the implication of interdependent or *covariant* features. Or to make it a bit easier, imagine that two features, A and B, are identical. After feature A has been considered by the model, feature B has nothing to contribute. It contains no new information. As builders of predictive models, the features you want are independent, and each one is at least a weak predictor of your target. If you have many weak predictors, so long as their predictions are better than random, in combination they gain strength. But this phenomenon, *the ensemble effect*, works only when features are independent.

Let's run SVD on our advertising data and have a look at the resulting singular values.

Listing 10.3 SVD on advertising data

```
user_idx, pub_idx = {}, {}                    <-- First substitutes
for i in range(len(users)):                       integer indices for user
    user_idx[users[i]] = i                        and pub symbolic keys
for i in range(len(pubs)):
    pub_idx[pubs[i]] = i

nTrainUsers = len(df.user_id.unique())              <-- Creates a sparse matrix
nTrainPubs = len(df.pub_domain.unique())                of user/pub interactions
V = sp.lil_matrix((nTrainUsers, nTrainPubs))
def matput(imp):
if imp.viewed:
            V[user_idx[imp.user_id], pub_idx[imp.pub_domain]] = 1

df5[df5.click == True].apply(matput, axis=1)

# run svds (svd for sparse matrices)

u, s, vt = svds(V, k = 1550)

plt.plot(s[::-1])
```

When you ran SVD, you used the k = *maximum singular values* parameter to limit the calculation to the 1,550 largest singular values. Figure 10.3 shows their magnitude;

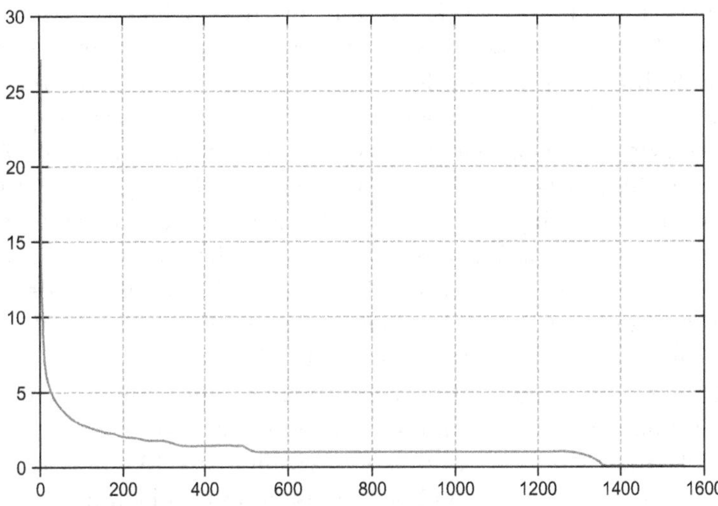

Figure 10.3 Singular values for advertising data

you can see that there are about 1,425 nonzero values, and that beyond the 450 most independent feature vectors, the rest are highly covariant. This isn't surprising. Although there are over 3 million users, remember that most of them interact with very few pubs. Consider that of these, 136,000 were observed exactly once (on ebay.com, by the way). So if each user vector is a feature of the pub, ebay.com has 136,000 features that are identical.

Our SVD reduced more than 3 million features to around 7 thousand, a 400:1 reduction. Knowing this, you have a much better sense of the resources that will be needed. In the next section, you'll look at ways to size and optimize the resources necessary to train your models.

10.6 Resource estimation and optimization

So far, you've looked at the cardinalities and distributions that characterize your data and done some feature engineering. In this section, you'll assess the task at hand in terms of the computational workload relative to the resources you have at your disposal.

To estimate resource requirements, you need to start with some measurements. First let's look at your available resources. So far, you've been using a single m4.2xlarge Amazon EC2 instance. Let's decode that quickly. EC2 is Amazon's *Elastic Compute Cloud.* Each instance is a virtual server with dedicated CPU, random access memory (RAM), and disk or solid-state online storage. The *m4.2xlarge* designation means a server with eight cores and 32 GB of memory. Disk space is provisioned separately. Our single instance has 1 terabyte of *elastic block storage (EBS).* EBS is virtualized storage, set up so that it appears that your instance has a dedicated 1 TB disk volume. You've set up your instance to run Linux. Depending on your needs, you can easily upgrade your single instance to add cores or memory, or you can provision more instances.

Next, let's have a look at your workload. Your raw data resides in transaction files on Amazon's *Simple Storage Service,* S3, which is designed to store large quantities of data inexpensively. But access is a lot slower than a local disk file. Each file contains around 1 million records. You can read approximately 30,000 records per second from S3, so if you process them one at a time, 10 billion will take about 92 hours. Downloading from S3 can be speeded up by around 75%, by processing multiple downloads in parallel (on a single instance), so that gets you down to 23 hours.

But speed isn't your only problem. Based on your earlier observation that 10 million records loaded into memory consume 53% of your 32 GB of memory, it would take 1.7 terabytes of memory to load your entire dataset. Even if you could afford it, Amazon doesn't have an instance with that much RAM.

Fortunately, you don't need all the data in memory. Furthermore, your requirement isn't just a function of the size of the data, but of its shape—by which we mean the cardinality of its primary keys. It turns out that there are 10 billion records, but only about 10 million users and around 300 thousand pubs, which means the user/pub matrix is around 3 trillion entries. But when you populated your sparse matrix, there were values in only about 0.01% of the cells, so 3 trillion is reduced to 300 million. Assuming one 64-bit floating-point number per value, your user/pub matrix will fit in about 2.5 of your 32 GB.

To cut processing time, you need to look at doing things in parallel. Figure 10.4 illustrates using worker nodes (additional EC2 instances, in this case) to ingest the raw data in parallel.

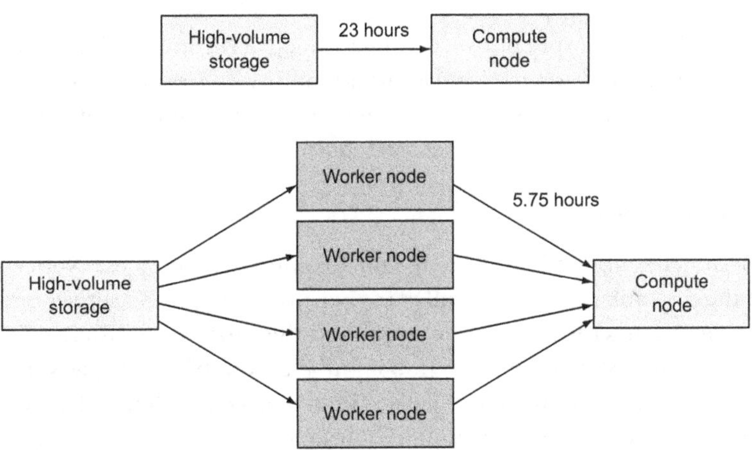

Figure 10.4 Parallel processing scales the initial data acquisition.

The worker nodes do more than read the data from S3. Each one independently builds a sparse matrix of users and items. When all the workers are finished with their jobs, these are combined by your compute node.

Chapter 9 described some big-data technologies: Hadoop, MapReduce, and Apache Spark. The processes described here are a highly simplified version of what happens in a MapReduce job. A large task is broken into small units, each of which is dispatched (mapped) to a worker. As workers complete their subtasks, the results are combined (reduced), and that result is returned to the requestor. Hadoop optimizes this process in several ways. First, rather than having the workers retrieve data over a network, each worker node stores part of the data locally. Hadoop optimizes the assignment of tasks so that whenever possible, each node works on data that's already on a local volume. Spark goes one step further by having the worker nodes load the data into memory so they don't need to do any I/O operations in order to process the tasks they're assigned.

Although this example problem is large enough to require a little parallel processing, it's probably not worth the effort required to implement one of these frameworks. You need to run your entire workflow only once per day, and you could easily add a few more instances and get the whole process down to an hour or less. But you can easily imagine an application requiring you to run a variety of processes at a greater frequency, where having the worker nodes retain the raw data in memory over the course of many processing cycles would boost performance by orders of magnitude.

10.7 Modeling

Your goal for the model is to predict CTR for each pub. You started with user interactions as features and used SVD to reduce the feature space. From here, there are several approaches to making predictions. Your first model will be a *k-nearest neighbors* (KNN) model. This is a simple but surprisingly effective recommender model.

You'll also train a *random forest regressor*. Random forests are a form of decision-tree-based learning; many random samples of data and random subsets of the feature set are selected, and decision trees are constructed for each selection.

10.8 K-nearest neighbors

Figure 10.5 shows simplified user/item and dissimilarity matrices. Notice that the diagonal of the dissimilarity matrix is all zeros because each pub's user vector (column in the user/item matrix) is identical to itself, and therefore zero distance from itself. You can see that the distance between pub3, pub4, and pub7 is zero, as you'd expect, because their respective columns in the user/item matrix are identical. Also note that pub1's distance to pub5 is the same as pub5's distance to pub1. In other words, dissimilarity is symmetric. Interestingly, some recommender algorithms don't define distance symmetrically. Item A may be like item B, but item B isn't like item A.

User / item matrix

	pub1	pub2	pub3	pub4	pub5	pub6	pub7
user1	0	0	1	1	0	1	1
user2	1	1	0	0	1	1	0
user3	1	0	0	0	0	1	0
user4	0	0	0	0	0	0	0
user5	1	1	1	1	1	1	1

Dissimilarity matrix

	pub1	pub2	pub3	pub4	pub5	pub6	pub7
pub1	0.0	1.0	1.7	1.7	1.0	1.0	1.7
pub2	1.0	0.0	1.4	1.4	0.0	1.4	1.4
pub3	1.7	1.4	0.0	0.0	1.4	1.4	0.0
pub4	1.7	1.4	0.0	0.0	1.4	1.4	0.0
pub5	1.0	0.0	1.4	1.4	0.0	1.4	1.4
pub6	1.0	1.4	1.4	1.4	1.4	0.0	1.4
pub7	1.7	1.4	0.0	0.0	1.4	1.4	0.0

Figure 10.5 The dissimilarity, or distance, matrix shows the extent to which user interactions are similar or different. In this example, the user/item matrix is binary, indicating whether the user has interacted with the pub.

You compute the similarity (actually, *dis*similarity, or distance) between each pair of pubs, using one of several available measures. You then choose the most common, the *Euclidean distance.*

After you've computed pairwise distances, the next step is to compute your predicted CTR for each pub. In KNN, the predicted target value is calculated by averaging the values of the target values for k-nearest neighbors, presuming that each example observation will be most similar to its nearest neighbors. There are several important questions at this juncture. First, what should you choose for the value of k? How many neighbors should be considered? Also, it's common to give greater weight to the closest neighbors, usually by weighting the calculation of the mean target value by $1/distance$ or $[1/distance]^2$.

Listing 10.4 shows a calculation of predicted values for a range of possible values of k by using scikit-learn `NearestNeighbors`. Here you try three weighting formulas, each of 20 values of k. Figure 10.6 shows that the best predictors are one or two nearest neighbors, and averaging over a larger range offers no real improvement. This is probably because our data is sparse, and nearest neighbors are often fairly distant. Note that the variation over the values of k is also small. In any case, the normalized RMSE for our test set predictions is in the range of 5%. Not bad!

Listing 10.4 KNN predictions

```
from sklearn.neighbors import NearestNeighbors

weightFunctions = {
    'f1': lambda x:  [1 for i in range(len(x))],      <- Equal weights
    'f2': lambda x:  1 / x,                           <- 1/dist
    'f3': lambda x:  1 / x ** 2                       <- 1/dist squared
}

for idx, f in enumerate(weightFunctions):             <- For each of the three weighting
    rmseL = []                                           schemes, computes predicted
    wf = weightFunctions[f]                              target values for k = 1 through 20
    for nNeighbors in range(1,20, 1):
        neigh = NearestNeighbors(nNeighbors)          <- Initializes

        neigh.fit(VT)                                 <- Finds k-nearest neighbors; VT is user/
        act = pd.Series()                                item transposed of the training set
        pred= pd.Series()

        for i in range(TT.shape[0]):                  <- TT is user/item transposed
            d = neigh.kneighbors(tt[i,:], return_distance=True)   of the test set
            W = pd.Series([v for v in d[0][0]])
            y = pd.Series(pubsums.iloc[d[1][0]].CTR)
            act.append(pd.Series(tsums.iloc[i].CTR))
            pred.append(pd.Series(np.average(y, weights = wf(W))))
    mse = act.sub(pred).pow(2).mean() / (pred.max() - pred.min())
    mseL.append(rmse)
    plt.subplot(130+idx+1)
    plt.plot(range(1,20,1), mseL)
    plt.tight_layout(pad=2.0)
```

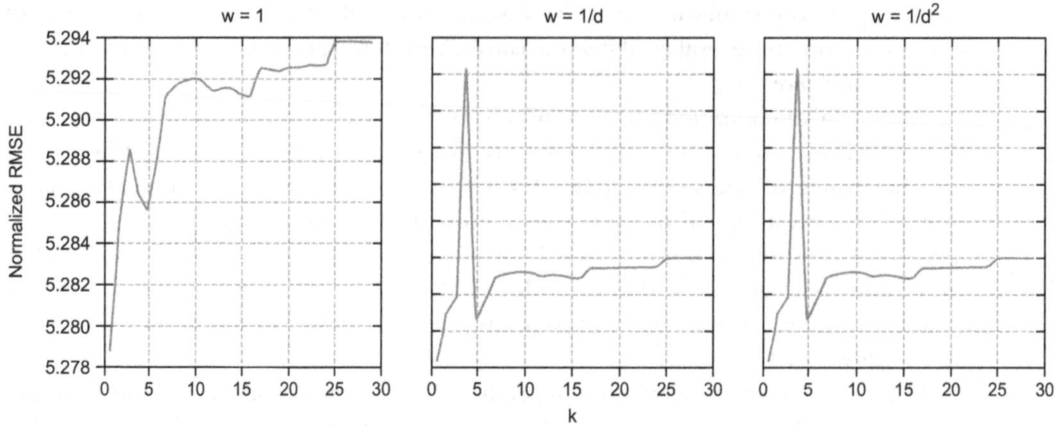

Figure 10.6 RMSE for three weighting functions and values of k = 1 to k = 30

10.9 Random forests

In the training phase of random forests, data is sampled repeatedly, with replacement, in a process called *bagging*, sometimes called *bootstrap aggregating*. For each sample, a decision tree is constructed using a randomly selected subset of the features. To make predictions on unseen data, each decision tree is evaluated independently, and the results are averaged (for regression) or each tree "votes" for classification. For many applications, random forests may be outperformed by other algorithms such as boosted trees or support vector machines, but random forests have the advantages that they're easy to apply, their results are easy to interpret and understand, and the training of many trees is easily parallelized. Once again, you'll use scikit-learn; see figure 10.7.

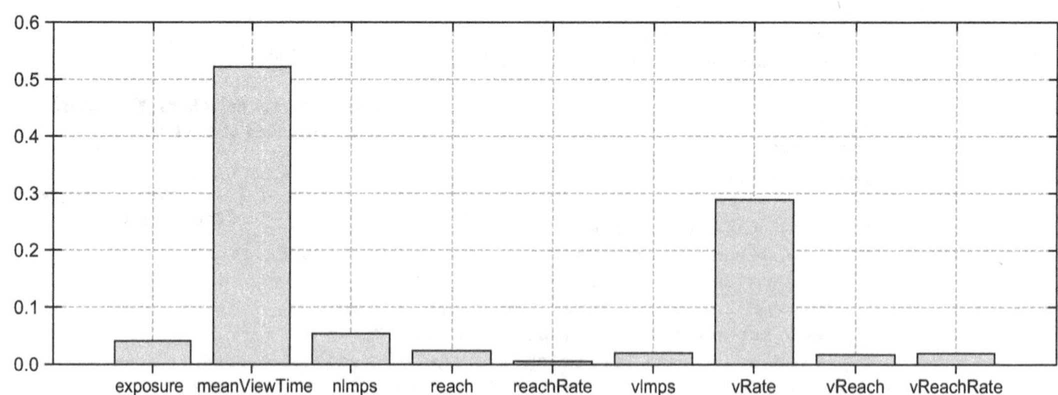

Figure 10.7 Variable importance for the random forest regression

Listing 10.5 Random forest regression

```
from sklearn.ensemble import RandomForestRegressor
from sklearn import cross_validation

features = ['exposure', 'meanViewTime', 'nImps', 'reach', 'reachRate',
                    'vImps', 'vRate', 'vReach', 'vReachRate']

X_train, X_test, y_train, y_test =  cross_validation.train_test_split(
               df[features], df.CTR, test_size=0.40, random_state=0)

reg = RandomForestRegressor(n_estimators=100, n_jobs=-1)
model = reg.fit(X_train, y_train)

scores = cross_validation.cross_val_score(model, X_train, y_train)
print(scores, scores.mean())

([ 0.62681533,  0.66944703,  0.63701492]), 0.64442575999999996)

model.score(X_test, y_test)

0.6135074515145226

plt.rcParams["figure.figsize"] = [12.0, 4.0]
plt.bar(range(len(features)), model.feature_importances_, align='center')
_ = plt.xticks(range(len(features)), features)
```

features are simple aggregates by pub

Splits data into test and train, features and targets; trains on 60% of the data, holds out 40% for test

Runs the random forest regression with 100 trees; n_jobs parameter tells RF to use all available cores

Cross-validation splits training set to evaluate the model

Runs the model on the test set

The optimized random forest regression provides a useful prediction of CTR, but it's not as good as the KNN prediction. Your next steps might be to explore ways to combine these, and possibly other, models. Methods that combine models in this way are called *ensemble methods.* Random forests are, in their own right, an ensemble method, as bagging is a way of generating multiple models. To combine entirely different models such as the two in this example, you might employ *stacking*, or stacked generalization, in which the predictions from multiple models become features that are combined by training and prediction using yet another ML model, usually logistic regression.

10.10 Other real-world considerations

You looked at the real-world issues that come with big data: high dimensionality, computing resources, storage, and network data transfer constraints. As we mentioned briefly, the entire process may be replicated for several species of digital ads: mobile, video, and native. Real-time bidding and user-level personalization have an entirely different set of concerns. The data at your disposal may vary widely from one program to the next, and the models that work perfectly in one situation may fail entirely for another.

In our example, we had a large historical dataset to start with. But our recommender-like approach has an issue known as the *cold-start problem.* When a new user or a new product enters the system with no history to rely on, you have no basis for building associations. For our purposes, a few unknowns don't matter, but when a new campaign starts from scratch, you have no history at all to work with. Models built on the basis of other similar campaigns may or may not be effective.

In the real world, there's a great advantage to having a variety of tools and models that can be employed. The larger and more complex the environment, the greater the benefit of having such a suite of feature-building, data-reduction, training, prediction, and assessment tools well organized and built into a coherent automated workflow.

Advertising is a great example of a business in which externalities may diminish the effectiveness of your predictive models. As technology and business practices change, behaviors change. The growth of mobile devices has changed the digital landscape dramatically. Real-time bidding completely changes the level on which you apply optimization. New forms of fraud, ad blockers, new browsers, and new web technology all change the dynamics that you're modeling. In the real world, models are built, tested, deployed, measured, rebuilt, retested, redeployed, and measured again.

Digital advertising is a multibillion-dollar business, and for the brands that rely on it, optimizations that reduce wasted expenditures, even a little, can have a significant return on investment. Each wasted impression you can eliminate saves money, but when replaced with one that results in gaining a customer, the benefit will be far greater than the cost savings—and will more than justify the effort to overcome the many challenges of this dynamic business.

10.11 Summary

This chapter covered elements of a real-world machine-learning problem somewhat more broadly than just choosing algorithms, training, and testing models. Although these are the heart of the discipline of machine learning, their success often depends on surrounding practicalities and trade-offs. Here are some of the key points from this chapter's example:

- The first step is always to understand the business or activity you're modeling, its objectives, and how they're measured. It's also important to consider how your predictions can be acted on—to anticipate what adjustments or optimizations can be made based on the insight you deliver.
- Different feature-engineering strategies may yield very different working datasets. Casting a wide net and considering a range of possibilities can be beneficial. In the first model, you expanded the feature set vastly and then reduced it using SVD. In the second, you used simple aggregations. Which approach works best depends on the problem and the data.
- After exploring a subsample of data, you were able to estimate the computing resources needed to perform your analyses. In our example, the bottleneck

wasn't the ML algorithms themselves, but rather the collection and aggregation of raw data into a form suitable for modeling. This isn't unusual, and it's important to consider both prerequisite and downstream workflow tasks when you consider resource needs.

- Often, the best model isn't a single model, but an ensemble of models, the predictions of which are aggregated by yet another predictive model. In many real-world problems, practical trade-offs exist between the best possible ensembles and the practicality of creating, operating, and maintaining complex workflows.
- In the real world, there are often a few, and sometimes many, variations on the problem at hand. We discussed some of these for advertising, and they're common in any complex discipline.
- The underlying dynamics of the phenomena you model often aren't constant. Business, markets, behaviors, and conditions change. When you use ML models in the real world, you must constantly monitor their performance and sometimes go back to the drawing board.

10.12 Terms from this chapter

Word	Definition
recommender	A class of ML algorithms used to predict users' affinities for various items.
collaborative filtering	Recommender algorithms that work by characterizing users via their item preferences, and items by the preferences of common users.
ensemble method	An ML strategy in which multiple models' independent predictions are combined.
ensemble effect	The tendency of multiple combined models to yield better predictive performance than the individual components.
k-nearest neighbors	An algorithm that bases predictions on the nearest observations in the training space.
Euclidean distance	One of many ways of measuring distances in feature space. In two-dimensional space, it's the familiar distance formula.
random forest	An ensemble learning method that fits multiple decision tree classifiers or regressors to subsets of the training data and features and makes predictions based on the combined model.
bagging	The process of repeated sampling with replacement used by random forests and other algorithms.
stacking	Use of a machine-learning algorithm, often logistic regression, to combine the predictions of other algorithms to create a final "consensus" prediction.

10.13 Recap and conclusion

The first goal in writing this book was to explain machine learning as it's practiced in the real world, in an understandable and interesting way. Another was to enable you to recognize when machine learning can solve your real-world problems. Here are some of the key points:

- Machine-learning methods are truly superior for certain data-driven problems.
- A basic machine-learning workflow includes data preparation, model building, model evaluation, optimization, and prediction.
- Data preparation includes ensuring that a sufficient quantity of the right data has been collected, visualizing the data, exploring the data, dealing with missing data, recoding categorical features, performing feature engineering, and always watching out for bias.
- Machine learning uses many models. Broad classes are linear and nonlinear, parametric and nonparametric, supervised and unsupervised, and classification and regression.
- Model evaluation and optimization involves iterative cross-validation, performance measurement, and parameter tuning.
- Feature engineering enables application of domain knowledge and use of unstructured data. It can often improve the performance of models dramatically.
- Scale isn't just about big data. It involves the partitioning of work, the rate at which new data is ingested, training time, and prediction time, all in the context of business or mission requirements.

The mathematics and computer science of machine learning have been with us for 50 years, but until recently they were confined to academia and a few esoteric applications. The growth of giant internet companies and the propagation of data as the world has gone online have opened the floodgates. Businesses, governments, and researchers are discovering and developing new applications for machine learning every day. This book is primarily about these applications, with just enough of the foundational mathematics and computer science to explain not just *what* practitioners do, but *how* they do it. We've emphasized the essential techniques and processes that apply regardless of the algorithms, scale, or application. We hope we've helped to demystify machine learning and in so doing helped to advance its use to solve important problems.

Progress comes in waves. The computer automation wave changed our institutions. The internet tidal wave changed our lives and our culture. There are good reasons to expect that today's machine learning is but a preview of the next wave. Will it be a predictable rising tide, a rogue wave, or a tsunami? It's too soon to say, but adoption isn't just proceeding; it's accelerating. At the same time, advances in machine-learning tools are impressive, to say the least. Computer systems are advancing in entirely new ways as we program them to learn progressively more-abstract skills. They're learning to see, hear, speak, translate languages, drive our cars, and anticipate our needs and desires for goods, services, knowledge, and relationships.

Arthur C. Clark said that any sufficiently advanced technology is indistinguishable from magic (Clark's third law). When machine learning was first proposed, it did sound like magic. But as it has become more commonplace, we've begun to understand it as a tool. As we see many examples of its application, we can generalize (in the human sense) and imagine other uses without knowing all the details of its internal workings. Like other advanced technologies that were once seen as magic, machine learning is coming into focus as a natural phenomenon, in the end more subtle and beautiful than magic.

Further reading

For those of you who'd like to learn more about using ML tools in the Python language, we recommend *Machine Learning in Action* by Peter Harrington (Manning, 2012).

For a deep dive with examples in the R language, consider *Applied Predictive Modeling* by Max Kuhn and Kjell Johnson (Springer, 2013).

Cathy O'Neil describes her and Rachel Schutt's book, *Doing Data Science: Straight Talk from the Frontline* (O'Reilly Media, 2013) as "a course I wish had existed when I was in college." We agree.

If you're interested in the implications of big data and machine learning for businesses and society, consider *Big Data, A Revolution That Will Transform How We Live, Work, and Think* by Viktor Mayer-Schönberger and Kenneth Cukier (Houghton Mifflin Harcourt, 2013).

Online resources include the following:

- www.predictiveanalyticstoday.com—For industry news
- www.analyticbridge.com and its parent site, www.datasciencecentral.com
- www.analyticsvidhya.com—Analytics news focused on learning
- www.reddit.com/r/machinelearning—Machine-learning discussion
- www.kaggle.com—Competitions, community, scripts, job board

appendix
Popular machine-learning algorithms

Name	Type	Use	Linear/ nonlinear	Requires normalization
Linear regression	Regression	Model a scalar target with one or more quantitative features. Although regression computes a linear combination, features can be transformed by nonlinear functions if relationships are known or can be guessed. R: www.inside-r.org/r-doc/stats/lm Python: http://scikit-learn.org/stable/modules/generated/sklearn.linear_model.LinearRegression.html#sklearn.linear_model.LinearRegression	Linear	Yes
Logistic regression	Classification	Categorize observations based on quantitative features; predict target class or probabilities of target classes. R: www.statmethods.net/advstats/glm.html Python: http://scikit-learn.org/stable/modules/generated/sklearn.linear_model.LogisticRegression.html	Linear	Yes

Name	Type	Use	Linear/ nonlinear	Requires normalization
SVM	Classification/regression	Classification based on separation in high-dimensional space. Predicts target classes. Target class probabilities require additional computation. Regression uses a subset of the data, and performance is highly data dependent. R: https://cran.r-project.org/web/packages/e1071/vignettes/svmdoc.pdf Python: http://scikit-learn.org/stable/modules/svm.html	Linear	Yes
SVM with kernel	Classification/regression	SVM with support for a variety of nonlinear models. R: https://cran.r-project.org/web/packages/e1071/vignettes/svmdoc.pdf Python: http://scikit-learn.org/stable/modules/svm.html	Nonlinear	Yes
K-nearest neighbors	Classification/regression	Targets are computed based on those of the training set that are "nearest" to the test examples via a distance formula (for example, Euclidean distance). For classification, training targets "vote." For regression, they are averaged. Predictions are based on a "local" subset of the data, but are highly accurate for some datasets. R: https://cran.r-project.org/web/packages/class/class.pdf Python: http://scikit-learn.org/stable/modules/generated/sklearn.neighbors.KNeighborsClassifier.html	Nonlinear	Yes
Decision trees	Classification/regression	Training data is recursively split into subsets based on attribute value tests, and decision trees that predict targets are derived. Produces understandable models, but random forest and boosting algorithms nearly always produce lower error rates. R: www.statmethods.net/advstats/cart.html Python: http://scikit-learn.org/stable/modules/tree.html#tree	Nonlinear	No

Name	Type	Use	Linear/ nonlinear	Requires normalization
Random forest	Classification/regression	An "ensemble" of decision trees is used to produce a stronger prediction than a single decision tree. For classification, multiple decision trees "vote." For regression, their results are averaged. R: https://cran.r-project.org/web/packages/randomForest/randomForest.pdf Python: http://scikit-learn.org/stable/modules/generated/sklearn.ensemble.RandomForestClassifier.html	Nonlinear	No
Boosting	Classification/regression	For multitree methods, boosting algorithms reduce generalization error by adjusting weights to give greater weight to examples that are misclassified or (for regression) those with larger residuals. R: https://cran.r-project.org/web/packages/gbm/gbm.pdf https://cran.r-project.org/web/packages/adabag/adabag.pdf Python: http://scikit-learn.org/stable/modules/generated/sklearn.ensemble.GradientBoostingClassifier.html	Nonlinear	No
Naïve Bayes	Classification	A simple, scalable classification algorithm used especially in text classification tasks (for example, spam-classification). It assumes independence between features (hence, naïve), which is rarely the case, but the algorithm works surprisingly well in specific cases. It utilizes the Bayes theorem, but is not "Bayesian" as used in the field of statistics. R: https://cran.r-project.org/web/packages/e1071/ Python: http://scikit-learn.org/stable/modules/classes.html#module-sklearn.naive_bayes	Nonlinear	Yes

Name	Type	Use	Linear/ nonlinear	Requires normalization
Neural network	Classification/regression	Used to estimate unknown functions that are based on a large number of inputs, through the back-propagation algorithm. Generally more complex and computationally expensive than other methods, but powerful for certain problems. The basis of many deep learning methods. R: https://cran.r-project.org/web/packages/neuralnet/neuralnet.pdf https://cran.r-project.org/web/packages/nnet/nnet.pdf Python: http://scikit-learn.org/dev/modules/neural_networks_supervised.html http://deeplearning.net/software/theano/	Nonlinear	Yes
Vowpal Wabbit	Classification/Regression	An online ML program developed by John Langford at Yahoo Research, now Microsoft. It incorporates various algorithms, including ordinary least squares and single-layer neural nets. As an online ML program, it doesn't require all data to fit in memory. It's known for fast processing of large datasets. Vowpal Wabbit has a unique input format and is generally run from a command line rather than through APIs. https://github.com/JohnLangford/vowpal_wabbit/wiki		
XGBoost	Classification/Regression	A highly optimized and scalable version of the boosted decision trees algorithm. https://xgboost.readthedocs.org/en/latest/		

index

F

G

H

I

K

L

N

O

P

Q

R

S

T

U

V

W